BUS-PASS BRITAIN

50 OF THE NATION'S FAVOURITE BUS JOURNEYS

edited by
Nicky Gardner, Susanne Kries
and Tim Locke

Edition 2
Bradt Travel Guides Ltd, UK

edition
2

(© Irish1983/DT)

🚌 *The circled number by each photo refers to the relevant bus journey.*

Nelson's Column towers 167ft above **Trafalgar Square** – the starting point for two of our journeys through the capital.

②

④

(© VisitEngland/Diana Jarvis)

①

You'll pass **St Pancras Station**, one of London's finest architectural offerings, on the journey from Paddington to Bow Church.

LONDON AND
THE HOME COUNTIES

Colourful graffiti decorates the streets of **Shoreditch** – the end of the line for the 35 bus.

③

(© DrimaFilm/S)

5 Charles Darwin spent the last years of his life at Down House in **Downe**, a village he chose due to its quiet, rural nature.

The view from **Box Hill**, Dorking. The 465 bus from busy Kingston upon Thames takes you through the heart of the Surrey countryside.

8 **Henley-on-Thames**, home to a famous annual regatta, is one of many riverside towns along the route between High Wycombe and Reading.

You'll spot open heathland and wild ponies along the Southampton to Lymington journey through the **New Forest National Park**.

SOUTHERN ENGLAND

The Isle of Wight is ideal for exploring by bus – you'll pass picture-perfect **Freshwater Bay** on our *West Wight* journey.

Hop off the Purbeck Breezer for a steam railway excursion to **Corfe Castle.**

11 The 49 bus through *Moonraker Country* passes **Silbury Hill**, the largest manmade mound in Europe.

12

Famous as the setting for ITV drama *Downton Abbey*, **Highclere** is one of the highlights of *The Secret Delights of North Hampshire* route.

Admire Dorset and East Devon's spectacular coastline on our two **Jurassic Coast** journeys.

SOUTHWEST ENGLAND

Catch a glimpse of the **Hardy Monument** on the way down to Abbotsbury.

We start our *Vintage Seaside* route at **Weston-super-Mare**, where the Grand Pier stretches 430yds into the sea.

17 The 319 makes a special detour to **Clovelly** – one of Devon's most picturesque villages – which tumbles down on to the coast.

18

Jump off the 178 at **Moretonhampstead** – a small town mixing old-world charm with modernity and home to an attractive church.

The beautiful curve of **Blackpool Sands** is well worth a stop on our Plymouth to Dartmouth route.

19

26

Hop off at **Hunstanton** on our Cromer to King's Lynn route and take a walk along the beach, where you'll find these quite spectacular banded cliffs.

MIDLANDS AND EAST ANGLIA

Our orbital route around **Birmingham** takes in the delights of the city's suburban web – a journey perfect for urban explorers.

21

25

On **Southwold** pier, you'll find Tim Hunkin's water clock, which you'll hear chiming (rather rudely, one might add) on the half hour.

(© VisitEngland/EnjoyStaffordshire)

Escape to **Cannock Chase** on our Stafford to Lichfield journey – a wild, open space that is a favourite weekend haunt for city dwellers.

Rolling hills and ironstone cottages are the backdrop for the 488 as it makes its journey through the **Cotswolds** to Chipping Norton.

(© Denis Kelly/DT)

With its rows of attractive Victorian villas and majestic cathedral, **Worcester** is an archetypal English county town – and the end point of our *Beyond Brummagem* route.

(© Brightskyvideos/DT)

The historic market town of **Aberystwyth**, with its Edwardian castle and old college, is the start and end point for two of our journeys.

WALES AND THE BORDERS

Alight at Hopton Heath on our Ludlow to Knighton journey for a lovely walk to the ruins of **Hopton Castle**, recently restored with the help of local residents.

The traditional seaside town of **Barmouth** – the end point of our *East to West Across North Wales* journey.

(© VisitBritain/Lee Beel)

With its half-timbered houses and pretty church, **Weobley** looks like something out of *Midsomer Murders*.

(© Arenaphotouk/DT)

Caernarfon is the first major stop on our Bangor to Aberystwyth route and is home to a UNESCO-listed castle.

Our route from Newtown to Cardiff is no ordinary bus journey, but a magic carpet ride through the **Brecon Beacons**, with an ever-changing vista of pastoral beauty and dramatic peaks.

(© Ch4chen/DT)

On our *Escape from Penrith* route, hop off at **Aira Force** for gentle walks, magnificent scenery and splendid views of the force itself.

At 1,696ft, towering **Mam Tor** is the spiritual focus of our route from Sheffield to Castleton.

THE PENNINES, CUMBRIA AND NORTHUMBERLAND

Muker is just one of the many traditional Dales villages that we pass on our Morecambe to Richmond journey.

40 Crossing the River Tyne on the Tyne Tees Express, this iconic view of **Newcastle upon Tyne** comes into sight, with the arching Millennium Bridge and futuristic Sage Gateshead.

The Honister Rambler service takes in some of the best scenery in the **Lake District**, where imposing Skiddaw dominates the landscape.

Bamburgh Castle is one of the highlights of our *North Sea Coastal Splendour* route – a Victorian structure with magnificent panoramic views.

43

Standing stones are a common sight on our *Jewel in the Clyde* journey – the **Isle of Arran** is littered with them, some dating back 4,000 years to the Bronze Age.

46

Make the effort to climb up to the Dugald Stewart Monument for great views over **Edinburgh** – final stopping point on Journey 43.

SCOTLAND

47

Our journey across the Sound of Islay passes the magnificent **Paps of Jura**, which dominate the spectacular landscape.

(45) Our *Essential Scotland* route whizzes along the shores of **Loch Lomond** on the way to Campbeltown.

(50)

With its sweeping silver sands, **Hushinish** is a breathtaking spot – the perfect place to end our last journey.

Kelso, the midway point on our Berwick-upon-Tweed to Galashiels journey, is one of the best-preserved historic towns in the Borders. (44)

Bus-Pass Britain
50 of the Nation's Favourite Bus Journeys

KEY
London and the Home Counties
Southern England
Southwest England
Midlands and East Anglia
Wales and the Borders
The Pennines
Cumbria and Northumberland
Scotland

LONDON

Orkney Islands

Outer Hebrides

Thurso
John o'Groats
48
50
Stornoway
Skye
49
Mallaig
Ben Nevis ▲
Mull
Oban
45
47
Campbeltown
Arran
46
Ayr
43
Stranraer

Fraserburgh
Inverness
Loch Ness
Moray Firth
Spey
Don
Dee
Aberdeen
GRAMPIAN MTS.
Pitlochry
Montrose
Tay
Perth
Dundee
SCOTLAND
Forth
Glasgow
Clyde
Firth of Forth
Edinburgh
44
Berwick-upon-Tweed
Tweed
Nith
Dumfries
CHEVIOT HILLS
The Cheviot
42
41
Tyne
Newcastle upon Tyne
Carlisle
Durham
40
39
Keswick
38
Middlesbrough
Isle of Man
37
Richmond
Scarborough
Swale
36
Morecambe
York
Leeds
Kingston upon Hull

NORTH SEA

IRISH SEA

N
Bradt

Manchester
Liverpool
35
Sheffield
34
Buxton
33
Skegness
Lincoln
Bangor
Wrexham
26
Snowdon ▲
Stafford
Derby
Crome
29
31
23
ENGLAND
Trent
Norwich
Newtown
Severn
Wolverhampton
21
King's Lynn
25
Birmingham
Leicester
Peterborough
Aberystwyth
30
WALES
27
22
Coventry
24
Cambridge
Ipswich
Cardigan
32
28
Worcester
Northampton
Wye
20
Gloucester
COTSWOLD HILLS
Oxford
Luton
Swansea
16
Thames
Swindon
8
London
Cardiff
11
Reading
6
Bristol
12
Canterbury
Barnstaple
Salisbury
Dorking
Dov
17
Taunton
Southampton
SOUTH
7
DOWNS
18
Exeter
9
Brighton
Eastbourne
DARTMOOR
14
15
Poole
10
19
Portland Bill
13
Isle of Wight
Plymouth
Penzance
Isles of Scilly

ENGLISH CHANNEL

0   100km
0   60 mile

LONDON
Cockfosters
4
Shoreditch
Paddington
1
Bow
2
Blackwall
3
Clapham
5
Bromley
Downe

FOREWORD

On a chilly morning in 2008, Janice Booth (who is a contributor to this volume) and I waited at the bus stop at Land's End clutching our bus passes. It was 1 April (no kidding!), the day that marked the launch of the concessionary bus-pass scheme for England. Other parts of the UK had long enjoyed such schemes. We had virgin bus passes in our hands.

'First ones I've seen!' said the bus driver cheerily as we climbed aboard. Janice and I took a week to travel from Land's End to Lowestoft Ness, respectively the westernmost and easternmost points of the English mainland. That journey, made by local buses, forged our love of bus travel and led to the previous edition of this book, *Bus-Pass Britain*, published by Bradt Travel Guides in 2011.

The popularity of that volume showed that we are not alone in our enthusiasm. Bus passes have given mobility to an older generation, but of course the majority of users of British buses are well below pension age. *Bus-Pass Britain* tapped a vein of enthusiasm for bus travel among travellers of *all* ages, so we published a second volume, *Bus-Pass Britain Rides Again*. In this new edition, we have updated the best journeys from both books, all written by ordinary members of the travelling public who have an extraordinary affection for their local bus routes.

Climb aboard and join us as we celebrate some of the nation's favourite journeys. Just be warned – bus travel can become seriously addictive!

Hilary Bradt

Second edition May 2016
First published 2011
Bradt Travel Guides Ltd
IDC House, The Vale, Chalfont St Peter, Bucks SL9 9RZ, England
www.bradtguides.com
Print edition published in the USA by The Globe Pequot Press Inc,
PO Box 480, Guildford, Conneticut 06437-0480
Text copyright © 2016 Bradt Travel Guides Ltd; except Journeys 21 and 30
© Nicky Gardner
Maps copyright © 2016 Bradt Travel Guides Ltd
Photographs copyright © 2016 Individual photographers

Book editors: Nicky Gardner, Susanne Kries and Tim Locke
Book design: Shane O'Dwyer
Cover illustration: Neil Gower (www.neilgower.com)
Colour map: David McCutcheon FBCart.S (www.dvdmaps.co.uk)
Route sketch maps: *hidden europe*
Typesetting and layout: Artinfusion and Wakewing, Chesham

ISBN-13: 978 1 78477 019 8 (print)
e-ISBN: 978 1 78477 164 9 (e-pub)
e-ISBN: 978 1 78477 264 2 (mobi)

British Library Cataloguing in Publication Data
A catalogue record for this book is available from the British Library

Some **photographs** have been sourced from photo agencies. Where this is
the case, the following abbreviations have been added next to the name of
the photographer: DT (Dreamstime.com), S (Shutterstock.com)

Production managed by Jellyfish Print Solutions; printed in India
Digital conversion managed by www.dataworks.co.in

Contents

WELCOME ABOARD

The numbers in parentheses below refer to the numbers of specific journeys in this book.

W e have always loved local buses. The bus that trundles from village to village is an antidote to globalisation, a chance to mark the importance of community in a frenetic world. We may be inclined to complain about the quality and frequency of our bus services, but Britain is blessed with one of the finest local bus networks anywhere in Europe. The humble omnibus has no pretensions to grandeur. That, for us, is part of its appeal. Most of the journeys we make on local buses are mundane, but venture beyond your home territory and the bus offers a chance to become an explorer.

At the heart of *Bus-Pass Britain* are 50 journeys that cover the length and breadth of Britain (including five routes on offshore islands). The routes reveal the variety of Britain's landscapes: from Dartmoor wilderness (18) to the gentle landscapes of the Tweed Valley (44); from the Fens (24) to the Outer Hebrides (49, 50). We map urban Britain too, taking local buses through our cities and their edgelands – the unsung spaces where town and country blur (see for example routes 5 and 21). Join us on forays through London and also through industrial regions from the West Midlands (22) to Teesside (40).

A COMMUNITY OF WRITERS

The really special thing about this book is the way it came to be. It resulted from a community-writing initiative in which members of the public were invited to write about their favourite bus routes. The writers who contributed to this book responded to our invites on Twitter and in other media, and many heard of the project from regional groups around Britain that encourage and support new writers. A particularly rich crop of potential contributors came through publicity in *hidden europe* magazine. We have journeys written by authors who, prior to the advent of this project, had never seen their names in print. Their texts sit alongside essays penned by writers who have enjoyed a long association with Bradt Travel Guides and have authored or edited many books.

The book is, first and foremost, a celebration of journeys that have meaning for the people who describe them. Many routes reveal something of the mind and soul of the writer. Read on and you'll discover numerous different voices, and 50 compelling reasons why we should cherish our local bus services as valuable community assets.

Freedom to roam

The concessionary bus passes introduced in England in 2008 (and earlier in Wales and Scotland) have energised an older generation, encouraging them to explore their home region and further afield. Yet you don't need to wait for retirement age to start exploring Britain by bus: in most parts of the country, good regional passes allow travellers of *any* age to benefit from the freedom to roam at will. We mention many such passes in this book.

Travellers once wedded to their cars are discovering that a ride on the village bus can be a very congenial experience. We have heard from readers of the first edition of this book who were initially sceptical, suggesting that they would prefer to travel by car rather than by bus. Some experienced Damascene conversions when they eventually joined the crowd at their local bus shelter, reporting back that local buses may win no prizes for speed, but they are invariably fun.

This book is thus full of intriguing characters. We run into an old soldier and the shadow of Tolkien in the suburbs of Birmingham (21), and we recall Kate Barton who, over one hundred years ago, became the first woman in Britain to become a bus driver (see page 144).

THE 50 JOURNEYS

This volume contains a wonderful variety of bus journeys. Some of the shortest (16, 27 and 34) are done and dusted within an hour. At the other extreme, we have routes that extend to over three hours, including journeys through the Scottish Highlands (48), Snowdonia (29) and the Yorkshire Dales National Park (36).

There are journeys through serenely beautiful countryside (37, 39 and 46 are all good examples) and we have routes that lead into forlorn and empty wilderness. For a taste of the latter, we particularly recommend the Hebridean itineraries which conclude the book (49 and 50).

Yet packed into these 50 essays you'll find more than merely a feast of fine landscapes. Some of our writers capture with great delicacy that distinctive end-of-the-road feeling. It is no surprise perhaps to encounter that at a remote headland in north Devon (17) or at the southern tip of the Mull of Kintyre (45), but we were greatly impressed to also encounter that sense of isolation in the tamer landscapes of southern England.

So much for the world beyond the bus window. For some of our contributors, the bus journey is more than an invitation to adventure: it is a gateway to the soul. A route that is at one level a prosaic trundle along the shores of the Bristol Channel (16) turns out to be a meditation on childhood. Another run, this time through the English Midlands (22), reflects on the new, the old, the lost and the foretold. One writer ponders on the strangeness of returning to old haunts (10), while many authors ponder on chances taken (and chances missed) on the top deck.

The landscapes through which we travel are indeed varied. But so too are the soulscapes and mindscapes captured in *Bus-Pass Britain*. So climb aboard and take a seat on the top deck as we set off to explore Britain by bus.

Nicky Gardner, Susanne Kries and Tim Locke
Editors, *Bus-Pass Britain* (2nd edition)

HOW TO USE THIS BOOK

This book is as easy to use as hopping on your local bus. We have divided Great Britain into eight regions. Well do we know that the coverage is not absolutely even, but we are keen to showcase the variety of bus journeys across Britain – and equally anxious to show the many ways in which even the most prosaic journey can inspire a good writer. Some texts are ones that you can easily follow yourself, and they were written with that intention in mind. Others attempt something more ambitious: they reveal how journeys are the midwives of thought. A bus journey can be a portal to the soul, an invitation to reflection. Those essays are perhaps best read in the comfort of an armchair on a winter evening.

You will find an index map showing the location of each of our 50 routes on the last of the colour pages at the start of this book. All but the shortest routes (and that includes most of the London journeys) are accompanied by a simple sketch map – nothing fancy, but just enough detail for you to identify the main *en route* points mentioned in the text. We give a typical travel time in minutes between each point on that map. Bear in mind that on some routes these average travel times can vary considerably from one trip to another. In urban areas, timetables often allow for longer journey times at peak hours. In rural areas, occasional buses may make deviations off the main route to serve villages that might otherwise have no bus service at all.

In the introductory notes at the start of each route, we give an indication of service frequency, an important consideration if you are planning to stop off along the length of a journey. Some of our routes run several times each hour, others as little as only once each week. Careful planning always pays off. We also always cite the Ordnance Survey 1:50,000 Landranger maps relevant to each essay in the order in which they occur if you follow the route as we describe it. And we mention the likely travel time if you follow the entire journey.

Our bus stop mini-features are just like bus stops: places to linger and ponder while you wait to embark on your next journey. We hope they'll make you think or smile – or both! In the postscripts section at the end of the book, you'll find some good tips on journey planning.

Finally, we should add a note of caution. Bus timetables are famously volatile. They often vary from season to season. Bus numbers and routings also change. Cuts in public subsidies mean that frequencies on some routes are being trimmed in 2016 and 2017; some services may be cut altogether. Not, as far as we know, any of those featured in this book. But it always pays to check the current situation before setting out.

50 BUS JOURNEYS

 Paddington to Bow Church Trafalgar Square to Blackwall Clapham Junction to Shoreditch Trafalgar Square to Cockfosters Bromley to Downe Kingston upon Thames to Dorking Horsham to Burgess Hill High Wycombe to Reading Southampton to Lymington Newport to Totland Trowbridge to Swindon Newbury to Andover Bournemouth to Swanage Exeter to Lyme Regis Lyme Regis to Poole Weston-super-Mare to Sand Bay Barnstaple to Hartland Okehampton to Newton Abbot Plymouth to Dartmouth Banbury to Chipping Norton Birmingham circular route Birmingham to Worcester Stafford to Lichfield Chatteris to Cambridge Great Yarmouth to Southwold Cromer to King's Lynn Ludlow to Knighton Hereford to Llandrindod Wells Bangor to Aberystwyth Aberystwyth to Tregaron Wrexham to Barmouth Newtown to Cardiff Derby to Bakewell Buxton to Macclesfield Sheffield to Castleton Morecambe to Richmond Leyburn to Gayle Penrith to Windermere Lake District circular route Middlesbrough to Newcastle upon Tyne Carlisle to Newcastle upon Tyne Newcastle upon Tyne to Berwick-upon-Tweed Dumfries to Edinburgh Berwick-upon-Tweed to Galashiels Glasgow to Campbeltown Brodick to Blackwaterfoot Feolin to Inverlussa Inverness to Thurso Berneray to Eriskay Tarbert to Hushinish

LONDON AND THE HOME COUNTIES

Londonʼs buses are the cityʼs most conspicuous ambassadors. They embody the spirit of London and, for many visitors to England, the capitalʼs red buses are as intimately associated with the city as Big Ben and Beefeaters. Time-worn London buses have proved to be a valuable export commodity, and the classic red double-deckers have made their way around the world. Weʼve heard of examples on the roads of Hong Kong, Patagonia and the French Riviera.

Londoners may be surprised to learn that the omnibus trade in their home city owes its origins as much to French as to English ingenuity. The mathematician Blaise Pascal had the idea of introducing shared *carrosses* running on set routes in Paris in the mid-17th century, but it wasnʼt a success – even the largest cities were very walkable in those days.

George Shillibeer, a Londoner by birth, worked in the coach trade in Paris in the 1820s. Shillibeer saw how successful the omnibus was in Paris and copied the idea for London. Along with the buses (of his own design) that Shillibeer imported from France, he brought the drivers and conductors, too. Londonʼs first buses were thus staffed mainly by Frenchmen, giving Londoners the chance to brush up their conversational French while trundling from Paddington to the City.

Nowadays, the London omnibus is still a place to catch snippets of many languages. Polish and Punjabi mingle. Join us on the top deck as we set off to explore London and its suburbs with a grandstand view of the capital. The cityscape has changed, but itʼs surprising how enduring some bus routes have been – there are some London bus routes that run today under the same number as they did a century ago.

We kick off our exploration of Britain's best bus journeys with five capital excursions through London, offering five very different perspectives on the city and its furthest-flung suburbs, including Journey 5's venture from Bromley to the village on the very edge of Greater London where Charles Darwin once lived.

Excursions beyond the capital

The very term 'Home Counties' imposes an amorphous uniformity on areas that are very different. Local bus services are a superb way of tapping into all that is distinctive in London's rural hinterland. The very fact that settlements nudge up against one another brings advantages: bus services are usually frequent and routes so interconnected that there are often multiple ways of getting from A to B.

The region should not be dismissed for want of remarkable scenery. You won't find great swathes of wilderness but, in the gentle valleys of the Weald and the Chilterns, you'll find landscapes of delicate beauty. Sussex-based Compass Travel leads us on a tour of the Weald in Journey 7, and Journey 8 picks up an old Alder Valley bus route – yes, there really was a bus company named after a non-existent valley. The Kingston to Leatherhead bus route served by Epsom-based Quality Line is described in Journey 6, a service that has been running for over 80 years. Only its number has inflated (from 65 to 465), and of course the service now runs on through the Mole Gap to Dorking.

Even if you do not have a concessionary bus pass, you will find rover tickets that allow inexpensive explorations. Particularly good value are the day 'Explorer' tickets allowing unlimited travel on buses run by a range of operators for east Hampshire, Surrey, Kent and Sussex; and for a sweep of territory around the north of London, extending from Reading in the Thames Valley through the Chilterns to Hertfordshire and Essex. ∎

A Divine Capital Taster

Fran Martin

1 Paddington

Service no. 205 | Journey time 60–90mins.

OS Landranger 176, 177. Daily, every 6–12mins
Operator: Stagecoach London.
Connects with Journey 4 at St Pancras, Journey 3 at Liverpool St
& Journey 2 at Whitechapel.

Bow Church

Let us start at the beginning. When George Shillibeer created London's first-ever omnibus service, he chose a route that ran east from Paddington towards the City. And the first part of London's 205 bus route, on its journey from Paddington to Bow, follows much the same itinerary.

The 205 is thus the lineal descendant of Shillibeer's pioneer service, which took to London's streets on 4 July 1829. Almost 200 years later, this is still one of the capital's premier routes. It serves a string of London's main-line railway stations which didn't exist in Shillibeer's day, and then concludes its journey at an East End church which has for over seven centuries echoed to the sound of the psalms.

There is a touch of the Divine about the 205. Few other London bus routes offer such an ecumenical mix of faiths and religions. Join me on the upper deck for a seven-mile ride that catches the spirit of a city that makes space for mosques and synagogues alongside churches representing a dozen shades of Christianity.

The route kicks off in humble manner. That somehow suits a journey that is a veritable pilgrimage to various temples of prayer. Our journey starts at a bus stop that is tucked away behind **Paddington Station**.

We are hardly on our way when we reach **Chapel Street**, which is oddly devoid of chapels. But, just off to our right, comes the first of many surprises presented by the 205: a church dedicated to an early 18th-century Swedish queen. The Ulrika Eleanora Church in Harcourt Street still caters to the Swedish Lutheran diaspora.

Then it's all stops east through more secular terrain, though **Madame Tussauds** (open 09.30–17.30 Mon–Fri, until 18.00 Sat–Sun) makes space for popes and a clutch of other religious leaders. It is surely the only place where you'll find archbishops rubbing shoulders with the goddesses of the silver screen.

Just past Tussauds, the conspicuous church on the right is dedicated to **St Marylebone**. It has given its name to this part of London. The foundation stone of this Anglican church was laid on 5 July 1813. Today St Marylebone's makes its mark on more than just the spirit. It also offers a healing and counselling service.

Of vices and virtues

Now we are in **Euston Road** and, as we shuffle east in crowded traffic, the landscape of faith is becoming more textured. The path of true dissent is represented by **Friends House** to our right, the headquarters of the Quakers in Britain. Its excellent café is a good spot for a break (open 08.00–20.00 Mon–Fri, 08.30–15.00 Sat).

Euston Road drops very gently downhill towards London's most ornate railway station at St Pancras. Just before this amazing

> ## FADING FAITH
>
> Not all London churches have been as successful as St Marylebone's. Just east of Nash's lovely Park Crescent, our bus passes Holy Trinity Church. From a distance, its Grecian lines and lantern tower look very fine, but close-up the appeal fades. The building is long abandoned and in a troubled state of disrepair.

Gothic extravaganza there is a temple of another kind on the left. Yes, those who regularly use the British Library speak with almost religious devotion of this testament to the written word.

I like the strong colours of the library building, but **St Pancras Station** just adjacent nudges the library into the architectural shadows. St Pancras is a temple devoted to trains, and it even comes with a lesson or two on faith, hope and charity. Climb up the grand staircase of the St Pancras Renaissance Hotel, part of the main station building, and you'll find the ceilings decorated with E W Godwin's tributes to various shades of virtue. Here we have a sermon, but one that is by no means crusty and conservative. It is light in touch, full of Oriental accents and whimsy.

Oriental accents of another kind feature in the next church on our ride. **King's Cross Methodist Church** is non-conformism with a twist. Sunday services are held in Cantonese and Mandarin, as well as in English, catering to the Chinese Methodist community.

The Methodist theme stays with us as we head east through twilight zones, the edgelands of the City that are punching their way back into fashion. We cut through Pentonville and soon we are slipping south down City Road, passing John Wesley's House and the **Museum of Methodism** (open 10.00–16.00 Mon–Sat, noon–13.45 Sun).

A PLURALITY OF FAITHS

Having been born and brought up as a Catholic, I have a soft spot for the next church on our pilgrimage. Most on the bus will miss **St Mary Moorfields** with its inconspicuous entrance on Eldon Street, but it is truly one of London's hidden gems. It is a very special haven of quiet and peace in the middle of the capital's bustling financial district.

The street names on this part of the 205 route recall lost meadows: here is Wormwood Street and there is Camomile Street. 'Yes, hop off here for **Bevis Marks**,' says a man on the top deck. So I take his advice. No-one should miss this opportunity, for

THREADS OF BELIEF

Route 205 serves Finsbury Square, a patch of green in the heart of London that might really claim to be the touchstone for English Methodism. John and Charles Wesley both preached here. This is a part of London that has always been receptive to new religious ideas. Finsbury Square has at various times been home to a rabbinical seminary and a Greek Orthodox church.

here is one of England's most beautiful synagogues. Just like that Catholic church we saw earlier, the synagogue is tucked away and not easy to spot.

Back on the 205, the double-decker nudges its way along **Whitechapel High Street**. Bangladeshi has eclipsed Yiddish, synagogues have made way for mosques. We cruise past the dramatic east London Mosque into Stepney. You'll have to look hard in Stepney nowadays to find any trace of the Huguenots who settled here in the 17th century. Subsequent waves of migrants have covered the traces of those French Protestants, and many of those migrants have reached out to touch the hearts and souls of all Londoners. So it's not just Buddhists who make their way to the **London Buddhist Centre**, which is in Roman Road just a short walk north of Stepney Green.

Our journey ends at **Bow Church**. The parish church at Bow was built to serve Catholics in what was then a rural hamlet. Shifting its pieties post-Reformation to Anglicanism, the church now serves as a focal point for one of London's most multi-cultural communities.

This bus route, which ends in the shadow of the **Olympic Park**, captures post-Olympic England – a country which has an extraordinary variety of faiths and cultures. ∎

ABOUT THE AUTHOR | **FRAN MARTIN** lives and works in London. Her first love is walking, but she makes time too for anything to do with visual arts.

SIMPLY RED: A CAPITAL ROUTE

Alastair Willis

2 Trafalgar Square 🚐

Service no. 15 | Journey time 35–55mins.

OS Landranger 176, 177. Daily, every 6–10mins.
Operator: Stagecoach.
Connects with Journey 2 at Whitechapel, Journey 3 at Monument &
Journey 4 at Trafalgar Square.

Blackwall ←

London's number 15 bus route really is capital. It is an artery linking the West End with the contrasting East End and Docklands, along the way passing some of London's finest buildings and vistas. Other services may have the edge when it comes to grand sights, but the 15 has a trump card that will appeal to bus travellers with a sense of transport history.

The busy section of the route from Trafalgar Square to Tower Hill benefits from extra daytime buses that ply just this part of the entire journey. The vehicles that operate those supplementary services are 50-year-old Routemasters (see box, page 13).

This is a chance for bus-pass holders to cast back to the days of their youth. Yes, we rode to school on open-platform double-deckers where we paid our fares to a conductor who sternly patrolled his or her vehicle and was quick to reprimand noisy and wayward passengers. I first rode a Routemaster in 1959, almost 60 years ago, a year when Max Bygraves was a hit at the London Palladium, and the Morris Mini-Minor made its debut at the London Motor Show.

This is definitely a journey where the best seats are upstairs at the front, rather than downstairs with the ebb and flow of visitors and Londoners who crowd the lower section of the bus.

ROUTEMASTER BUSES

Routemaster buses were introduced in 1956, and nearly 3,000 were built. Retired Routemasters are a popular export product, and over 1,000 survive in all corners of the world, many now deployed on sightseeing tours. You'll still find one heritage route in London, run by five iconic 50-year-old AEC Routemasters. They run every 20 minutes from Trafalgar Square to Tower Hill (part of the number 15 service, as described in this article) between 09.30 and 18.30. Please note that these buses are exempt from wheelchair accessibility legislation due to their heritage nature.

There's about a fortnight's holiday's worth of things to see and do along route 15. I use it most frequently as a 'gallery hopper' service that conveniently links the National Gallery (and its near neighbour the National Portrait Gallery), the Courtauld Gallery, Tate Modern and Whitechapel Gallery.

TRAFALGAR SQUARE TO ST PAUL'S CATHEDRAL

Trafalgar Square, with Nelson commanding proceedings from 167ft aloft, is the point from which mileages in London are traditionally measured, meaning that in many ways it is the city's central point. I'm always intrigued to see the latest commissioned artwork on the formerly empty northwest plinth in Trafalgar Square.

The 15 Routemaster service still runs from Trafalgar Square to Tower Hill (© Ciolca/DT)

TWO CATHEDRALS WALK

St Paul's Cathedral (☎ 020 7246 8348; open 08.30–16.30 Mon–Sat, Sun for worship only) is worth a visit in its own right, but for me there is another good reason for hopping off the 15 bus at St Paul's. It is the start of a short walk that nicely captures many flavours of London life. From the south entrance of St Paul's head down the wide walkway over the London Millennium Footbridge. Stop now and then to look back over the Thames at the cathedral dome, the infamous Gherkin and other architectural landmarks that dot the London skyline. The Tate Modern (☎ 020 7887 8888; www.tate.org.uk/modern; open 10.00–18.00 Sun–Thu, 10.00–22.00 Fri–Sat; the Tate Café has won a best-family-restaurant award) is the former Bankside Power Station, full of compelling contemporary art. Then walk east to Shakespeare's Globe (☎ 020 7902 1500; open 09.00–17.30 daily, depending on theatre performances), the beautiful 1980s reconstruction of a 20-sided oak-framed galleried courtyard.

Go along past Clink Prison Museum, Vinopolis and The Golden Hinde, through the narrow warehoused streets. The lively Borough Market foodstalls are worth sampling. Southwark Cathedral (☎ 020 7367 6700; open 08.00–18.00 Mon–Fri, 08.30–18.00 Sat–Sun; excellent, friendly refectory) is a hidden, tranquil gem, Gothic and of medieval origin. Either return by the same route or catch bus RV1 to Tower Gateway (to join route 15 eastbound) or back to Aldwych (to rejoin route 15 westbound).

There's a glimpse of the Savoy, the grand old dame of London hotels, as we drive along the Strand. Gilbert and Sullivan's operettas were first produced in the theatre next door, and indeed it was profits from opera that allowed theatre impresario Richard D'Oyly Carte to fund the building of the Savoy hotel.

A little further east, our bus pauses by the late 18th-century **Somerset House**, which was England's first purpose-built government office block. Nowadays it is a place not just for bureaucrats but for art, for it houses the Courtauld Gallery with its outstanding collection of Impressionist and post-Impressionist art.

Grand buildings follow in quick succession as our driver navigates the busy London traffic. The cathedral-like **Royal Courts of Justice** are Victorian Gothic in style. When high-profile court cases are heard it's interesting to watch the television crews, busily filming the comings and goings at the courts. This area, and nearby **Fleet Street**, are great places to wander. The Inner and Middle Temples, full of little courtyards and alleys, are a respite from the noise of busy streets. These lanes and squares seem unchanged for decades, though the same cannot be said of Fleet Street. Once busy with journalists, editors and printers, but no more! The great newspapers have forsaken Fleet Street, moving east along route 15 to the Docklands.

DOCKLAND BOUND

Then it's all stops east as our bus glides past **St Paul's Cathedral** and along Cannon Street to the Monument. The 202ft tall **Monument to the Great Fire of London** is a fluted Doric column, built in 1671 to commemorate the fire that, five years earlier, had so devastated the City of London. There is a marvellous view from the top of the column.

The next major landmark is the **Tower of London**, where I always break my journey for the picture-postcard views of **Tower Bridge** from St Katharine's Docks. The docks are Thomas Telford's most notable work in London, and they once specialised in handling high-value imports like brandy, spices and perfumes. These were the first of the London docks to be rehabilitated, back in 1973.

It is well worth heading on to the end of the route, which continues past Aldgate into **Whitechapel**. This is a very different London, an area once afflicted by great poverty, and even today conspicuously less affluent than many other parts of the city. Limehouse, Poplar and Blackwall are quite another world from where our journey started on Trafalgar Square just an hour earlier. Yet urban regeneration in the Docklands is changing this area fast, a reminder that our capital city is continually evolving.

Don't miss the **Museum of London Docklands** (open 10.00–18.00 daily), which tells the story of 2,000 years of history of the Thames and its dockland districts from the time when this was a small Roman port to the present day. For an easy way back to the City, opt for the **Docklands Light Railway** (DLR). The trains are driverless, so grab a front seat for superb views from the elevated railway tracks across an urban area that has utterly reinvented itself. ■

ABOUT THE AUTHOR

ALASTAIR WILLIS lives in Leicestershire and visits London frequently. He often joins the 15 at St Paul's, after travelling by train via St Pancras International to City Thameslink.

LONDON BUS INFO

Just as with trains, there are many enthusiasts who know far more about buses than we could ever capture in this book. Robert Munster is just such a man. For the last 16 years, Robert has run the amazing www.londonbusroutes.net website, which is the absolute bible for devotees of London buses, their routes and their timetables. If there is a broken gas main at Elephant and Castle, or road works in Hampstead, this website has it mapped. It is regularly updated to include current diversions and route alterations. For London, we find the timetable information on Robert's website is better than that available from any other source.

Francesca Rushton and
Gregory Gardner

3 · Clapham Junction 🚐

Service no. 35 | Journey time 50–80mins.

OS Landranger 176. Daily, every 8–12mins (at night every 15mins).
Operator: Abellio London.
Connects with Journey 1 at Liverpool St & Journey 2 at Monument.

Shoreditch ←

There are quicker routes from Clapham Junction to Shoreditch, and the 35 wins no prizes as a route for classic sightseeing in the capital. Yet this journey is a favourite of ours because it affords awesome insights into the lives of real Londoners as the residents of contrasting boroughs hop on and off. Aboard the 35 – which runs seven days a week – you'll see Clapham's yuppies, the bustle of Brixton and Camberwell, the suits of the City and the hipsters of Shoreditch.

The bus stops behind **Clapham Junction Station** are on the proverbial wrong side of the tracks. Inauspicious though the spot may be, it is the place to catch the spirit of the 35. A fractured view of tower blocks to the northwest, the rumble of trains from the bridge overhead, and scents of fast-food chicken from across the road are the sights, sounds and smells at the starting point of our journey on the 35. Grab yourself a seat near the front of the top deck and watch the social landscape change.

You'll soon be marvelling at the grand town houses and upmarket eateries as you head east towards **Clapham Common**. Look right on a summer's weekend and the Common, the biggest park *en route*, will be buzzing with picnickers, footballers and dog walkers among others. The picnics might not be suited to winter but a small café (open 09.00–17.00 daily) close to the bandstand can warm you up with cups of tea and a decent bacon sandwich. Regardless of season, the bars, Irish pubs and chain restaurants around the Common's tube station are often full of young professionals enjoying their weekends.

Clapham's residents are typecast as rich, sporty and/or Australian, while The Clash's 'The Guns of Brixton' typifies the associations of the 35's next significant stopping point. The stereotypes may be overblown – particularly given Brixton's recent gentrification – but make your own inferences as the 35 heads into **Brixton** along Acre Lane, the scene of social unrest and riots in 1981 and again in 2011. The bookies, kebab stores and nail parlours have replaced the glass smashed by looters in August 2011. This really is another world from Clapham.

CHANGING DECKS

Beyond Brixton, the 35 is best sampled from the hustle and bustle of the lower deck. Prepare to be barged by buggies, squeezed by shopping bags, and silenced by sirens – not a relaxing ride perhaps but the reality of south London.

Brixton market (© Savo Ilic/DT)

Alight at Brixton Station for a wander through the lively markets and arcades that showcase the area's rich Afro-Caribbean heritage. This is the area settled by the migrants from the West Indies who in 1948 arrived on the *Windrush* – many of whom found their first jobs working on London's red buses. Coffee shops and trendy cafés are nudging in among the fishmongers and butchers. In this compact area, food from almost every continent is showcased, so a stroll through Brixton can easily morph into a culinary tour.

An Afro-Caribbean mood prevails along Coldharbour Lane towards **Camberwell** with numerous jerk chicken outlets and an improbable number of Afro hair and nail salons that, despite the plentiful competition, all seem to do a roaring trade. The notable exception is Sunday when the congregations of the area's many churches don their finest and you're more likely to hear a gospel choir than gossip from the salons.

Turning north at Camberwell, the bus jostles with cyclists, shoppers and other double-deckers along **Walworth Road**. The stop-start pace may frustrate the hurried traveller, but it gives time to survey the passing balconies, which are a window into the world of those who live in the apartment blocks. Some balconies are used as miniature gardens with potted plants and deckchairs, others double as bike racks or even laundry rooms. Coloured sheets flapping in the wind give a tapestry of colour to the estates.

CHANGING MOODS

Closer to **Elephant and Castle** new private apartments targeting students and young professionals start to appear and, in 2015, after its closure, the Elephant and Castle pub that gave the area its name was occupied by squatters in a protest against the area's gentrification.

The stretch from Elephant and Castle to London Bridge takes only five minutes but a glimpse of the Shard – London's tallest building – hints at a shift in the economic and social mood. Gritty south London morphs into **the City**. Gone are the grey residential tower blocks, replaced by greyer, taller office blocks. Gone are the fried-chicken joints, replaced by corporate Britain and Starbucks.

Rufus, a regular driver on the 35, candidly remarks in his Caribbean twang that 'driving is hell' around here on weekdays – the lack of respect shown to him by passengers supposedly only matched by the disregard of cyclists for their own safety.

Beyond Monument, the bus tracks north along **Bishopsgate**, affording neck-straining views of the Cheese Grater, Heron Tower and the Gherkin. These tall glass-fronted buildings stand alongside historic stone buildings. The Bank of England is just down Threadneedle Street, on the corner of which you'll see the engravings on the façade of **Gibson Hall**, which represent the industries and crafts for which finance is supplied. Take a look and see if you can spot the various trades, and statuary representing the arts, commerce, science, manufacturing, agriculture, navigation and shipbuilding.

Tourists slowly disembark at **Liverpool Street Station**, holding up the businessmen rushing to meetings at RBS's sparkling headquarters. The bohemian Spitalfields Market is a stone's throw to the east but Bishopsgate feels decidedly unbohemian with its endless glass-fronted offices.

Then the 35 crosses an invisible boundary line, this time into **Shoreditch**. Suddenly a pinstripe suit would look decidedly conspicuous as skinny jeans and vintage shirts dominate hipster cafés, where east London's traditional jellied eels have been usurped by organic fruit smoothies and soya lattes these days. Lively **Brick Lane** is a short walk from the last stop of the 35, which offers the best choice of curry houses in London. Barter well and you'll surely save yourself a couple of quid for the return trip to Clapham. ∎

ABOUT THE AUTHORS | **FRANKIE RUSHTON** and **GREG GARDNER** have recently moved from South Africa to Brixton for their careers in international development and are glad to live a stone's throw from the 35 route once more.

RED BUS AT NIGHT:
CLUBBER'S DELIGHT

Rebecca Reynolds

Trafalgar Square

Service no. N91 | Journey time 62–70mins.

OS Landranger 176. At night, every 15–30mins.
Operator: Metroline.
Connects with Journey 1 at St Pancras.

Cockfosters

Cast back many years and London Transport promoted their night buses as 'a welcome sight on a dark night'. That old tag line still rings true for me after dancing late-night salsa in town, when the N91 is my preferred option for the journey back to my north London home.

The N91, a sort of nocturnal stand-in for the Piccadilly Line, departs from **Trafalgar Square** and ends up an hour later on the edge of Hertfordshire fields. But this late-night foray through London is no grit-your-teeth necessity – on the contrary, it is a marvellous opportunity to see another side of the city I call home.

It is two on a Sunday morning. From the bus stop in Northumberland Avenue (just off Trafalgar Square) I can just see the white cables of the **Hungerford Bridge** walkways and the illuminated dome of the National Gallery. I swap my plastic perch at the bus stop for a seat on the top deck. We glide along the Strand, the glitzy Savoy to the right and sparkling signs advertising musicals on the left.

Then we sweep past King's College and on to **Bush House**, one-time home of the BBC World Service. Even in darkness, Malvina Hoffman's classic sculpture above the portico of Bush House stands bold and clear, a striking silhouette in the London night. Now the N91 sails north up Kingsway – a road once judged so stately that Elgar wrote music to honour it. And so to **Bloomsbury**, which tonight is notable not for its literary connections but for the rickshaw rider who speeds towards the small-hours trade in Covent Garden or Soho.

We pass the dirty caryatids of St Pancras Church, the modern red-brick British Library and taxis waiting in a curve outside the cathedral-like **St Pancras Station** with its happily refurbished hotel. The famous clock above the great Gothic feast of Victoriana records the passing minutes of the night.

THE MOOD ON THE BUS

At **King's Cross** the bus takes on the biggest load of the journey. 'The only problem with London is that it's too far to walk,' I overhear. 'In Leeds, when one nightclub is dead, you can just walk to the next one.'

A soundtrack of sorts develops. There is the tinny rhythm from headphones, talk on mobiles, the scrape of a ring pull, along with the disembodied voice of an announcer reciting a litany of bus stop names. On the top deck, different languages mingle – three long-haired women flip between French and American

GOTHIC STYLE

The ghost of 19th-century train travel lingers in the Booking Office Bar (☎ 020 7841 3566; open 06.30–01.00 Mon–Wed, 06.30–late Thu–Sat, 06.30–midnight Sun) of the St Pancras Renaissance Hotel. The bar is part of the original neo-Gothic station building, and the menu includes intriguing Victorian-style drinks, some sounding like a cross between a cocktail and a cup of tea. Eat oysters and drink Charles Dickens' Memorial Punch amidst leather armchairs, dark wood panelling and high ceilings and travel back to a time when a train journey was a luxury adventure. The staff are welcoming, and live music is played on Thursday, Friday and Saturday evenings.

English, an Indian language is spoken by two men behind me, and there's something that sounds like Turkish spoken into a mobile opposite.

I talk with 23-year-old Simon White, sitting at the front of the top deck with friends he has met at the airport. He tells me he often gets the bus after a night out. 'It's always a bit dodgy,' he says. 'By day no-one's going to get on smoking, with loads of beers. But the rules are different at night. It's sometimes funny to watch drunken people.'

So what about the hard-core clubbers, shift workers, transvestite DJs and other colourful denizens of London's dark underbelly? Well, I can only say that for me the N91 has always been a distinctly unedgy experience, and as a lone woman traveller I have always felt safe. That is an underrated aspect of London's night bus network.

We travel on. Lights rule. A ripped advert at a bus stop exposes fluorescent tubes beneath the plastic. A red back light flashes as a cyclist overtakes, high up are crane lights, traffic lights punctuate the journey. We go past Pentonville Prison, black pollarded trees outlined against its white bulk. Further on three blonde women cross the street, heading home with blue plastic bags. Men standing outside a restaurant turn their heads unashamedly. Looking back over the city from the top of **Crouch End Hill**, I can see the lights of Canary Wharf winking next to the newer vertical of the Shard.

Courting the Piccadilly Line

From Crouch End, we go down Turnpike Lane and emerge on to **Wood Green High Road**. This is a more desolate place than nearby Green Lanes, where jewel-like oranges are displayed outside Turkish and Cypriot greengrocers until the early hours. Here the stores include Poundland, downmarket jewellers, cinema multiplexes and, incongruously, an adventure travel shop with shadowy lumps of rucksacks hanging on the walls. Night brings respite from the crowds, and the shop windows are blank squares.

From now on the bus calls at the Piccadilly Line tube stations. After **Bounds Green** we cross the North Circular, London's inner ring road, where power station rings frame the sky.

We pause by London's most stylish tube station: **Southgate**, a perfectly circular Art Deco building standing on its own roundabout, banded in white, glowing in the dark, crowned by an audacious, illuminated, vertical stick with a white ball on the top. Charles Holden's ingenious 1933 design engineered its roof to be supported from a central column inside the ticket hall.

The route becomes distinctly suburban. We quietly go past large homes where families are sleeping; a synagogue; a primary school. The occasional wall-wide plasma screen can be glimpsed through maisonette curtains. Then along **Cockfosters Road**, lined with banks, restaurants and slightly frumpy boutiques, the better-heeled cousins of the Wood Green stores. Shop signs call: Sweet Cherry; Moonlight; Anuraag; Kalamaras. The bright vertical spear of the Cockfosters tube sign appears. We halt here at the edge of the city, the dark fields of Hertfordshire beyond. ∎

ABOUT THE AUTHOR

REBECCA REYNOLDS is a freelance museum educator. She also teaches museum studies and creative writing at various universities.

Brian Grigg

5

Bromley

Service no. 146 | Journey time 25mins.

OS Landranger 177. Daily, once an hour.
Operator: Stagecoach.

Downe

I don't know whether the former BBC radio programme *Down Your Way* ever went to the village of Downe. This community was surely a worthy candidate for inclusion in the show. For here is a fragment of London that has all the rural flavours so cherished by that perennial classic of the airwaves.

As London bus routes go, service 146 is one of the capital's shortest, yet one of the most extraordinary. It kicks off as just another red bus route in busy Bromley, but within half an hour morphs into a country bus journey along narrow leafy lanes. It is a route that dates back to before World War II – for many years numbered 146A but changing to 146 in 1952.

Londoners of a certain age will well remember the traditional colour coding of local buses: red for those that stayed within the city, green for those that bravely ventured out into London's rural hinterland. And this route from Bromley to Downe was always determinedly red, even though the southern part of the route was most decidedly green in character.

The starting point is **Bromley North Station**, definitely the lesser-known of the town's two railway stations. With its classical lines and copper-domed cupola, it is a handsome piece of Southern Railway architecture from the 1920s, though nowadays sadly bereft of useful trains, having merely a weekdays-only shuttle service to Grove Park.

Bromley deserves a better press. Its most distinguished sons and daughters have fled, among them Enid Blyton and David Bowie. The market square has a blue plaque marking the birthplace of H G Wells who wrote none-too-lovingly of Bromley in his novels.

HEADING SOUTH

Visitors are more likely to board the 146 at **Bromley South Station** (17 minutes from London Victoria). The bus stays within the London Borough of Bromley, offering passengers a ride through what was originally Kent (and still is in postal address terms) before London became Greater!

With the hustle and bustle of Bromley left behind, some minutes are spent going through suburban commuter territory before reaching open country at **Hayes Common**. Keston village follows soon thereafter. When returning across Hayes Common on a clear day, there is a fleeting reminder, just before the traffic lights, of the approaching metropolis. Look north for a view over the great monuments to money at Canary Wharf. If you blink though, they will be obscured by trees and out of sight.

One can walk from **Keston**, using parts of the London Loop footpath over Keston Common with its Iron Age earthwork and large ponds. Once across Westerham Road, the path

KESTON

This village is also served by the 246 from Bromley, Biggin Hill and Westerham. Fiona's Pantry (☎ 01689 638910) is a small café and delicatessen open daily. There are also two pubs and a restaurant by the green. A couple of times I have enjoyed meals at The Fox Inn (☎ 01689 852053; open from noon daily). Most conveniently, Bromley-bound buses stop immediately outside.

goes on to skirt the private Holwood Estate, now made up of luxury apartments as well as the original mansion, to the so-called 'Wilberforce Oak' and continues to **Holwood Farm** (☎ 01689 638381; open 09.00–17.00 Tue–Sat, 10.00–16.00 Sun), a splendid barn conversion with a delicatessen and coffee shop specialising in quality produce.

The 146 has strong scientific and political credentials. William Wilberforce discussed the abolition of the slave trade with Prime Minister William Pitt the Younger under the **Wilberforce Oak** near Pitt's home on the Holwood Estate. Today an old stone bench with an inscription from Wilberforce's diary marks the spot, although precious little remains of the actual oak tree due to the ravages of the weather on this exposed location.

If you walked from Keston, you can reboard the 146 at Holwood Farm. This is lovely rolling countryside, wooded for some distance. Once out of Cuckoo Wood, flints can be seen in the soil.

THE DARWIN CONNECTION

Charles Darwin, author of *On the Origin of Species*, lived at **Down House** (no letter 'e') from 1842 to 1882. This followed a five-year world voyage as a young man aboard HMS *Beagle*, most famously including the Galapagos Islands. When London became

Downe village sign (© Brian Grigg)

a bit too much for Darwin, especially given health considerations, he chose Downe because of its quiet and rural nature – yet within reach of the capital. This description is still largely true although today occasionally light aircraft from nearby **Biggin Hill** can be heard.

Darwin was able to do his work in peace at Down House, observing flora and fauna and conducting many experiments while he and his wife Emma brought up their children in the area's idyllic surroundings. Nowadays those parts of Hayes and Keston commons which Darwin explored are designated 'Sites of Special Scientific Interest'.

Many local buildings along the bus route are constructed with flint stones, for example the churches at Keston and Downe and Downe Village Hall. In the centre of Downe, a tree with a circular wooden seat forms the turning circle for the 146. St Mary's Church, by the bus stop, has evidence of the Darwins: Emma and some of the couple's children are buried here. A sundial on the tower was placed here in memory of Charles, who is buried in Westminster Abbey.

Right in the centre of the village are two pubs, The Queen's Head with its Darwin Bar (☎ 01689 852145) and the George & Dragon (☎ 01689 889030). The latter has a nice old photograph of a double-decker bus on the Downe route. Just before its final stop, the 146 passes the **Tea Shop at Downe** (☎ 07787 423558; open 10.00–16.00 Wed–Sun), which is well worth a visit – look out for the day's special sandwiches.

A little way from the village centre – and reached by the R8 bus from the middle of Downe or on foot, taking care on the narrow road – Down House is open to the public by English Heritage (☎ 01689 859119; www.english-heritage.org.uk/darwin). It makes for a rewarding visit, showing an insight into family and working life in authentic room settings.

I think readers will enjoy the 146. It is a London bus route with a difference. Return buses from Downe usually have some local passengers on board who are, no doubt, very pleased to have retained a regular bus service for their special village. ∎

ABOUT THE AUTHOR | **BRIAN GRIGG** has had a lifelong interest in public transport. He travels at home and abroad by bus, coach and train.

Martin Stribblehill

Kingston upon Thames

Service no. 465 | Journey time 55–75mins.

OS Landranger 176, 187. Every 30mins Mon–Sat, hourly on Sun.
Operator: Quality Line.

Dorking

I moved to Surbiton over ten years ago. Among the red buses I used when too lazy to cycle to and from the station was a clear interloper. Much of its journey is in leafy Surrey, yet the entire journey is still covered by a London Travelcard. Since then I've used the 465 bus for various journeys: getting home from work, shopping in Kingston, weekend jaunts to Box Hill and excursions to the pubs of Leatherhead and Mickleham.

THE KING'S TOWN AND THE QUEEN OF THE SUBURBS

Board the bus in Eden Street in **Kingston** town centre. As the bus navigates the streets, you'll catch a glimpse of the busy marketplace, the old town hall and the 1930s-style Guildhall. In front of the last-named is the Coronation Stone. The story is that seven Anglo-Saxon kings were crowned on it. You can see why later kings of England preferred a more comfortable coronation throne at Westminster instead.

The view quickly opens out, with the river on our right. This is the last run for the clean, flowing Thames before it hits the mud, salt and worse of the upcoming tide. On a summer's day it is full of boats – from kayaks to fake paddle steamers – on their way to

Hampton Court Palace. This is where Jerome K Jerome's three men in a boat began their journey with Montmorency the dog in tow. In winter the river is a ribbon of calm belonging only to the swans and the coots.

The river setting is rudely snatched away as the bus turns left and weaves through suburban streets. This is the cue for the gleaming-white centre of **Surbiton** life: the railway station. In the 19th century, the people of Kingston didn't want the noise and fuss of the London to Southampton railway line going through their town. Instead, a village to the south found itself a short train ride from central London. The imposing Art Deco station building reflects its importance to the thousands who sigh and shuffle on the Waterloo-bound platform each day.

The bus ducks under the railway to emerge in leafy **Southborough**. A fellow passenger once saw me envying the grander houses, and assured me that while they look good, the roofs leak. You can peer up the side roads and speculate on which one might have been home to the '70s sitcom *The Good Life*. But you'll not spot it – the series was filmed in northwest London, though Surbiton got the credit. Accelerating south after crossing

TAKING A HORSE TO WATER

There are a number of good pubs, cafés and restaurants on the route. My favourite is the Running Horse (☎ 01372 372081; open 11.30–23.00 Mon–Sat, noon–22.30 Sun) by the river in Leatherhead. This is a traditional English pub with a low-ceiling, excellent beers and locally sourced food. Inside are pictures showing the history of the area, and an unexpected display of spigots. For something more gourmet, go plural. The Running Horses (☎ 01372 372279; open noon–23.00 Mon–Sat, noon–22.30 Sun) props up the bus stop opposite the church in Mickleham. The food in its restaurant is excellent (open daily from noon for lunch and supper, but closed between 15.00 and 18.00 Mon–Fri; no food Sun evening but served all day Sat).

the A3, you may spot the blue plaque on the left marking where Enid Blyton lived as a governess in the 1920s.

Leaving suburbia

There is still plenty of suburbia before the edge of London's sprawl. The first clue to its end is the sight of wooded **Winey Hill** beyond the playing fields on the right, contrasting with the industrial estate on the left. After Malden Rushett, the bus then climbs and passes outside the control of the Mayor of London, but not of the Lord Mayor. The lightly wooded nature reserve on the left is Ashtead Common, owned by the Corporation of London.

You know you have properly escaped London's clutches as the bus crosses the eight lanes of the M25. The route into **Leatherhead** town centre isn't particularly picturesque, but after the crooked Running Horse pub (see box, page 30), look right as you cross the River Mole to see the viaduct that carries the Leatherhead to Dorking railway. The company would have liked to keep it functional, but the landowner insisted on something more ornate.

Now the landscape becomes more three-dimensional and our bus climbs a steep hill. On the left is our first view of the **North Downs**, with their wooded heights overlooking the neat fields of Bocketts Farm Park. Generously, the bus almost turns back on itself, giving passengers a second look.

Between the Downs

South from Leatherhead, we follow the ancient Mole Gap through the Downs, with our bus happily eschewing the main A24 and sticking to the old road through **Mickleham**. This narrow country

Kingston

12 mins

Surbiton N

16 mins

Chessington

12 mins

Leatherhead

9 mins

Mickleham

12 mins

Dorking

IN AMONG THE DOWNS

Box Hill has many walks popular with Londoners escaping the city. Alongside the zigzag road is the straighter military road to the top. Or from the bus stop at Burford Bridge there is a good path up the hill, climbing steeply alongside the escarpment's edge with excellent views south. From the North Downs Way bus stop, a path goes down to a set of stepping stones across the Mole, part of the Pilgrim's Way from Winchester to Canterbury. A final suggestion is a walk among the grapes of Denbies Vineyard, perhaps followed by a glass of something local.

lane is a happy contrast to the earlier suburbs. On the right you get a quick peek at the red-brick mock-Tudor and Gothic grandeur of Box Hill School. Then the white half-timbered sprawl of the village centre. Opposite is its Norman church. Some churches stand out because of their soaring spires, but St Michael's takes a different approach, squatting beneath the trees. The wooden grave markings are a local tradition in an area lacking suitable stone.

The next stop is at the bottom of the zigzag route up **Box Hill**. This road is Surrey's Alpe d'Huez, a particular favourite with cyclists. It was so popular with the organisers of the 2012 Olympic road race that riders had to haul themselves up it nine times. It is also a favourite for motorcyclists, and you often see rows of gleaming machines outside Ryka's Café at the following stop.

The bus rejoins the main road. The trees fall away and no longer hide the hills rising on either side. To the right are the regular rows of Denbies Vineyard above **Dorking**. As the bus enters the town, it has a final treat. A detour through the station car park means it turns for one last look north, where there is a panoramic view of Box Hill's steep southern slopes. This is a far cry from the busy streets of Kingston upon Thames. ∎

ABOUT THE
AUTHOR | **MARTIN STRIBBLEHILL** is a civil servant. He lives in Chessington.

A SUSSEX CENTURION

Brian Grigg

Horsham

Service no. 100 | Journey time 2hrs 20mins.

OS Landranger 187, 197, 198. Hourly Mon–Sat, no Sun service.
Operator: Compass Travel.

Burgess Hill

Sussex has its fair share of memorable bus journeys. The one-day Discovery ticket is a fine way of exploring routes over and around the South Downs area and beyond, being valid on the 100 and most other local bus services. But as author Tim Locke reminds us in his book *Slow Sussex* (also published by Bradt Travel Guides), there is more to the county than chalk. The bus route from Horsham to Burgess Hill captures a great variety of Sussex landscapes, traversing a segment of the Weald that boasts sandy ridges, clay vales and culminating in some very fine views of the South Downs. In the latter part of the journey, the route dances along the northern border of England's newest national park.

You really have to be a bus enthusiast to ride the number 100 without a break of journey from end to end.

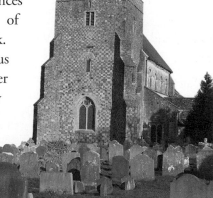

Steyning — definitely a worthy stopping-off point on this Wealden bus journey (© Brian Grigg)

It takes over two hours, and there are certainly quicker ways of getting from Horsham to Burgess Hill. The two communities are just 15 miles apart, but Compass Travel's service 100 contrives to cover over thrice that distance. The entire route is a charming ride through the Weald, but the real highlight is the section from Pulborough to Henfield where the South Downs are never far away to the south.

That part of the journey takes just under an hour, and with buses running along the route generally every 60 minutes, there is every opportunity to just hop off to take the pulse of some of the small Sussex villages along the route.

Take time before setting off to explore Horsham. The Causeway is the place to start. With its fabulous mix of traditional Wealden building styles, it is no surprise that this road is the most photographed in town. With its handsome lime trees, it is a lovely place to wander. On the Causeway you'll also find the town's visitor information centre and the free Horsham Museum and Art Gallery (☎ 01403 254959; open 10.00–17.00 Mon–Sat).

CENTURIONS OF YESTERYEAR

Our bus ride starts at **Horsham**'s small modern bus station but also stops in cobbled Carfax by the bandstand as well as opposite the railway station. The single-decker bus slips out of town, crossing

---

ARUN VALLEY WALKS

Visits to Pulborough Brooks or Parham House can be combined with an Arun Valley walk, perhaps venturing as far as the village of Amberley with its Museum and Heritage Centre (☎ 01798 831370; open mid-Mar until Nov 10.00–17.00 Wed–Sun, daily in school holidays). The museum is dedicated to the industrial heritage of the southeast, and its many reassembled buildings include a vintage Southdown Bus Garage. Walkers can return by train from Amberley to Pulborough to join the 100 again.

the River Arun and turning left onto the A29 at **Slinfold**. No ordinary highway this one, for it traces the line of a Roman road called Stane Street. So the 100 bus follows the ghosts of centurions of old, rumbling south through pleasant

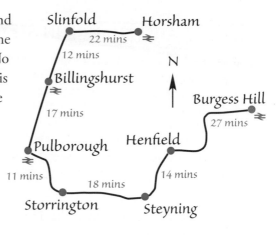

Sussex countryside. Indeed, we follow Stane Street all the way to Pulborough. The only place of any significance along the way is **Billingshurst** where, on occasion, the bus may have to pause at the recently modernised level crossing to let a train pass.

Pulborough is a pleasant little town on the north bank of the River Arun. The bus gives a chance to see the town from all angles, running along the high street in both directions. We pause for a few minutes at the railway station, before heading east out of town. There are fine views of the River Arun, in rainy times often topping its banks and flooding the surrounding water meadows.

Now comes the finest stretch of the route, where it makes sense to grab a seat on the right side of the bus. We pass **RSPB Pulborough Brooks**, which offers some lovely walks through woods and down towards the Arun, with the possibility in spring and summer of hearing and even seeing the reclusive but vocal nightingale. Further along, shortly before Storrington, is the Elizabethan **Parham House** with its deer park and gardens (☎ 01903 742021; see www.parhaminsussex.co.uk for opening times & admission fees). There are request bus stops near both these attractions.

Now heading more decisively east, we go through the heart of **Storrington**, then hug the foot of the Downs. Trees surround the Iron Age fort at Chanctonbury Ring high on the ridge above.

There is evidence of the Romans having been here too and maybe more centurions. But beware: it is a formidably steep hike up to Chanctonbury from the bus stop.

The next place of any size is handsome **Steyning** (pronounced Stenning), surely the jewel in the crown of this route. This lovely old borough, so full of Saxon and Norman history, was once an inland port on the River Adur. The 100 stops by the clock tower. Walking along High Street, turning into Church Street, there are fine timbered flint-and-brick buildings. The road continues past the 12th-century St Andrew's Church, the library and museum leading to the River Adur and the Downs Link path.

From Steyning the 100 still has some way to go. The adjoining villages of **Bramber** and **Upper Beeding** are divided by an old brick and stone bridge over the River Adur. The ruins of the Norman Bramber Castle, seen from the bus, are looked after by English Heritage. Timber-framed St Mary's House (☎ 01903 816205) dating from the 15th century is open to the public.

Then we detour to serve **Henfield**, before returning to the shadow of the Downs. There are fine views south to Devil's Dyke. But that's the last we see of the hills as the bus heads north through Hickstead, before ending its journey in **Burgess Hill**. It is a town that sprawls. The best that can be said of it is that it has a great range of onward bus and rail connections. ■

ABOUT THE AUTHOR | Brian Grigg has had a lifelong interest in public transport. He travels at home and abroad by bus, coach and train.

THREE COUNTIES
RIVER RUN

Kate Booth

⑧ High Wycombe 🚌

Service no. 800 | Journey time 1hr 23mins.

OS Landranger 175. Daily, once an hour (no evening services).
Operator: Arriva.

Reading ◀

Remember mild-mannered Mole? His spring-cleaning done, he ventured to the bank of the river. Kenneth Grahame captured the moment in *The Wind in the Willows*: 'He sat on the bank, while the river still chattered on to him, a babbling procession of the best stories in the world.' If like Mole you love the river, then this route that takes in part of three counties – Buckinghamshire, Oxfordshire and Berkshire – is most surely for you. Along the way, we encounter some delicious scenery as the River Thames nudges against the Chiltern Hills. With a high frequency of buses, there is ample opportunity to hop off along the way. The riverside towns of Marlow and Henley-on-Thames both warrant a stop.

We leave from the clean and modern bus station in **High Wycombe** and almost immediately the bus staggers uphill to the highest point of the journey where the Chilterns spread out before us. Look back for views of urban sprawl in the valley of the River Wye, and ahead for a glorious swathe of Chiltern countryside. The Arriva 800 bus dips down towards **Marlow**. Keep an eye open for red kites with their distinctive forked tail and 6ft wingspan.

Marlow is an amiable small town that attracts a moneyed crowd. No surprise perhaps that the first gastropub to secure two Michelin stars is here: the Hand & Flowers on West Street

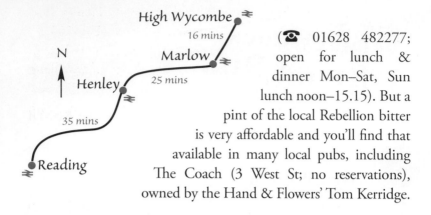

(☎ 01628 482277; open for lunch & dinner Mon–Sat, Sun lunch noon–15.15). But a pint of the local Rebellion bitter is very affordable and you'll find that available in many local pubs, including The Coach (3 West St; no reservations), owned by the Hand & Flowers' Tom Kerridge.

Of boats and toads

If you do stop, take a peek at Marlow's famous bridge over the Thames. Like Henley, a shade upstream, the river here is prime water for rowing, and the two towns vie for superiority. Both have produced Olympic oarsmen. Marlow is especially proud of Sir Steve Redgrave whose statue has pride of place in Higginson Park.

For the best views of the river, sit on the left as the bus heads west from Marlow. We pause by the entrance to Danesfield House Hotel, and a handful of regulars disembark. They look as though they are staff at the hotel. I guess that the guests probably don't arrive with Arriva. Indeed, I wonder if those guests even know what a bus is. As we set off again, don't miss a fine example of a wattle fence on the left, complete with a stylish thatched top.

When we arrive in **Mill End** and get the first proper view of the river, some might wish to break their journey with a walk in the picturesque Hambleden Valley. This gentle chalk vale tracks north from the river. It is much used in film and television productions.

Just beyond Mill End, you see an extraordinary road sign, one that advises of an upcoming toad crossing. Springtime is the season for the toad patrol. A toad tunnel under the road was designed to smooth the route of toads from woods on one side to their spawning ponds on the other. The tunnel has proved not to be to their liking, so a few weeks each spring volunteers escort toads across the road here. Over the last five years the Henley Toad Patrol has helped tens of thousands of toads across the A4155.

The part of the run after the toad crossing is at its best in springtime when there are bluebells in abundance in woodland on the right-hand side. On the left there are fine views of **Fawley Court**, a country house designed by Christopher Wren with gardens landscaped by Capability Brown.

Henley-on-Thames

Once in **Henley**, the bus loops round the one-way system through town ending up by the side of the river – it's helpful if the traffic lights are red as it gives more time to absorb the views. Across the river is the Leander Club whose members have won more Olympic rowing medals than any other single-sport club in the world. It is Britain's oldest rowing club, founded in London in 1818 and then moving to Henley in 1896. Those who like to mock the Leander crowd are quick to note that the club's emblem is a hippo – the only other aquatic creature apart from Leander members to keep its nose permanently in the air!

Henley's famous regatta takes place over a five-day period in early July followed immediately by an arts festival, and in

EATERIES ALONG THE ROUTE

In Henley, the River and Rowing Museum has an excellent café serving a selection of homemade dishes throughout the day. For a quirky and intimate café, you can't do better than relax at Hot Gossip with the newspapers (7 Friday St, Henley; ☎ 01491 414070; open 08.30–17.30 Mon–Fri, 09.00–17.30 Sat, 10.30–16.00 Sun) with its retro 1960s atmosphere, outdoor and indoor seating and a cosy log fire in the winter. In Marlow, Burgers is a must (The Causeway; ☎ 01628 483389; open 08.30–17.30 Mon–Sat, 11.00–17.00 Sun). This artisan bakery has been family run for three generations since 1942. Everything is freshly baked on the premises and you might as well abandon the diet for the day.

A HENLEY HIGHLIGHT

The River and Rowing Museum in Henley is certainly worth a visit (Mill Meadows; ☎ 01491 415600; www.rrm.co.uk; open 10.00–17.00 daily). The building itself has won awards and the museum has a constantly changing calendar of exhibitions, adult lectures, workshops and children's events. The three galleries are dedicated to rowing, rivers and the history of Henley. Visit the magical 'Wind in the Willows' exhibition (more toads of course), which brings to life the much-loved story with 3D models, lighting and music.

September there is a hugely popular literary festival with many daytime events. For those wishing to emulate the regatta's rowers, boats can be hired from Hobbs of Henley (☎ 01491 572035).

The current bridge was built from 1776 to 1786 by Thomas Hayward who died before it was finished, supposedly having caught a cold after giving up his place inside a coach to a lady.

Leaving Henley, the 800 bus gives us a good view of Victorian terraced cottages before heading towards **Shiplake** which featured in Jerome K Jerome's *Three Men in a Boat*. The river disappears from view, but the ride through the village is attractive and continues so as the bus takes us through Binfield Heath, Playhatch and on to Caversham where we cross over the river into Berkshire. It's a short ride over the bridge to journey's end at Friar Street in **Reading**. This is a town which has happily rediscovered its river in recent years and some imaginative urban renewal has opened up walks along the canalised River Kennet which joins the Thames here. Reading deserves a better press than it often gets. If you are inclined to linger, Reading Museum on Blagrave Street is a first-class diversion, housing a stunning Victorian replica of the Bayeux Tapestry (☎ 0118 937 3400; open 10.00–16.00 Tue–Sat). ∎

ABOUT THE AUTHOR

KATE BOOTH has spent almost all her life in the Chilterns. Now semi-retired, she is equally happy continuing to explore the area on foot or by bus.

There was a moment in the opening ceremony of the 2012 Summer Olympics that nicely recalled the history of bus travel in and around London. Isambard Kingdom Brunel, played by the actor Kenneth Branagh, arrived in the stadium on a horse-drawn bus. The vehicle was in the distinctive green livery of the London General Omnibus Company (LGOC).

For those who know their buses, the symbolism was immense. Here was a London bus, presented in a scene rich in nostalgia, but the colour of the bus was a reminder of London's links with its hinterland. As Brian Grigg reminds us in Journey 5 in this book, the colour coding of London buses was for decades very clear. Buses that stayed in the city were red; those that ventured into the hinterland were green. Brunel arrived in a green bus.

LGOC had its fair share of 'red' routes, but the company was a pioneer in developing 'green' services that crossed the London boundary. The last horse-drawn LGOC vehicle ran in 1911. A brand-new fleet of LGOC motor buses were transforming bus travel. In summer 1911, LGOC launched a monthly guide highlighting the many places that could now so easily be reached by bus.

The following year, LGOC offered its first regular route into the Home Counties, providing a Sunday service to Windsor Castle. Other routes for excursionists quickly followed, and by September 1912, Londoners could take the bus out to St Albans on any day of the week. If there was a golden age of buses in London and the Home Counties, it was in these couple of years just prior to World War I. New routes were being launched every week.

These early LGOC ventures beyond the boundaries of London were the precursors of the Green Line network launched by LGOC in 1930, taking advantage of a period in which new services in the region could be introduced without prior permission from the Traffic Commissioners. Green Line developed into a powerful transport brand. There were some extraordinary routes that went right across London, eg: from Hitchin to Reigate and Harpenden to Great Bookham. They have long gone, but the name Green Line lives on in about a dozen bus services, mainly to the north and west of London. Happily, one of those routes is the 702 which still ferries Londoners every day of the week out to Windsor. ∎

SOUTHERN ENGLAND

The real joy in exploring southern England by bus lies not merely in unusually long journeys but in less demanding explorations. In this chapter, we present five varied routes, all taking less than two hours. At the southern extremity we include the Isle of Wight, a scenic microcosm remarkably well served by buses, with local operator Southern Vectis, which takes the second half of its name from the Roman word for the island. Wight's capital, Newport, is the main bus hub, with services fanning out in all directions. Our featured Journey 10 to Totland can easily be extended by taking a northern route back to Newport via Yarmouth, or by starting from Sandown, on the east side of the island, and heading down to Ventnor and up to Newport, or by taking the bike-carrying Island Coaster buses along the southern coast and combining bus travel with a cycle ride.

By sharp contrast, over on the mainland, the New Forest – Britain's smallest national park – seems like a different world. The views on Journey 9 morph abruptly from the edgelands of Southampton into the primeval, pony-nibbled heathy expanses and rolling forests that in some respects haven't changed very much since William the Conqueror established it as a royal hunting forest back in 1079. The far side of the New Forest almost touches eastern Dorset, where the landscape again reveals an extraordinary change of mood. Here, the Purbeck Breezer (Journey 13) ventures through Bournemouth's supremely affluent suburbs to use the bus-carrying ferry – the only one featured in this book – across Poole Harbour to a wild-looking heath landscape evocative of Thomas Hardy's writings, and down to the seaside resort of Swanage, in the Isle of Purbeck's southeastern corner. One of many reasons to linger there is to take a journey on a steam train on the Swanage

Railway to Corfe Castle, where the jagged pinnacle of the castle ruin towers over the eponymous grey-stone village.

Further north, Stagecoach services take us into the chalk downlands of Hampshire and Berkshire on Journey 12 and past some of the great archaeological riches of the Wiltshire Downs in Journey 11. There's abundant scope for prolonging these excursions and taking a walk on the way: a saunter along the Kennet and Avon Canal from Devizes past an astonishing series of locks that was one of the wonders of the canal era; a ramble along the chalk escarpment to the grisly gibbet near the summit of Inkpen Hill; and an exploration from Avebury taking in the stone circle, East Kennet Long Barrow, and Silbury Hill.

Remember that, even without a bus pass, travel by local buses in this region can be cheap. Last year we rode local buses from Southampton to Oxford via Salisbury and Hungerford using a Wiltshire Day Rover ticket, paying less than a tenner each for the entire journey. Like so many rover tickets in England that take their name from a county, the Wiltshire Day Rover is in fact valid on many bus routes that extend well beyond the county boundaries. ∎

Journey 13 is the only route to feature a bus-carrying ferry – the Purbeck Breezer (© Angela Simpkins)

Into the Magic Forest:
Pony Country

Jane Westlake

9 Southampton

Service no. 6 | Journey time 70mins.

OS Landranger 196. Hourly Mon–Sat daytime, 5 journeys Sun.
Operator: Bluestar.

Lymington

On this bus trip it is the ponies that have the right of way. The West Quay shopping mall in **Southampton**, often with a visiting ocean liner as backdrop, is our starting point. Along the way, we delve right into the heart of the New Forest, once a royal hunting ground where commoners still exercise their rights and the animals roam free. Wonderland continues with the opportunity to see the original Alice's grave and once out of the woods we're deposited in the yachting haven and former smugglers' port of Lymington.

The good-natured queue at the bus stop just outside **West Quay** is growing steadily as it's a Saturday – market day in Lymington. If you are here at the right time you may hear a hymn by local lad Isaac Watts sounded by the Southampton Civic Centre clock. It is the old favourite 'Oh God, Our Help in Ages Past'. However, there's no need for divine intervention as Bluestar has laid on one of their finest blue double-decker buses. So today there's room for everyone and with a flurry of shopping trolleys we clamber aboard.

Once we're clear of the scruffier part of the city, where I used to live as a student in the 1970s, a glance to the left reminds me that Southampton is still a major passenger and cargo port.

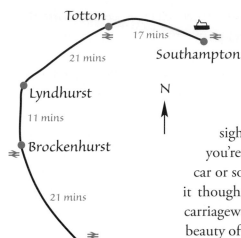

Totton

17 mins

21 mins

Southampton

Lyndhurst

N

11 mins

Brockenhurst

21 mins

Lymington

Cranes stoop over the vast Western Docks as we glide past the container port towards the Millbrook Industrial Estate. The latter isn't a sight to lift the spirits unless you're in the market for a new car or some kitchen tiles. Stick with it though as the tedium of the dual carriageway and flyover make the beauty of the New Forest all the more magical when it appears.

A bridge over the River Test leads us to **Totton** where we exchange a few passengers opposite the church of St Theresa. The soft yellow building with a statue of the 'Little Flower' seems out of place next to a Chinese take-away.

INTO THE WOODS

The bus is now weaving on and off the A35, here and there serving the edgeland sprawl of estates of bungalows. This land of one-storey dwellers gives way to big trees, long drives and smart homes hidden away in woodland glades.

Bob, a fellow passenger who makes full use of his bus pass, is on his way to Lyndhurst to top up his stamp collection. He tells me about his old job delivering furniture, before the days of mobile phones. 'Addresses in the New Forest were often a challenge,' he recalls. 'We couldn't find them. It was just a house name, no street or number.'

We've passed The New Forest pub at **Ashurst** and woods are now hugging either side of the forest road. We're looking out for ponies and deer but instead we spot walkers appearing and disappearing like a magic trick among the oak and beech glades. A group of them hail the bus and scramble upstairs. The woodland then morphs into heathland, which changes colour with the seasons: vibrant yellow gorse, purple heather or burnt orange as the bracken dies down.

Bob is on his feet as we pass on the left a **Lyndhurst** landmark, Bolton's Bench, a handsome yew-topped hill. Hop off at the Lyndhurst Park Hotel (now closed for business) bus stop if you want to visit the village. Don't miss St Michael and All Angels, the village's Victorian red-brick church. It has a large painted fresco recalling the parable of the wise and foolish virgins by Frederic Leighton and glorious stained-glass windows. Behind the church you'll find the grave of Alice Liddell who, as a little girl, was the inspiration for Alice in *Alice's Adventures in Wonderland*. She grew up to be Mrs Reginald Hargreaves and that's the name on her grave.

If you fancy a tea or coffee while curled up on a big settee, opposite St Michael's is Crown Manor House Hotel (☎ 023 80282922) where non-residents are welcome in both the lounge and the bright restaurant. The Greenwood Tree café and restaurant down the other end of High Street (65 High St; ☎ 023 80282463; open 08.30–17.00 daily) is a good place to refuel whether you want a homemade main course, cream tea or their speciality, waffles, before you're back on the number 6, heading south towards the coast.

This next stretch of the route is one of my favourites with the Lymington River flowing nearby. We pass the Balmer Lawn Hotel which was used during World War I as an army hospital

NEW FOREST INFORMATION

Whatever information you seek the New Forest Visitor Information Centre and Museum with its well-informed staff is a good place to start (Main car park, Lyndhurst; ☎ 023 80282269; www.thenewforest. co.uk; open Nov–Easter 10.00–16.00 daily, Easter–Oct 10.00–17.00 daily). They have books, maps and walking guides for sale. There is also information on horseriding and cycling and there's a gift shop.

VERDERERS AND AGISTERS

There are ten Verderers who regulate and protect the commoners' interests and preserve the natural beauty of the New Forest. They appoint five Agisters who help with the management of the commoners' livestock in the Forest. The Verderers sit in open court on the third Wednesday of each month at the Verderers' Hall in Lyndhurst. The hall isn't open to the public except on court days, but the Clerk to the Verderers (☎ 023 80282052) is often willing to give visitors access on weekdays if advised in advance. Look out for the Rufus's Stirrup, used to determine whether a dog would be a threat to royal hunting. If a dog couldn't pass through the stirrup the animal's toes were cut off, or the owner paid a fine.

for wounded Indian and New Zealand troops. As we draw into **Brockenhurst**, we see a pony trimming the grass around the war memorial.

We pass, and some may be tempted to stop, at a pub with a story. The Snakecatcher at Lyndhurst Road in Brockenhurst (☎ 01590 622348; open noon–21.00 daily) was originally called the Railway Inn, but was renamed after Harry 'Brusher' Mills who used to drink here. He lived in a charcoal burner's hut in the New Forest and made his living from catching snakes, some of which he was said to have sold to London Zoo.

We're now driving slowly across heathland under the watchful gaze of the ponies. They're mooching about in convivial groups and although they appear to be wild they are owned by commoners exercising their rights to use the common pasture. Another common right, called Mast, lets the owners turn out their pigs to gobble up acorns and beechmasts. There are about 700 commoners; the rights attach to the land they own or rent.

A mother and foal meander across the road and our driver brakes gently. A child who's been kicking the back of my seat is thankfully transfixed by them. The deer are more skittish and tend to occupy quieter parts of the forest; sadly there's a problem throughout the forest with drivers who hit animals but fail to stop. William the Conqueror designated the New Forest a royal hunting ground more than 900 years ago. It's now a national park but still maintains its tradition of Verderers and Agisters (see box opposite).

There's a small detour for the modern Lymington New Forest Hospital which is set next to a retail park. It's a shock to the senses after the soft lawns, forest glades and heath. Ultimately, though, it is a reminder of the appeal of the New Forest. It is an area of England which has not kept modernity at a distance. It's there but in its place. So there's still space for ponies.

Georgian delight

Daniel Defoe described the main commercial activities of the people of **Lymington** as 'smuggling and rogueing'. There's little evidence of this as we pass St Thomas's Church with its elegant cupola. The bus is making slow progress and restless passengers, keen to enjoy the market, descend before the final stop. The wares reflect local concerns and pastimes: fishing rods and waders, golf clubs, local fish, meat and cheese, beautiful handmade crafts and of course – there being lots of dog owners – items for their pets to chew, eat or sleep in.

The last stragglers and I thank the driver as we descend at the final stop on the high street. Lymington is ever pleasant but positively bustles on market days. Much of the architecture is Georgian. The high street slopes down to a cobbled area, Quay Hill, where many shops have bow-fronted windows. Just beyond is Town Quay by the Lymington River which is still used as a base by commercial fishing boats and the town's popular sailing centre. ■

ABOUT THE AUTHOR | **JANE WESTLAKE** is a former BBC producer. She used to travel this route regularly with her mother who, like Jane, enjoys a good piece of cake.

Beautifully Bleak: Visiting West Wight

Emily Bullock

10 Newport 🚐

Service no. 12 | Journey time 48mins.

OS Landranger 196. 5 journeys daily Mon–Fri, 4 on Sat.
Operator: Southern Vectis.

Totland

Tourists are attracted by the Isle of Wight's sandy beaches, local ice cream, adventure parks, and watersport activities. But my quest is rather different. Southern Vectis's bus number 12 goes to West Wight – and that's the part of the island where I was born. Ignoring warnings about the possible dangers that attend trips down memory lane, I found myself queuing for the bus and realised how times have changed. Nowadays, you have to get there early if you want a front window seat on the top deck.

This is a journey that recalls my childhood, holidays and family visits. We would get the bus from the brick-and-stone sprawl of Newport; head out along the salty rush of the Military Road to the Needles at the westernmost extremity of Wight. It has an end-of-the-world feel with its lighthouse and white rocks, threading sea and sky together.

I have moved away, grown older, but the island hasn't changed. It is still populated with tea rooms and ice-cream vans. Taking my seat on the top deck, I imagine I'm wearing long socks and hand-knitted cardigans again, mouth itching for a lick of sugary rock. The Isle of Wight is often both praised and dismissed for being wedged in the 1950s – austerity Britain and technicolour hopes for the future. So this is the perfect moment to revisit my childhood.

But nostalgia comes at a price. Almost a fiver for a 48-minute journey.

Island roads are different. Street signs remind drivers of this but it isn't until the bus starts that I remember it really is so. The driver isn't off-roading or aiming for cars on the other side – he is avoiding pot-holes. Perhaps the ride is rougher upstairs, but sit downstairs and the only view would be high hedges and cycle helmets. The bus leaves **Newport** bus station, leading me through the town like a giant in a miniature village. The top floor of the buildings have evidently not changed over the centuries while the high street shop façades reinvent themselves every season.

My first disappointment comes as the bus climbs west towards Carisbrooke and I realise none of the schools I attended still exist. But not everything has changed. We pass Spring Lane which leads to **Carisbrooke Castle** (open 10.00–16.00 daily). The ford on that lane was the perfect place to float in an upside-down umbrella!

Cutting through the Downs

It is a cold day but sun fills the upper deck, the heating is pumping, and coats are coming off. This is the scenery I remember: patchwork downland on all sides as the bus travels the Bowcombe Road between Carisbrooke and Shorwell. There are aerodynamic displays by low-flying seagulls as we glide past working farms and forgotten farms. Although not completely forgotten, the route passes through many small villages ending in 'stone' – a suffix declaring it is a farmstead. Maps don't forget.

The winter scene outside the window has the faded feel of a bleached-out photograph. Perhaps the memories are a little older than I would want to admit. Can I still claim to be a true islander if I haven't lived here for over 18 years? No-one knows me on the bus, but a few faces have nodded recognition to each other. Have I finally become a grockle (an island word for a holidaymaker)?

Cheverton Farm comes up on the left, open for lambing days and cycle events. I am taken back to summer holidays: driving along these roads, the bus smelling of wild garlic as it brushed past the hedgerows. Going under the wooden footbridge at Shorwell Shute feels like entering a fairytale land: thatched cottages and stone walls mark the way. The bus also stops for its first walkers, carrying wooden sticks as they come down from Brighstone Forest.

On the horizon above the village of **Shorwell** the coast emerges, reminding me this is an island. Sea running into sky until it is hard to tell which is which. A buzzard watches from a tree, then flies off towards Limerstone; the bus follows.

To the seaside

Brighstone with the old St Mary's Church, village shop, local museum and small cottages, conforms to most people's imaginary village of the 1950s: the shop has goods stacked outside in baskets and an array of primrose plants for sale – a nice hint that spring is on the way. I want to stop just to touch such brightness. A chalkboard lists island produce for sale: honey, milk, cheese, garlic. Plenty to fill a lunch box before setting off along a footpath; with names like Hunny Hill or Strawberry Lane.

We pass **Mottistone Gardens** (☎ 01983 741302), a place for floral magic with herbaceous borders and hidden pathways. The bus reaches **Hulverstone** and I get my first glimpse of the white cliffs of Tennyson Down. This is a journey full of literary connections. Moments later we pause at Brook, one-time home to J B Priestley: novelist, playwright and broadcaster.

The bus turns right at Brook Chine onto Military Road. **The Chine** itself is worth a visit, with the chance to see surfers, dogs chasing big waves and children hunting in rock pools. I remember the smell of coconut from summer days here, rising off the sun worshippers stretched out on the beach.

The Military Road sounds like a harsh place to be; the twisted trees whisper of icy winds and thundering rain. The bus slows as it climbs the downs; rabbit warrens have eaten into the sandy earth. But as it reaches the top, Freshwater appears, rolling green down to the pebble beach. The sun comes out and sparks across

Lighthouse at the Needles (© Simon Greig/DT)

the sea on my left. This road and these rocks will work their way out there too; there is only so long the Isle of Wight can hold onto this route. Frequent landslips can result in road closures. When we were young, my sister and I thought lying in the middle of the road (when it was closed, of course) was the funniest thing to do, made even more ridiculous by sharing a box of After Eights at the same time. So if the bus is diverted you might like to try this out; I can recommend it. But for now, Military Road spreads itself out along hills and knolls.

Standing sentinel above **Freshwater Bay** is Tennyson's Monument, a stone cross pointing up through the blue. The grockles decant, evidently keen to see the coloured sands and rocket launch test site at the **Needles**. Our bus continues to Freshwater town centre, with its tiny parade of shops, such as Val's Collectables and the RocknRose tattoo parlour.

The last stop is **Totland War Memorial** where I am the only person to get off the bus. End of the line. The woman occupying the front seat since Newport is in no mood to give it up and stays on board. The driver wishes me a good day and circles around the memorial heading back to Newport.

As a child, I recall many a bright afternoon on **Totland**'s pebbly beach. I turn right down Madeira Road towards Turf Walk and the promenade. Battered by winter storms and the economic downturn, Totland stands precariously, like the pier that for years has been crumbling into the sea, on the point of being bypassed by tourists. Perhaps this is its aim because the tranquillity of grass and sea and pebbles and nothing else, is peaceful – beautifully bleak indeed. Perhaps I am still an islander because when I close my eyes I smell sea salt on wood. And still I hear the beat of the waves against the struts of Totland Pier. Yes, this really is like coming home. ∎

ABOUT THE AUTHOR | **EMILY BULLOCK** is a writer and university lecturer. You can find out more about her work at www.emilybullock.com.

Moonraker Country

Vicki Messam

Trowbridge

Service no. 49 | Journey time 1hr 25mins to 1hr 30mins.

OS Landranger 173. Runs hourly Mon–Sat, hourly between Devizes & Swindon on Sun.
Operator: Stagecoach.

Swindon

I awoke one night some years ago with one of those Eureka moments. I realised that I really know more about Wiltshire bus timetables than one might sensibly admit to. Indeed, I knew some timetables off by heart. The Wilts & Dorset bus to Salisbury… the APL Travel link to Marlborough… and a dozen more besides. Armed with this deliciously eccentric intelligence, I founded a little group composed of folk who, like myself, love both walking and bus journeys. This Devizes-based group operates under the aegis of the University of the Third Age (U3A).

If you are based in Devizes there is one bus route which is truly a mainstay of everyday life: the Stagecoach 49, often called the Trans-Wilts Express, which links Trowbridge with Swindon via Devizes and Avebury. Don't be misled by the title. This bus journey is hardly an express. Occasional trains will speed you from Trowbridge to Swindon in 40 minutes. The Trans-Wilts Express is a bus option geared to those who like to travel slowly. Our U3A group has explored various sections of the 49 on many occasions, and it has always been memorable, whether we have rain, sun, wind, sleet or snow. Perhaps the secret is that we always walk to a pub for a well-deserved lunch.

DEVIZES

The local council styles Devizes as 'Wiltshire's hidden gem'. Being bang in the middle of the county, and at the intersection of two major routes across Wiltshire, Devizes can hardly claim to be hidden. The name derives from the Latin *castrum ad devisas*, meaning 'the castle at the boundaries', alluding to the place where three manors met. The first castle was built in 1080 and the town's road layout still follows the lines of the inner and outer baileys of that early castle. It is good to find a town that is still shaped by distant history.

The Market Cross bears an interesting inscription commemorating Ruth Pierce, a local resident who, in 1753, claimed that she could not pay her dues for a bag of corn. When accused of not paying she said, 'I am honest, I will drop down dead if I am not.' She promptly dropped down dead with the money in her hand!

Wadworth Brewery, founded in 1875 and brewing 6X beer since 1921, has an excellent visitor centre on New Park Street (open from 09.30 daily). Beer is delivered to local pubs in the town by dray and on most days of the week the brewery's two shire horses, Max and Monty, can be seen pulling their welcome loads around Devizes.

Devizes visitor centre has sadly closed, but information is available at Devizes Library.

East from Trowbridge

Trowbridge is Wiltshire's county town, a little surprisingly perhaps. Sedate Salisbury and upstart Swindon both think they have better claim to the privilege, but Trowbridge it is. The bus starts at the local Tesco supermarket – but don't judge Trowbridge just on that detail. Once famed for its textiles, the town has more to offer. The first 30 minutes of the journey are a pleasant run east with, at several points, good views north over the Kennet and Avon Canal. There are place names that ooze history: Semington Turnpike and Seend Cleeve. Approaching Devizes, Caen Hill Locks are on the left. This spectacular series of locks, over 29 of them packed into a two-mile stretch of canal, was judged an engineering miracle when completed in 1810.

Arriving in **Devizes**, the bus stops in the marketplace – so much better than relegating buses to supermarket car parks. Costa Coffee is popular with passengers waiting for the 49, and is particularly busy on Thursdays, which is market day. 'Here she comes,' says a keen-eyed observer in the window and suddenly all the world is on the move as shoppers gather up their bags and head out to the bus. There is no need to rush; the timetable always allows the bus a four-minute pause in the market square.

A STORY ABOUT SMUGGLERS

The stretch of route from Devizes to Avebury is the finest of the entire journey. Grab one of the front seats on the upper deck if you can. These seats offer the best view of the unfolding journey into the Wiltshire landscape. Sit comfortably, off we go!

Leaving Devizes the bus travels along Long Street, a beautiful conservation area with tall 18th-century town houses. The Wiltshire Museum and the 12th-century St John's Church are on your right. The church retains much of its Norman architecture and was the place where General Hopton and the Royalists took refuge when surrounded by the Roundheads during the English Civil War in 1643. Three medieval churches stand in Devizes, and two of them still show the cannonball holes sustained during the bombardment of the town.

A couple of bends later and to your right is Crammer Pond, about which there is a lovely local tale. Wiltshire folk lived well from smuggling and they would stash their contraband in Crammer Pond for safe keeping. When returning one moonlit

Swindon

21 mins

Wroughton

12 mins

Avebury

5 mins

Beckhampton

19 mins

N

28 mins   Devizes

Trowbridge

SILBURY HILL

To the right, on the journey from Beckhampton to Avebury, is Silbury Hill. Some 120ft high, this Neolithic manmade mound is an utter mystery. Back in the 1980s, it was still permissible for the public to climb to the top, and I shall never forget once doing that, on an especially wild and windy night. The experience was made all the better by the company of a rather good-looking boyfriend. It is estimated that 500 men might have toiled for half-a-dozen years to create this magnificent artificial mountain. And every time I ride by on the bus to Avebury I still ponder why they spent so much time and energy on that project.

night to retrieve their liquor, a policeman passed by and enquired curiously of the smugglers 'What's going on here then?'

'We're fishing for cheese,' said the men, pointing to the moon's reflection in the pond. Evidently bemused but satisfied by the explanation, the policeman continued on his way, reflecting on the utter stupidity of these country locals. Those born and bred in Wiltshire are now often dubbed Moonrakers.

Crossing the Kennet and Avon Canal, the road climbs very slowly up on to the downs. The prominent hill to the left is **Roundway Down**, site of a major Civil War battle. A marked trail (called Battle Walk) tours the hill, with an elevated viewpoint and signs giving vivid, bloody accounts of the battle.

The **Millennium White Horse** is carved into the chalk here. A local farmer gave land to the local council and the horse was carved into the hillside by volunteers to mark the millennium in 2000. It is one of a number of Wiltshire White Horses, most of which face to the left. This one is unusual, for it gallops to the right.

SACRED SPACES

We detour off the main road to serve **Bishops Cannings**, a village with a church that boasts a dramatic slender spire. Now comes four miles of sheer magic: a journey through the rolling Marlborough Downs into a prehistoric landscape. We pass Wansdyke, a strange earthwork defence built in the 5th or 6th century, and Shepherds Shore, the site of an old coaching inn.

You may be able to count the bell barrows that stand on each side of the road. These little round burial mounds, some individual and others in clusters, are easy to make out. They are a reminder that, for the prehistoric residents of Wiltshire, the downs were sacred territory.

To the left on the hilltop is the **Lansdowne Monument**, built by Lord Lansdowne of Bowood House to remind himself that there were not many more miles to go on his homeward journey. At **Beckhampton** the Swindon Road crosses the A4 Bath Road. It is said that Beckhampton gave rich pickings for a notorious gang of highwaymen who robbed the mail coaches. Locals recount that the last highwayman to be hung in Wiltshire met his death in the middle of what is now the A4 roundabout.

From the junction we continue straight on towards Avebury. To the left are Adam and Eve, two distinctive longstones that act as heralds for Avebury Stone Circle, still about a mile away.

Silbury Hill (see box, page 57) stays a companion on our right for a mile as we continue towards Avebury, a village at the heart of a great complex of prehistoric monuments which in 1986 was inscribed (along with Stonehenge, 30 miles away to the south) on the UNESCO World Heritage List. **Avebury Henge** contains three stone circles, one of them the largest in Britain. The bus follows the road that goes through the middle of a stone circle. But seeing the stones is not enough; definitely plan to stop for an hour or two. The village is justifiably popular in the tourist season. But if you can contrive to visit on a quiet midwinter day, you are in for a treat, as it is mysterious Avebury at its best. Take a walk around the stones. Try some stone cuddling if you wish. I've been tree and stone cuddling for years and it is very therapeutic. Many of the individual stones have names and some I feel I know like old friends. You can find out more in the museum (open from 10.00 until dusk daily).

What a bus ride! Where else can you view from a double-decker such great sweeps of chalk downland and such a feast of prehistoric burial sites? And ride through the centre of a World Heritage Site? It is no surprise perhaps that the final leg of the journey on to Swindon is something of an anticlimax. But it is not without interest. There are pleasant north Wiltshire villages with a liberal dose of thatched roofs. Then, as the bus drops down from the hills towards **Swindon**, one of Britain's most important libraries: the archives of London's Science Museum are kept in **Wroughton** and are open to the public. Shortly after Wroughton, the bus crosses the M4, from where it is a few minutes through uninspiring suburbs to the end of the journey. Ride the whole route from Trowbridge to Swindon, and then you can say you have seen the best of Wiltshire – the land of the Moonrakers. ■

ABOUT THE AUTHOR

In 2007 ex-potter **VICKI MESSAM** formed the 'Bus-Pass Walking Group' for Devizes U3A. The twice-weekly walks involve using public transport. The Trans-Wilts Express journey is a firm favourite.

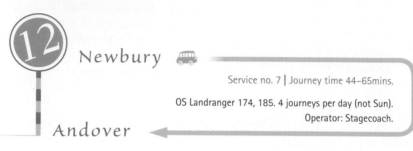

THE SECRET DELIGHTS OF NORTH HAMPSHIRE

Pauline Phillips

12 Newbury

Service no. 7 | Journey time 44–65mins.

OS Landranger 174, 185. 4 journeys per day (not Sun).
Operator: Stagecoach.

Andover

The historic market town of Newbury is just 60 miles from London. It is a thriving place situated at the junction of the A4 and the A34, and served by direct trains from London. It lies at the hub of a wonderful network of local bus routes that include three really first-class journeys: the number 4 over the Berkshire Downs to Lambourn; the 3 that serves villages south of the Kennet Valley on its run west to Hungerford; and the journey south into Hampshire on the number 7 – the one described here. This last route crosses beautiful, untroubled scenery sheltering hidden delights that tempt you to alight and explore, and with four buses a day there is scope for stopping off along the way. The trip begins in **Newbury** (see box, page 61), at the bus station situated in Market Street, next to the West Berkshire Council offices and opposite the splendid new cinema.

Newbury to Highclere

Climbing out of the Kennet Valley, we follow the A343 southwards, under the busy Newbury bypass, and continue through **Great Pen Wood**. This is a good spot for forest walks.

NEWBURY

The River Kennet flows through Newbury, running east to join the Thames at Reading. In the late 18th century the new Kennet and Avon Canal provided a waterway through Newbury linking London with Bath and Bristol, later to have its fortunes clipped by the arrival of the Great Western Railway. You can follow the old canal towpath west to Bath and east to Reading. Newbury has a good range of shops, from smaller independent stores to the larger high-street brands, eating places galore and a famous racecourse served by its own railway station. The open-air market, dating back to 1204, is held on Thursday and Saturday and a farmers' market on the first and third Sunday of each month.

A couple of buses each day detour along the Enborne Valley to serve the villages of Ball Hill and Woolton Hill.

This is border country, the territory where Berkshire quietly slips into Hampshire. **Highclere** is the first place of any size in Hampshire. The village is noted for its extraordinary castle, which is in truth more a palace. It is a fine piece of Renaissance Revival architecture, adapted in the early Victorian period but styled in a manner that affects to be much older. The architect responsible for this dramatic remodelling was none other than Charles Barry who moved to the Highclere project after reconstructing the Houses of Parliament in London. It is interesting to compare the two buildings. If Highclere seems a little familiar, it is probably because you have seen it on television. It served as the fictional Downton Abbey in the popular period drama of the same name, which aired between 2010 and 2015.

Note that public openings at **Highclere Castle** are very irregular, with about 60 public days scheduled per year (a spell around Easter, bank holidays in May, then June to mid-September; details on www.highclerecastle.co.uk). Even if the castle is closed, Highclere warrants a stop. The Red House, on the main road, is a reliable spot for lunches (☎ 01635 255531; open noon–21.30 daily).

Beyond Highclere, our bus climbs gently to **Three Legged Cross**, a former pub but now a private residence. This is a place for keen walkers to alight (see box opposite).

Bowling along the road surrounded by green rolling hills, we pass a turning on the right beckoning to the secluded village of Ashmansworth, where the composer Gerald Finzi once lived. One bus a day makes a little detour into the village, a reminder that for those without cars the local bus really is a lifeline link with the wider world.

The next highlight is **Hurstbourne Tarrant**, a charming village surrounded by high chalk downland, threaded by the Bourne, a stream which flows only in winter. A plaque on the George and Dragon pub (☎ 01264 736277; open 08.00–23.00 Mon–Sat, 11.00–22.00 Sun) reveals that Hurstbourne Tarrant was the home of the famous Shakespearean actor Donald Wolfit. The village was also a favourite of William Cobbett, author of *Rural Rides*. 'This, to my fancy, is a very nice country,' wrote Cobbett. 'It is continual hill and dell.' We get a sense of what Cobbett meant as the bus climbs steeply out of Hurstbourne Tarrant on the main road towards Andover.

Views over the downland and meadows surrounding Andover prevail as we approach **Enham Alamein** (rivalling Three Legged Cross as the oddest place name on this bus route). The name alone is an incitement to alight at the thatched bus shelter, but the place also has an interesting history. In 1919 a consortium of London businessmen purchased Enham Place, a country house that then dominated the hamlet of Enham, and started a rehabilitation centre for ex-servicemen with disabilities arising from World War I.

Newbury

N

18 mins

Highclere

10 mins

Hurstbourne
Tarrant

6 mins

Enham Alamein

14mins

Andover

DOING THE WAYFARER'S WALK

At Three Legged Cross our bus route crosses the Wayfarer's Walk, a well-signed footpath that meanders for 70 miles through the chalk vales and downlands of Hampshire. The five-mile walk northwest to Walbury Hill and Inkpen Beacon is superb – the former is the highest point in Berkshire and southeast England (at 297m), and also has an Iron Age fort. From the ridge there are stunning views over Hampshire and Berkshire, and hang-gliders and kites (the feathered kind and the recreational variety!) can often be seen. Inkpen Beacon is close to the prominent landmark of Combe Gibbet. The original gibbet was destroyed many years ago and has been replaced several times. Walking southeast from Three Legged Cross along the Wayfarer's Way another splendid vista opens up across Beacon Hill (accessible to the public from the A34) to Watership Down, the location of Richard Adams's eponymous book.

Enham Place was demolished in 1939, but the village had established a reputation as a community that helped those with disabilities reach their full potential. Purpose-built housing, much of it in a style redolent of the early garden cities, makes Enham somewhere special. The village became Enham Alamein in 1945 following a substantial gift by King Farouk on behalf of the Egyptian people in gratitude for Allied help in the victory of the Battle of El Alamein. The entire village today still continues its mission of helping folk with disabilities. You can find out more at www.enhamalameinpc.org.uk.

After Enham Alamein, you come to **Andover**, home to the Museum of the Iron Age (☎ 01264 366283). But it is the end of the road for the number 7 and time to alight. It is worth strolling round the town before making the return journey to Newbury. ∎

ABOUT THE AUTHOR | Originally from the Potteries, **PAULINE PHILLIPS** has lived in Newbury since 1973 and seen it grow from a quiet market town to a prosperous, bustling place. Pauline loves walking in the west Berkshire countryside while observing the wildlife and photographing its beauty.

THE
PURBECK BREEZER

Angela Simpkins

Bournemouth

Service no. 50 | Journey time 1hr 10mins.

OS Landranger 195. Hourly Mon–Sat, 6 services on Sun.
Operator: More.

Swanage

The Purbeck Breezer is aptly named, as during the spring and summer months it is operated by open-top buses, and offers a chance to cruise the coast cabriolet-style. For the best seats, board the bus at **Bournemouth Station** where the route starts. The atmosphere on the top deck is one of excitement and holiday fun, which nicely infects even those who are merely making routine journeys to work or the local shops.

It was an inspired moment when local bus operator Wilts & Dorset decided in 2009 to swap time-worn old vehicles for brand-new open-top buses on the route to Swanage. Suddenly, folk started to ride the route for fun. Rebranded the Purbeck Breezer (for Swanage is on the Isle of Purbeck, which oddly is not an island at all) and now run by More, this is a British bus success story. It happens also to be the only bus route in this book where you get a ride on a ferry as part of the journey.

TOWARDS SANDBANKS

Travelling through Bournemouth you will get a first glimpse of the sea. The bus heads out through the smart residential areas of

Westbourne and Canford Cliffs. At **Branksome Chine** you might be tempted to hop off to enjoy the beautiful beach, but stay aboard for this is a route that just gets better and better. At Sandbanks Road, there is a splendid panorama over **Poole Harbour**. 'That's the second-largest natural harbour in the world,' says the bespectacled young lad in the front seat. Who knows if that is really true, but the harbour is certainly lovely. It is blessed with several islands, the most celebrated of which is Brownsea Island (see box below).

The road out to **Sandbanks** takes us along a little thread of land with the sea on one side and the harbour on the other. At the end the ferry awaits, ready to take our bus and its passengers on the short voyage across the mouth of Poole Harbour.

PURBECK BOUND

Well, an ocean cruise it is not, but the five minutes afloat on the **Sandbanks ferry** are always interesting. The sheer density of shipping is remarkable so the ferry master has to be very attentive. There are yachts and motorboats, even a huge catamaran leaving Poole Harbour to travel to the Channel Islands.

The ferry docks at **Shell Bay**, starting point of the South West Coast Path. 'At 630 miles, the longest national footpath

BROWNSEA ISLAND

The largest of Poole Harbour's several islands, Brownsea boasts 500 acres of beautiful woodland, heath, shore and wetland. Unusually for southern England, it has a thriving colony of red squirrels. Dorset Wildlife Trust manage a nature reserve on the island. The island as a whole is under the care of the National Trust, which levies a small landing fee to visitors arriving on Brownsea who are not members. You can catch a boat from the jetty next to the Sandbanks ferry (Brownsea Island Ferries; ☎ 01929 462383). The island has many striking buildings, including a fine Victorian Gothic church, a fake castle and picturesque clusters of cottages.

in the United Kingdom,' intones the boy with the professorial demeanour in the front seat. Should you fancy a shorter walk, it is about two miles along glorious sands to **Knoll Beach** where you can get refreshments at the National Trust café (☎ 01929 450259; open daily).

For something a little different, pause for a swim at the naturist beach on the way. Don't worry – even if skinny-dipping is not for you, the naked souls on

Steam survives on the Isle of Purbeck: the Corfe Castle to Swanage railway (© VisitEngland/VisitDorset)

the beach will not mind you wandering past. Otherwise, there is an alternative walk to Knoll Beach leading over heath and sand dunes. Known as the Heather Walk, this well-marked trail is a riot of colour when the Calluna is in flower.

The bus rolls south over Studland Heath – Brand's Bay on your right – to **Studland** village (see box opposite), which is worth a wander. There is a fine Norman church and plenty of tempting walks. Ballard Down, immediately south of the village, is one of my favourites. From the crest, you can survey the entire Purbeck Breezer route, with views over a great sweep of coastline north to Bournemouth. Then turn and look south to Swanage.

Swanage

Back on the bus, it is a pleasant 15-minute journey from Studland to **Swanage**. This is a classic seaside town, and in high season the town's many bars, cafés and fish and chip shops can be full to overflowing. My favourite Swanage diversion is Chococo (Commercial Rd; ☎ 01929 421777), a place dedicated to chocolate lovers. Try their ice-cream sundaes or, on winter days, they do scrumptious hot chocolate, and good tea, coffee and homemade cakes.

Swanage has a lot to offer: another wonderful Dorset beach, a Victorian pier, a steam railway for excursions to nearby **Corfe Castle**, and plenty of boat trips. At the end of the day, just hop on the Purbeck Breezer for the ride back to Bournemouth. ∎

ABOUT THE AUTHOR | **ANGELA SIMPKINS** retired to Dorset in 2004 and has been lucky enough to spend much of the time since exploring this beautiful county – on many occasions with the aid of the Purbeck Breezer.

ARE BUSES BORING?

'Is this the world's most boring blog?' queried a national daily in 2011 when one of the paper's reporters stumbled on Gerald Fletcher's blow-by-blow account of happenings on the X1 Lowestoft to Peterborough bus route. True devotees of the absurd need only click through to http://fecx1news.blogspot.com for some fine entertainment.

Yet buses are not boring. History was made on buses. Rosa Parks struck a major blow for civil rights in the United States when in 1955 she sat on a seat designated for white passengers while riding home from work on the bus in Montgomery, Alabama.

Even in Britain buses can inspire revolutionary fervour. The Bristol bus boycott in 1963 was a protest by Bristolians to contest the Bristol Omnibus Company's refusal to employ non-white workers. For five months the company management held out until at last the company's own workers voted against the ban on 27 August 1963. Just three weeks later, a local Sikh gentleman took up a position as Bristol's first non-white bus conductor. The Bristol protest evoked such considerable public sympathy that it paved the way for the 1965 Race Relations Act.

Nowadays, it seems our revolutionary zeal on buses is directed more at self-interest than the betterment of society. In April 2011, a Gloucester pensioner chained herself to a bus in protest at her local council's attempt to tinker with the rules governing the use of concessionary bus passes.

No, buses are certainly not boring, but they do have a knack of bringing out the best and worst of human emotions. George Orwell, a man with such sound socialist credentials that we might have expected him to be a great supporter of buses, was terribly impatient with bus conductors, never seeing them as potential allies in his efforts to denounce capitalism.

They may not be essentially socialist, but buses are essentially social. Ride with Colin Thubron on the bus to Samarkand (in *The Lost Heart of Asia*) and you will never forget the ride. Just as we hope the image of Mrs Lewis and her tangerines in Journey 30 will rest with you long after you have finished reading this book. Buses are fascinating. So much so that we really think that the proverbial Clapham omnibus might well be the most interesting aspect of Clapham. ∎

SOUTHWEST ENGLAND

It was the unbridled enthusiasm of Hilary Bradt for one particular bus route, namely the X53 Jurassic Coaster service from Exeter to Poole, that really convinced us of the clear potential in a book celebrating Britain's favourite bus routes. You don't need to have Hilary's commitment to bus travel to realise that southwest England is ideal for exploring by bus.

The Jurassic Coast route is the only journey in this book we have split into two sections. Hilary introduces us to the western section (Journey 14), although the once regular service all the way from Exeter to Poole has now been reduced to just one a day off season – a cost-cutting exercise that is affecting many of the region's buses. In Lyme Regis she hands over the baton to Ronald Lee to escort us eastward to Poole (Journey 15). The full 5½-hour trip is one of Britain's finest bus adventures, taking in the remarkable coastline of East Devon and Dorset, an area so intimately associated with the early history of geology that in 2001 UNESCO added the Jurassic Coast to its Natural World Heritage Site list.

Other journeys in this region cover coastline and moors, market towns and prehistoric settlements. We explore a fragment of the Somerset coast (Journey 16), and ride along the Atlantic Highway of north Devon on a trip from Barnstaple to Hartland (Journey 17). We encounter the open moors and lushly wooded river valleys of Dartmoor (Journey 18), and we head through Devon's South Hams district between two nautically minded settlements of very different characters, Plymouth and Dartmouth (Journey 19).

Yet still there were routes for which we had no space. In particular Cornwall has plenty of scope for bus connoisseurs,

who are well served by an excellent bus map on www.
cornwallpublictransport.info. We'd particularly recommend a tour
of the Penwith Peninsula, a terrain of prehistoric stone circles and
standing stones, ruined engine houses of long-defunct tin mines,
rugged cliffs and austere moors. Penzance makes the obvious
starting point, with First bus services taking you by bus 1/1A to
Land's End via Porthcurno, and bus 16/16A via Zennor to St
Ives. Check details before setting out. Bus services in Cornwall in
particular are in a state of flux, following the sudden bankruptcy in
2015 of Western Greyhound, a company that had a good network
of routes in Cornwall and beyond.

Other journeys in this region cover coastline and moors,
market towns and prehistoric settlements. We roam along the
Somerset coast in an encounter with sands and the Severn Bridges
(Journey 16), and along the Atlantic Highway of North Devon on
a trip from Barnstaple to Hartland (Journey 17). We encounter
the open moors and lushly wooded river valleys of Dartmoor
(Journey 18), and we head through Devon's South Hams district
between two nautically minded settlements of very different
characters, Plymouth and Dartmouth (Journey 19). ■

SEND US YOUR SNAPS!

We'd love to follow your adventures using our *Bus-Pass Britain* guide –
why not send us your photos and stories via Twitter (@BradtGuides) and
Instagram (@bradtguides) using the #BradtBus.

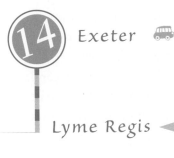

THE
JURASSIC COAST: WEST

Hilary Bradt

14 Exeter 🚍

Service no. X53 | Journey time 2hrs 15mins.

OS Landranger 192, 193. 1–3 buses daily.
Operator: First.
Connects with Journey 15 in Lyme Regis.

Lyme Regis ◄

This is a bus with attitude; it squeezes cars up on to the pavement in the narrow streets of Beer, Colyton and Lyme, and persuades even pushy Land Rovers to reverse out of its way. The X53 is justifiably self-confident; it's the **Jurassic Coaster**, a double-decker with its name and 'One bus, millions of years of history' branded on its sides and jungle-like, prehistoric leaves painted on the windows. And it's my local bus. As it slows to the bus stop I check whether my favourite seat at the front of the top deck is still empty and clamber up the stairs to join shoppers, walkers and sightseers. We all want to sit where we can watch the Devon countryside slowly unfold; much of the route is, after all, an Area of Outstanding Natural Beauty.

HERITAGE

The Jurassic Coast was accorded the status of a UNESCO World Heritage Site in 2001 and several towns have scrambled for the honour of being its 'gateway'. Lyme Regis, long known for its fossils, has the historic claim, but Seaton, with its new Jurassic Centre, can justifiably edge its way to the front. All along the coast

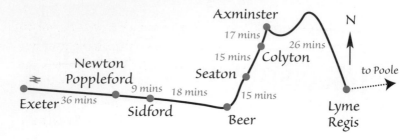

there are noticeboards explaining the geology, and a careful search along the pebble beaches may yield a fossil, though the 'ammonite graveyard' to the west of Lyme Regis is there for all to see.

This is a route made for walkers, and between Exeter and Lyme Regis are some of the best stretches of the South West Coast Path, varying from the easy 30-minute stroll from Beer to Seaton to the seven-mile walk from Donkey Sanctuary down to Weston Mouth and along the cliffs to Beer.

Leaving Exeter

Famous for its splendid cathedral, **Exeter** was thoroughly bombed in World War II and suffers from 'clone Britain' shops and architecture. To escape the glass and metal of the high street head for the quayside where small traditional shops and workshops front the river, and life is led at a slower pace. The cathedral also deserves at least an hour's visit.

EATERIES

The Cathedral Café (☎ 01392 285988; open summer 09.00–17.00 Mon–Sat, winter 09.30–16.00 Mon–Sat) in Exeter, just a couple of steps from the cathedral, has very good lunches and tasty snacks. The Anchor Inn (☎ 01297 20386) in Beer has outdoor seating in the summer and cosy fires in the winter plus good food. In Axminster, Hugh Fearnley-Whittingstall's River Cottage Canteen (☎ 01297 631715) is always popular, or try Hix Oyster Fish House (☎ 01297 446910) in Lyme Regis, a nationally famous seafood restaurant.

The bus station (scheduled for redevelopment) is well organised and has a convenient café. Once on its way, the bus soon leaves the city behind, and the first place to catch your interest is the **Countess Wear** roundabout, curiously named after Isabella, a wealthy and idiosyncratic countess who, in the 13th century, allegedly responded to some insult by building a weir across the River Exe to block off shipping to the city.

Soon the Jurassic Coaster approaches **Aylesbeare Common**, a blaze of yellow in the spring from the gorse that flanks the road. There are walks a-plenty on this pebblebed heath where wildlife enthusiasts may find adders sunning themselves and the rare Dartford warbler. As the bus approaches **Newton Poppleford**, look out for the cheerful family of wooden bears fishing in the stream on the right; they receive Christmas cards from visitors each year. Just beyond these, in a garden, is a large clock face set into a red telephone box. These eccentricities are the work of two brothers. The village itself is typical inland Devon, with a pleasing

collection of cob-and-thatch cottages, including what is arguably the oldest toll house in the country (1758).

Stopping along the way

Sidford is next, squeezed into the valley of the River Sid which reaches the sea at the Georgian resort of Sidmouth. The next bus stop serves the area's most famous attraction, the **Donkey Sanctuary** (☎ 01395 578222; open 09.30–16.00 daily). Spending two

Retro-style on the Seaton Tramway
(© David Hughes/S)

hours visiting the donkeys and having coffee in the tea room is enjoyable at any time of year, and, although the place is free, any money you spend in the shop goes to a good cause. The sanctuary works with impoverished donkey owners overseas, mostly in Africa, to help them improve the care of their animals.

A mile or two beyond Sidford the route starts to get more interesting as the bus plunges into the network of narrow lanes that lead to Beer. Buses are not permitted to reverse, so we passengers on the top deck watch with some relish the discomfiture of the oncoming drivers as they weave their way backwards to the nearest passing place or try to squeeze by on the grass verge. It gets worse in the narrow streets of Beer itself where drivers find themselves between a bus and a hard place.

Beer is a delight, a working fishing village with boats drawn up on the pebble beach and a curving bay dominated by the white chalk (Cretaceous) cliffs; these are an anomaly along the Jurassic Coast where the older, red Triassic rock dominates. Beer is the perfect place for a break: it's four hours before the next Jurassic Coaster comes along, about the right amount of time to enjoy the beach, art galleries and restaurants before walking the coastal path to Seaton, or visiting **Pecorama** with its miniature railway.

Seaton deserves as much time as you can give it. The long expanse of beach is cut by the River Axe, which brings birdwatchers flocking to the estuary and its wetlands, but it is the new **Seaton Jurassic Centre** that is the must-visit attraction here (see box opposite). Another Seaton speciality are the colourful old trams

LYME REGIS

Steeped in history, famed for fossils, this small town rightly attracts a large number of visitors in the summer when crowds throng 'The Cobb' and the sandy beach and fill the tea shops. Lyme Regis takes culture seriously, and there is a lively bookshop as well as a small theatre and cinema. Fossil walks are offered on a regular basis by the Lyme Regis Museum (☎ 01297 443370) and are well worth joining for a thorough understanding of what makes the Jurassic Coast special.

which trundle up to Colyton where you could pick up the next bus. In 2015, the Jurassic Coaster's route was changed; it veers inland from Seaton and takes an equally scenic route through rolling hills and pasture, via Colyton and Axminster, to Lyme Regis. This has added half an hour to the journey and at present it's not known whether the old route via Rousdon will be restored.

The new route has plenty of incidental interest. Note, for instance, the unusual octagonal church tower in **Colyton**, and the traditional Devon longhouse in the village of **Whitford**. Enjoy the views of the River Axe as you cross and recross it, and if you're continuing east to Poole, as was my neighbour on my most recent journey, ask the driver if you can fit in a toilet break at **Axminster** station; there are few such opportunities.

Lyme Regis is the end of this journey, but why not continue eastward? The X53 bus runs from Exeter to Poole, and that eastern section of the route is described in Journey 15. ■

ABOUT THE AUTHOR | **HILARY BRADT** MBE is founder of Bradt Travel Guides and has rejoiced in bus travel since the introduction of the all-England bus pass in 2008.

THE JURASSIC COAST: EAST

Ronald Lee

15 Lyme Regis 🚌

Service no. X53 | Journey time 3hrs 20mins.

OS Landranger 193, 194, 195. 1–3 buses daily.
Operator: First.
Connects with Journey 14 in Lyme Regis.

Poole ⬅

The previous journey in this volume is the run from Exeter to Lyme Regis on the famous X53 Jurassic Coaster bus service. 'A bus with attitude', wrote Hilary Bradt in her account of that route. But it is also a bus with stamina for the stretch from Exeter to Lyme Regis is merely the first third of the long X53 journey from Exeter to Poole. So why not stay aboard the X53 and join me on the continuing journey as we head east from Lyme Regis along the Dorset coast? Climb aboard and let me show you the stretch of coast I now call home.

BRIDPORT BOUND

Lyme Regis post office is good for more than stamps. Here, at the top of Broad Street, you join the Jurassic Coaster bus for Poole. Front-seat passengers may fear they are heading for an unfortunate encounter with the local tourist information centre, but don't worry – the X53 drivers are adept at managing Dorset's challenging roads, and our bus makes a very tight left turn without harming buildings that are merely inches away. An earlier generation of Dorset architects didn't reckon on modern buses

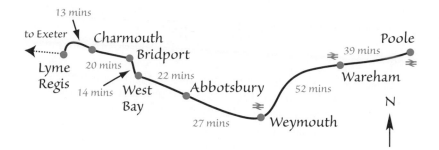

13 mins

to Exeter   Charmouth   Poole

◄┄┄┄┄┄┄   Bridport   39 mins
Lyme   20 mins   Wareham
Regis   14 mins   West   22 mins
                    Bay   Abbotsbury   52 mins
                                                              N
                              27 mins   Weymouth   ↑

having to navigate between their buildings, and first-timers on the X53 are often in awe of the bus driver's skill in avoiding the medley of architectural hazards that jut out assertively into Lyme's narrow streets.

Charmouth is the first spot on the route along the coast. It is a quiet little town that makes the most of having been the place where Mary Anning, the early 19th-century fossil collector, made her most celebrated discoveries. Charmouth vies with Lyme Regis in claiming to be the fossil capital of the Jurassic Coast and, like Lyme, offers a variety of fossil-hunting walks. The Charmouth Heritage Coast Centre provides an excellent introduction to the fossil scene.

The tourist images of Dorset may have seduced you into thinking that this is a county of quaint cottages, cobbled lanes and beautiful vales. But the X53, heading east from Charmouth, reveals another side of the Dorset coast: ugly caravan sites. Lots of them. I am afraid you cannot miss them. But let's agree to look the other way and I'll not mention them again.

Charmouth claims to be the fossil capital of the Jurassic Coast (© Mark Charles/S)

Back on the main A35, we climb to **Morecombelake**, the original home of Moores Bakery, the dark building which you will see on the right. Devotees of good old-fashioned biscuits make pilgrimages here to see the place where, way back in 1880, the Dorset Knob was invented. Nowadays this acclaimed Dorset delicacy is baked in a modern Bridport factory, but happily they are still packed in very retro-styled tins – a nice deference to tradition.

We are now cruising down towards **Chideock**. Suddenly on the left there are signs announcing an 'escape lane' – hopefully not used too often, but no doubt a lifesaver when drivers of heavy trucks (or even buses) suddenly find their brakes have failed. With Chideock behind us our next stop is **Bridport**. The town is noted for the manufacture of rope and nets and for its traditional market, which in truth is what prompted me to settle in Bridport. The market is as good as ever, and if you are passing through on a Wednesday or a Saturday, do stop. You'll be in for a treat.

After leaving the bus station the road rises to the red-brick Georgian town hall, supported on pillars, with a butcher's shop below, built in 1786 for £3,000. It is a gem of a building, refurbished in 2011 with some much-needed tender loving care. We turn right at the traffic lights and down to the left we see Bucky Doo Square, not a square at all but a triangular area of granite setts. It is Bridport's equivalent to the village green, but without the burden of having to cut the grass. As we continue east we see **Palmers Brewery** – the only thatched brewery in England.

Chesil country

We ride south, the River Brit on our right, to **West Bay**, a place that until the mid 19th century was known as Bridport Harbour. But West Bay wanted to be something more than merely an adjunct of nearby Bridport and asserted its own identity, although it is now better known as Broadchurch since the ITV drama was filmed there. West Bay marks a dramatic change in the character of the Dorset coast, as rugged cliffs give way to the long shingle ridge known as Chesil Beach.

We then go through Burton Bradstock and Swyre, skirt Limekiln Hill and then, far away to the left, we get a glimpse of the **Hardy Monument** – in honour of Vice Admiral Thomas Hardy, flag captain of HMS *Victory* at the Battle of Trafalgar, not Thomas, of literary fame. Then comes one of the most magnificent vistas on the entire X53 bus route. As we drop down towards **Abbotsbury** (see box, page 78), there is a superb panorama that takes in Chesil Beach, the stretch of water behind the beach known as West Fleet, and the starkly beautiful ruins of St Catherine's Chapel. In the distance is the Isle of Portland.

From Abbotsbury, we continue southeast with occasional views of West Fleet and East Fleet, and Chesil Beach beyond, until we reach **Weymouth**, where the bus stops by a striking statue of King George III. It was the king's patronage of Weymouth that brought fame and fortune to the seaside town.

The final act: Poole

Skirting Weymouth Bay, we pass through **Osmington**, a busy place in smuggling days, and turn inland past Poxwell Manor House on our left (reported as 'faire and newe' in 1625), sheltered behind its walls and an attractive gatehouse. The scene is idyllic

WAREHAM

One of King Alfred's burghs, with walls on three sides, on one of which there is a Saxon church. There is a very impressive sculpture of T E Lawrence (of Arabia fame) at the church. Lawrence is appropriately depicted in Arab clothing. Clouds Hill, the one-time home of Lawrence, is a few miles west of town. Wareham was once a noted port, and the quay is still a nice spot to wander. But the River Frome eventually silted up, and Wareham's water-borne trade declined (much to the advantage of nearby Poole). Wareham has a second river, often shown on maps as 'River Piddle or River Trent' – almost as if the cartographers have never managed to agree on this little stream's rightful name.

Dorset, with little ponds, a gentle river and four Purbeck stone cottages with impressive thatched roofs.

Now we have a sharp change in mood. Modernity intrudes with a light-green building in the distance, just before the small town of Wool. This is **Winfrith Atomic Energy Research Establishment**, now in the process of being decommissioned. We pass signs to Lulworth to the right, a famously beautiful village with its castle and cove. In the distance are the Purbeck Hills.

Continuing east via Wareham, it is a short run to **Poole**, with a large inlet called Holes Bay on our right. At low tide Holes Bay, which is really an extension of Poole Harbour, is an expanse of mudflats. But the twice-daily tides bring Holes Bay to life, subtly transforming it into an appealing stretch of water. The final approach to Poole shows two sides of the community. Busy working docks and, by contrast, a boatyard that builds luxury yachts. So there is still some money out there. But I doubt whether the yacht owners take time to ride the X53. ∎

ABOUT THE
AUTHOR
Born in Plymouth some 70-plus years ago, with chemistry and history interests, **RONALD LEE** finds the Dorset coast has everything he needs. He hopes it brings pleasure and challenge to others who travel the route.

VINTAGE SEASIDE:
OFF TO SAND BAY

Fraser Balaam

16 Weston-super-Mare

Service no. 100 | Journey time 20–30mins.

OS Landranger 182. Daily every 30mins, hourly on Sun in winter.
Operator: Crosville.

Sand Bay

When I was a boy, few things felt quite as daring as dangling an arm over the edge of the top deck of the open-top bus in Weston-super-Mare. Knowing that there was nothing but air between my fingers and the ground so far below added a frisson to the ride. Twenty years ago, as the wind whipped the curls of my hair across my eyes, my dad would clasp the toggles of my coat to rein me in as my spread hand reached for any overhanging branches that flicked by. Before my attention was stolen by trains, rockets and race cars, nothing was quite as captivating as sitting on a bus that exposed me to the summer drizzle. Nowadays, I'm dusted with a light nostalgia whenever an open-top bus rattles by, its passengers craning out of the upper deck, and that boyhood fascination belongs to the coastal route between my home town of **Weston-super-Mare** and its sedate neighbour, Sand Bay.

Departing from the railway station, the service winds quickly through Weston's town centre and on to the sea front. Weston's waterfront and promenade have had a thorough makeover since the turn of the century. Brushed stonework, new sea walling and an added gleam to the pier help undermine the common perception that the traditional seaside town is little more than peeling paintwork and crumbled paving. On a summer day, when the route to Sand Bay has open-top buses, this is a journey that is fun for all on board – and for me it is a journey that excites a few good memories.

Excited children on the seafront trade in the prospect of a donkey ride on the beach for a ride on the open-top bus. That the queue for the bus is so much shorter than the queue for the donkeys surely plays some part in the calculus. Up on the top deck, life is a treasure. Childhood is shorter than the kids realise. They smile, and so too do their parents and grandparents. For all on the top deck this is more than merely the bus to Sand Bay. It is a journey through childhood, one that for older travellers invites reflection on summer holidays of yesteryear.

A BUS WITH A VIEW

Slowly we get beyond the garish bars and penny arcades of the town centre. As **Knightstone Island** and **Marine Lake** appear, many passengers turn to take a look back towards the town, catching the smack of salty sea air in their faces. This is the classic view of Weston. Old picture postcards catch the sun creeping over the Grand Pier and Brean Down. The latter is the rocky peninsula which juts out into the Bristol Channel well south of the town. The grey, wave-like structure of the pier, much closer to hand,

THE GRAND PIER

Stretching for 430 yards out to sea, Weston's Grand Pier dominates the promenade and is arguably Weston's statement to the wider world (☎ 01934 620238; www.grandpier.co.uk; open from 10.00 daily except Christmas Day; entry £1). Well that, and the fact that this is the home town of John Cleese. Ripples of laughter from Weston-super-Mare have certainly made the world smile. First built in 1904, devastated by fire in 2008 and reopened two years later, the new-look pier squeezes in a medley of attractions from 4D cinema to go-karting.

WESTON WOODS

Weston is lucky to have a fabulous spread of woodland so close to its centre. The 130ha of Weston Woods make it easy to escape the fever of the town. Footpaths snake through dense woodland; some of them are wheelchair-accessible. For younger visitors there's an adventure playground in a clearing with wooden fixtures including a particularly jerky zip line (tested in the name of research, of course). The conifers of Weston Woods were used to shore up the trenches of the Western Front during World War I, and in the heart of the woods are the remains of an Iron Age hill fort, with its crumbling ramparts and deep-storage pits visible. On many of the paths you'll be able to hear the sound of waves smoothly folding against the nearby shore.

gives a sense of scale. It's bold and almost overbearing in the way it overlooks the town and demands attention (see box opposite).

Passing Knightstone Island, the bus breaches a gentle crest and Birnbeck Pier comes into view. Opened in 1867, this largely derelict pier has long lost its seaside charm. It recalls the heyday of Victorian seaside tourism, when visitors to Weston would often make a day trip by steamer over to the Welsh coast. Today, Birnbeck rusts in isolation. Beyond the old pier, the Bristol Channel is interrupted by **Flat Holm Island**, which edges above sea level like a rising submarine. Flat Holm has an intriguing history – it was, for example, used as the site for an isolation hospital to protect mainland Britain from cholera in 1883. Sixty years later it had been fortified to provide protection against potential invasion in World War II. Its hump-shaped sister island Steep Holm, five miles from Weston, is also visible.

THE TOLL-FREE TOLL ROAD

Quickly leaving the town behind, the atmosphere changes as the bus approaches **Kewstoke Road**, which is commonly referred to locally as the toll road. A cliff-top stretch, the toll road is flanked on the left by a steep drop to the sea and on the right by the brooding dankness of **Weston Woods** – a place that in my imagination as a lad was definitely full of all manner of wild things (see box, page 83). We have swapped one Weston for another. The hue and cue of the brash seafront has been eclipsed by imposing nature. Occasionally, the toll road – which, incidentally, no longer charges a toll – gives views across Sand Bay. When I was young, it seemed so huge and I surely gasped at the sight. But beaches shrink as a boy turns into a man.

Thus, catching views and reaching out for overhanging branches, we weave our way through Kewstoke to reach **Sand Bay** – which is both a beach and a community. It is, however, a timid neighbour to bold Weston. It is a place to look across the water to Wales and to be battered by the winds that sweep up the Bristol Channel. The north end of Sand Bay is Sand Point, owned by the National Trust. It is an easy half-hour walk from the bus terminus to the grasslands of Sand Point from where one can look up the **Severn Estuary** to the two Severn bridges. To the northwest, there are clear views to the south Wales coastline, with the spikes of Cardiff's Millennium Stadium punching the horizon.

From bitter personal experience, **Sand Point** is a lousy place from which to launch a message in a bottle with any prospect of receiving a reply. I tried many times. But my most positive memory of that bus journey, beyond the breezy dangers of life on the top deck, is just the moment of arrival at Sand Bay. The mustard shore unfolded by the roadside. We'd run downstairs and hop off. My dad would put me on his shoulders and carry me down to the water's edge, where I'd meekly skim shells at the surface and collect sticks as if they had a resale value. Sand Bay is surely a good place to think about yesterday. ∎

ABOUT THE AUTHOR | **FRASER BALAAM** grew up on the Somerset coast. Once, he was fined $100 for riding without a ticket on a bus in Sydney, Australia. He has learnt his lesson.

By Bus Along the
Atlantic Highway

Nicky Gardner

Barnstaple

Service no. 319 | Journey time 70–90mins.

OS Landranger 180, 190. 4 journeys daily Mon–Sat, no service on Sun.
Operator: Stagecoach.

Hartland

Buttered toast and crumpets are staple fare at the bus station in Barnstaple. Edith opts for a cuppa ('two sugars, please') and a round of toast ('extra butter if you don't mind, love'), then points out the sign that recalls the Barnstaple elephant. 'They dug up the poor beast over there. Just where that 319 to Hartland is waiting,' says Edith with evident Devon pride.

Actually, it was way back in 1844 that workmen unearthed a fossilised elephant, long before Barnstaple had buses. Long before the 319 ever ran out to Hartland. The story of Barnstaple's most famous fossil done and dusted, Edith turns her attention to the destination of the 319. 'I cannot imagine who goes all the way to Hartland,' she reflects. 'I've heard say it's like the end of the world out there. Very wild, so they say.'

My idea had been to head northeast from Barnstaple to the Exmoor coast. Odd, isn't it, how a chance meeting at a bus station can change your plans? Were it not for the elephant and Edith, I would never have boarded bus number 319 bound for Devon's Atlantic extremity.

Since then, I've thoroughly explored that route to Hartland, which several times each weekday and Saturday is served by one of the smart double-deckers operated by Stagecoach. There are bus routes in England which distil greater social magic, and there are journeys which take in more dramatic scenery. But the 319 captures quite perfectly the sense of heading out to the end of the world. Hartland is just as Edith suggested: very wild.

CROSSING THE TAW

North Devon has two great tidal estuaries: the Torridge and the Taw. Route 319 takes in both of them before sweeping west to Clovelly and Hartland – high ground to port, the sea off to starboard. Grand stuff, but the departure from **Barnstaple** is more prosaic. The bus tussles with Barnstaple traffic, eventually making its escape from the town centre across Long Bridge which has for over 700 years escorted travellers across the River Taw – though presumably medieval man did not plan the original structure with double-decker buses in mind. No doubt the bridge's 16 masonry arches have been many times widened and strengthened over the centuries.

'An ancient and respectable market town', I read of Barnstaple in a 200-year-old copy of *Crosby's Gazetteer*. The editors then go on to praise the town's 'handsome piazza, ornamented with a statue of Queen Anne'. Cast a glance back, as the bus purrs over **Long Bridge**, and Barnstaple looks handsome enough. Look forward to the far bank of the Taw and I am confronted by quite another Barnstaple. Where once the woollen industry was diligently prosecuted, now there is an urban wilderness of vast supermarket sheds and DIY stores. Come, come now! This is not the Devon of the tourist brochures, but rather a soulless Tescoland, a triffid sprawl impertinently casting a maze of modernity over the banks of the River Taw.

Our bus driver rather depressingly follows the road sign marked 'superstore', though this turns out to have one building of interest. Buried away amid the shopping park (a scarred wasteland that is anything but park-like) is **Barnstaple Station**, a little gem of antique railway architecture that is mightily inconvenient for travellers bound for the middle of Barnstaple.

Bideford and beyond

A few more passengers join at the station, and we are now on our way. The driver manoeuvres the double-decker into the fast flow of traffic on the Atlantic Highway, a road so over-engineered as to defy the warp and weft of Devon topography. It is a fast dash, and those on board are distracted by their mobile phones. 'No Tipping' proclaim the signs in a lay-by. No-one notices **Kittymoor Brake** or **Huish Moor**: the cool analytics of cartography are reduced to a blur on the top deck as our driver rushes to reclaim minutes lost in that loop through Tescoland.

You meet all sorts on the top deck. Today, the star of the show is a retired engineer from London, on holiday in Devon, who is making a quick hop from Barnstaple to Bideford. 'Just to see the Torridge Bridge,' he says. I make the dreadful mistake of assuming that the **Torridge Bridge** is the venerable old stone bridge that crosses the Torridge in the heart of Bideford. 'No, no. That's the old

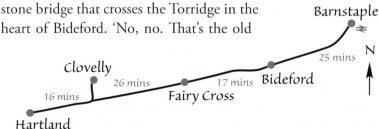

one,' he says. 'I'm more interested in new bridges.' He tells us how back in the 1980s he helped design the Torridge Bridge. 'It perfectly combined aesthetics with economy,' he adds with a smile and proudly recounts how the new bridge won an award from the Concrete Society.

Within a few minutes we are cruising over that new bridge. It is wonderful, a delicate span over a silken estuary. Downstream there are views over tidal sandbanks towards **Appledore**, while upstream there is a glorious vista of Bideford, hugging the west bank of the river. There the old stone bridge is the centrepiece.

Bideford is as good close-up as that first glimpse from the new bridge promised. The bus route nicely contrives to reveal Bideford from all angles. The 319 stops on the quayside, where there are signs for the ferry connection to the Isle of Lundy. It sweeps past the town hall, a fussy mock-Tudor creation, then up through back streets to regain open country.

We pass through a medley of Devon villages and then, back on the A39, head west to **Fairy Cross**. A few years ago, few travellers on the A39 even noticed Fairy Cross. It was just one of dozens of inconsequential hamlets on the Atlantic Highway. That was before the inhabitants of Fairy Cross hit on the inspired idea of embellishing their village with the finest bus shelters in England. Each side of the road, there is a striking hexagonal stone shelter with a slate roof. Those waiting for the bus to the coast at Hartland enjoy aquamarine décor. Move to the other side of the road for buses to Bideford and Barnstaple and the design theme is orange. The latter shelter is dedicated to the memory of local farm manager Robert Davies who died in an accident in 2005. 'Make time to stand and stare. Bob Davies would have appreciated this,' reads the inscription.

I am in luck. Two villagers are waiting for our bus. They climb aboard and join us on the top deck. 'Ah, yes, the bus shelters,' says the younger of the two women, sensing my interest in these fabulous structures. 'Caused a lot of problems hereabouts, they did,' she explains, going on to recount the story of how other villages on the A39 thought they might copy the example set by Fairy Cross. I wondered if armed brigades went out from Fairy Cross by night to destroy rival bus shelters. 'There was talk for a while of bus-stop wars,' says the woman but declines to elaborate.

To the coast

The bus dips down past Hoops Inn (☎ 01237 451222). This old pub, a labyrinth of a place, makes a good spot to break the journey to Hartland for a couple of hours. Then it detours to the coast to serve **Clovelly**, a wee slip of a village that tumbles down to the coast. It is mightily popular with tourists, and levies a hefty entrance fee. Its crowded car park suggests that there are plenty of visitors willing to pay to see Clovelly.

The route of the 319 beyond Clovelly seems almost to have been designed as a reaction to the village. Now it is time to really get off the beaten track. We leave the A39 for the last time and take to back lanes for the final part of the journey to Hartland. The landscape suggests that Cornwall cannot be far away. It is suddenly altogether bleaker. This is territory where, over the centuries, life has often been a struggle. Farmers and peasants turned to God for support, and this corner of Devon boasts large churches that once gathered huge congregations. The Church of England and

The 319 in front of Hoops Inn (© *hidden europe*)

BUS NOTES

Hartland may seem like the end of the road, but there is a good connection with the Stagecoach South West services that run south across the Cornish border to Bude. The last bus of the day from Barnstaple to Hartland continues through to Bude without any need to change vehicles. The short hop onward from Hartland to Bude takes an additional 30 minutes.

Methodism tussled for the souls of folk in and around Hartland, both leaving a strong imprint on the landscape. Devonians in the remote northwest of the county were seduced by neither, looking instead for a compromise. They discovered in the Bible Christian Society a home-grown Church that took elements of Anglican and Wesleyan liturgical practice and threw in a dose of Quaker piety to create a uniquely local religion.

Our bus slows to allow a passenger to alight at the **Providence Chapel**, built in the 19th century by the Bible Christian Society. The stern building bears the bold inscription: 'I believe in Church and State and all other religions that do good.' No mention of God, strangely.

We roll down into **Hartland**, the village's irregular main street made all the nicer by the raised pavement on the north side. What did Edith say back in Barnstaple? 'It's like the end of the world out there.' And it is. A fierce west wind funnels through Hartland. Undeterred, I take to footpaths to explore the old port and the imposing cliffs. Offshore lies Lundy, serenely beautiful. 'Make time to stand and stare' was the wording on that dedication to Bob Davies on the bus shelter back at Fairy Cross. Here, at the very edge of England, where Devon meets the sea, that maxim seems like very good advice. ∎

ABOUT THE AUTHOR | **NICKY GARDNER** is a Berlin-based travel writer. She is co-editor of *hidden europe* magazine (www.hiddeneurope. co.uk).

Dipping into Devon's Past

Janice Booth

Okehampton

Service no. 178 | Journey time 1hr 50mins.

OS Landranger 191. Once daily Mon–Sat, twice daily between Moretonhampstead & Newton Abbot, no service on Sun. Operator: Country Bus.

Newton Abbot ←

I love the rural Devon roadsides on this route! Hedges and verges vary with the seasons, from scatterings of snowdrops in early spring through primroses, daffodils, foxgloves, wild roses, to nettles and bramble blossom. Finally we get the blackberries, hips and fading foliage of autumn. Here and there a gnarled tree survives in a hedgerow, an ancient stone wall underlies a bank, or a stream bubbles beside the road. Sheep and red Devon cattle graze in the fields, and crops ripen through deepening shades of green to dusty gold. Between gaps in the trees, the hills and tors of Dartmoor appear as a distant backdrop.

Landscapes of this kind have endured for millennia, and are so rich in history. In this case the medieval thatched cottages, centuries-old inns and much-loved little village churches are in areas where prehistoric monoliths, hut circles and burial cairns once stood, and the footprints of their early people stretch back a long, long way.

The 178 bus takes an indirect route through villages on its way from Okehampton to Newton Abbot, much of it within the boundaries of Dartmoor National Park. Its lunchtime departure gives you time to explore **Okehampton** before setting off; the town centre has some historic old buildings. A few high-street stores have closed but several small independent shops are flourishing, and a little shopping arcade that replicates London's Burlington Arcade, but in miniature, is an unexpected treat. If you fancy buying a homemade snack for your journey, just follow the smell of fresh baking. The ruined Okehampton Castle, crouched on a hillside about a mile from the centre, was once Devon's largest castle and is mentioned in the Domesday Book.

Okehampton
12 mins
13 mins
Stickle-
path
South Zeal
21 mins
14 mins
Chagford
Moreton-
hampstead
15 mins
Lustleigh
10 mins
Bovey
Tracey
22 mins
Newton
Abbot
N

GETTING UNDER WAY

At its starting-point in Market Street, the single-decker bus fills up quickly with local passengers, some of them shoppers and others off to visit friends. Sit on the right for the best views; Dartmoor is visible on this side as the bus emerges from the town into open countryside.

Shortly afterwards it plunges abruptly downhill to cross the River Taw in **Sticklepath**, an attractive village with some fine thatched cottages. It's one of Dartmoor's four 'beacon villages' (South Zeal, South Tawton and Belstone are the others) located at the base of Cosdon Beacon, a broad 1,804ft hill where signal fires were lit in medieval times and on which are many prehistoric remains. Sticklepath is also home to the Finch Foundry (☎ 01837 840046; open mid-Mar–Oct 11.00–17.00 daily), the last working water-powered forge in the country, now managed by the National Trust.

From Sticklepath, the bus heads for **South Tawton** and stops near its surprisingly large church of St Andrew. South Tawton was a royal manor at the time of the Domesday survey and its fertile land made for successful farming. Wealth from the wool trade expanded a smaller, probably 11th-century chapel into the mainly 15th-century granite church that dominates the village today. The historic thatched **Church House** beside it was built soon after 1490 as a parish centre where communal feasts and functions were held (☎ 01837 840418; open May–Oct on Sun or other times by appointment).

More narrow, winding roads and thick hedges lead on through open country until the bus dips sharply down into **South Zeal**; watch out for the 16th-century King's Arms on the left and then, on the right, the 14th-century market cross in the churchyard of little St Mary's Chapel, with its distinctive turret for two bells. Directly after these comes the Oxenham Arms (see box below), where Charles Dickens stayed while writing *The Pickwick Papers*. Then soon you're climbing steeply out of the village again, with the outline of Dartmoor emerging distantly on the right. Sharp, blurred, misty, grey, calm, menacing – it's never the same two days running.

Continuing southward, the bus crosses the watershed into the Teign Valley and then heads to **Chagford** along a lovely open

SOUTH ZEAL

There's so much history here. Long ago, the village was on the main road from Exeter to Cornwall, and back in 1298 was granted a royal charter for a weekly market. The Oxenham Arms (☎ 01837 840244), an imposing listed building looking more monastery than pub, was probably built by lay monks in the 12th century. It is one of Devon's oldest inns. Extraordinarily, set into the wall of one of its inside rooms is a huge prehistoric standing stone, supposedly about 5,000 years old. Another room has a similar stone supporting the ceiling. The menu is somewhat more modern – I've had an excellent meal there – and the bedrooms are beautiful.

BREAKING YOUR JOURNEY

With only one daily 178 service running the full length of the route in each direction, you can't just hop off it to explore a tempting village and then continue on the next bus. But other services do operate in the area; Chagford, for example, is linked by Dartline bus number 173 to Moretonhampstead and Exeter, while if you leave the 178 at Moretonhampstead or Bovey Tracey (and both towns are worth a visit), you have links to Exeter via Country Bus number 359 from the former and the hourly Stagecoach 39 from the latter.

Many bus times and routes change seasonally, and country buses are vulnerable just now, so you do need to check the current situation. Devon County Council produces a set of six printed timetables that cover the whole county; this particular journey is in the one for Teignbridge. You can also access the timetables online at www.journeydevon.info, which includes a helpful interactive bus map.

road with views of gentle countryside and Dartmoor's rounded hills; glimpses of Chagford ahead show how tightly it is cradled by the moor. It's a delightful little town, with twisty streets, a mix of old and new buildings and some good independent shops and eateries, including the Devonshire Dairy which offers honey and local lamb, an extensive hardware store selling far more than just hardware, handicraft shops and a busy central market. The striking 13th-century church of St Michael the Archangel, built with wealth from the tin trade, has been considerably restored but retains some appealing carvings, such as an angelic St Michael with flowing locks slaying a rather small demon.

SOUTHWARD BOUND

Back on the main road beyond Chagford, the journey is faster and less strikingly rural for a while, although the traditional countryside still unfolds pleasantly. **Moretonhampstead** is a busy small town mixing old-world charm with modernity; it has some attractive old buildings and an atmospheric centre, but the bus allows only a few glimpses as it rattles through. After some rather tatty industrial buildings on its outskirts, the scenery becomes prettier, with flowers in the verges, open views, woods and – when I last was there – a lone buzzard surveying the landscape from a treetop. Then the bus veers round a very sharp right turn and down a steep lane as it heads towards **Lustleigh**; don't miss the beautiful thatched cottage tucked away on the right at the top of the lane.

To Lustleigh's benefit, although not to yours, the bus stops well short of the centre. After a switchback approach along narrow roads it drops passengers and turns round at two small restored gatehouses. Thus if you stay on board you'll miss a true picture-postcard village, with an array of thatched cottages and a 13th-century church. Or, if you're energetic, tired of the bus and have a suitable map, you could alight here and do an easy walk (roughly three miles, along lanes) from Lustleigh to Bovey Tracey, where there are buses to Exeter.

DRAWING TO A CLOSE

Back on the A382 after retracing the route from Lustleigh, the 'village' part of your journey is over, although the views are still pleasantly rural. **Bovey Tracey** is a friendly town, part traditional and part modern, notable for the wonderful gallery of the Devon Guild of Craftsmen at the Riverside Mill (☎ 01626 832223; open 10.00–17.30 daily) and the House of Marbles with the world's longest marble run. I would be inclined to end the journey here, rather than continuing to Newton Abbot – which is nice enough, but much busier and noisier than the places you've been visiting. However, **Newton Abbot** does offer you rail links to Plymouth or Exeter (sit on the right for Exeter to get wonderful views across the Exe Estuary) and good bus services in either direction. ■

ABOUT THE AUTHOR | **JANICE BOOTH** lives in Devon, within sound of the sea. She has co-written Bradt guides to Rwanda and South and East Devon, and edited numerous others.

BRITAIN'S RAREST BUS

As bus stops go, the one at Dawlish Green on the coast of Devon is pretty handsome. There is the salty tang of sea air, and a cosy bus shelter that affords a little protection when a sharp east wind comes in off the bay. It is at this bus shelter that every afternoon a National Express coach decants the Midlands holidaymakers who come to Dawlish for a few days of sun, sea and sand.

The 337 is the most distinguished arrival of the day at Dawlish Green. 'That one is Rugby to Paignton. Quite a long haul,' says Fred who used to work on the buses and now sits in summer sunshine to watch the comings and goings at Dawlish Green. The 337 pauses at the bus shelter just after four every afternoon – an hour shy of the end of its long journey across England.

On this summer Saturday, there are many new arrivals. A single mum attends to a mountain of luggage, while one of her three charges makes a bid to escape. Fred helpfully goes to the rescue, restraining the toddler who is keen to catch a glimpse of the sea. The newcomers disperse, and we start to head off too.

'Don't go yet,' calls Fred. 'You'll miss the 113. She's due off the Green at half past four.' So we wait. And the 16.30 departure to Tavistock is indeed a rare sight to behold, for this is Britain's least-frequent bus service. It runs from March to October – but only on the fifth Saturday of each month. So in 2016 it will run just three times – on 30 April, 30 July and 29 October.

The two-hour journey to Tavistock crosses the very heart of Dartmoor. The 113 is run by Tavistock Country Bus, a community transport association founded 35 years ago by Tavistock locals who felt that their area deserved better bus services (www. tavistockcountrybus.co.uk). Nowadays the association runs routes around the town and to nearby villages in the Tavy Valley. They run a route from Tavistock to Launceston in Cornwall, and from March to October they run special once-a-month Saturday routes to Exeter, Truro, Plymouth, Torquay and – when there is a fifth Saturday in the month – to Dawlish.

This suite of Tavistock services is run entirely by volunteers. Concessionary passes are accepted on all services. All services are advertised as regular scheduled bus routes, so they run even if nobody turns up for the ride. ∎

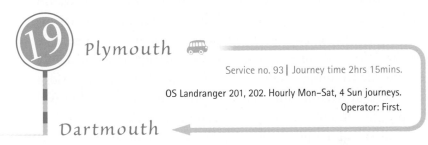

SAUNTERING THROUGH THE SOUTH HAMS

John Deacon

19 Plymouth

Service no. 93 | Journey time 2hrs 15mins.

OS Landranger 201, 202. Hourly Mon–Sat, 4 Sun journeys.
Operator: First.

Dartmouth

This route takes us through the rolling countryside of the South Hams with its old thatched cottages – an exploratory journey across the southernmost portion of Devon. It takes in dramatic headlands, attractive coves, and some seductively beautiful inlets before culminating in the lovely ancient town of Dartmouth. The thing I like about the 93 is that, Sundays apart (when the service is sparse), it runs sufficiently frequently that one can break one's journey on a whim. The next bus always comes along an hour later for you to continue your journey.

Hop on the top deck and map the progress of the Devon seasons – from lambs and primroses in spring to pheasants and blackberries in autumn. The great plus of the upper deck is that one can see over the thick Devon hedges into fields and gardens along the way.

OLD MOTHER HUBBARD AND MORE

Our journey begins at **Plymouth**'s Bretonside bus station and after crossing the River Plym we head east out of the city to Yealmpton. Old Mother Hubbard's thatched cottage is on the right, opposite the Rose and Crown (☎ 01752 880223), one of the new generation of gastropubs. Look for tasty Devon fish specialities. Food is served from noon daily.

Yealmpton takes its name from the River Yealm, which we cross just east of the village. The old toll house by the bridge nicely records the toll charges of yesteryear. Then it's on through fields with red soils and reddish cattle to Modbury and **Aveton Gifford**, both spots where our bus squeezes through narrow streets. The top deck is great for people-watching in these little communities. There is a good view west along a road open only at low tide (running beside the River Avon) from the long bridge just beyond Aveton Gifford. More often than not, the bus will stop at the end of the bridge to drop off or pick up hikers. It is a good spot for walkers wanting to connect on to the nearby South West Coast Path.

Devon's rivers certainly make a dramatic impact on the county's topography, so it is a long climb up from the River Avon to Churchstow and Kingsbridge. The timetable is such that buses normally stop a while at **Kingsbridge Quay** to change drivers, so take a moment to pause for an hour as Kingsbridge has a lot to offer.

KINGSBRIDGE

Kingsbridge is the centre for the local area with a wide variety of shops, pubs and cafés. But the real attraction is the Cookworthy Museum (in the old Grammar School on Fore St; ☎ 01548 853235; www.kingsbridgemuseum.org.uk; open 10.30–17.00 Mon–Sat, shorter winter hours), which charts the history of the entire South Hams area. Kingsbridge has a very good tourist information office (☎ 01548 853195) on Kingsbridge Quay. Those of the bus-pass generation will find a good cup of tea at the Pensioners' Rest Centre (open 10.00–noon daily), reached through the gate marked 'Kingsbridge UDC' beside the bus stops at the quay; next door, Age UK does cheap lunches on Wednesdays for the same age group.

I sometimes use a break in Kingsbridge to make a little side diversion down Kingsbridge Estuary to Salcombe. The beautifully named Tally Ho Coaches, a Kingsbridge-based bus operator, run an hourly service (not Sundays or bank holidays) down to Salcombe, just 25 minutes away. Even better, take a boat to **Salcombe**. Services depart twice or thrice daily in the season, but the times do vary with the tides. The tourist information centre will have details of current times.

On to Dartmouth

The scenery changes, becoming less hilly as we head east out of Kingsbridge and cross over the single-track bridge to follow the head of the estuary, passing more traditional Devon thatched cottages. We get a chance to admire the skill and patience of the driver as he manoeuvres his vehicle along these twisting and narrow roads. On the way through the villages of Charleton, Frogmore and Chillington there are road signs pointing the way to hamlets and ancient churches hidden away in the deep Devon lanes. After passing through Stokenham, where a right turn would take us south towards the isolated communities around Start Point and Prawle Point, we finally emerge on the coast at **Torcross**.

On leaving Torcross, the bus runs for about two miles between the beach and the freshwater lake of Slapton Ley, a popular spot for birdwatchers. Then on through the straggly village of Strete to the beautiful cove of **Blackpool Sands**. The latter is worth a stop. It has a Blue Flag beach and the Venus Beach Café (☎ 01803

TORCROSS

This little village with the Start Bay Inn (☎ 01548 580553) and several cafés is at the southern end of the sweep of Slapton Sands. It is a good jumping-off point for several fine walks. One of the best is south through Beesands and Hallsands to the lighthouse at Start Point and then on to Salcombe. These paths are all marked with the acorn symbol of the South West Coast Path and more information regarding them and the rest of the route can be found at www.southwestcoastpath.com.

770209; open 08.30–17.00 daily, shorter hours in winter), which is open in even the worst of winter weather and is good for snacks or a light meal.

Leaving Blackpool, it is 20 minutes of hill and dale, until eventually we drop down into Dartmouth. But if you want a more dramatic finale to your journey, alight from the bus at the Village Hall in **Stoke Fleming**. From here it is possible to walk around the top of the cliffs following the signed coast path through Little Dartmouth. There are glorious views of the River Dart and the Day Mark navigation tower on the opposite hill, before you descend through the woods, full of bluebells in season, to reach **Dartmouth Castle** (☎ 01803 833588; open 10.00–18.00 daily in summer 0, but shorter hours otherwise). From here there is a choice of a ferry or the road for the mile into town.

Dartmouth is the ultimate town for boat lovers. Dartmouth harbour is effectively the town's main street. Don't miss the Cherub Inn (☎ 01803 832571) and surrounding Tudor buildings in Higher Street and The Butterwalk. One of the great pleasures in Dartmouth is just to take a seat along the waterfront and relax while watching the action on the river, with ferries and pleasure craft always on the go. ∎

ABOUT THE AUTHOR | **JOHN DEACON** is a retired engineer from Plymouth who has travelled along this road for over 50 years, watching the changes along the way.

MIDLANDS AND EAST ANGLIA

This swathe of central England extends from the Malvern Hills to the North Sea and includes the one-time industrial hubs of the English Midlands. Not always the promising areas for local bus journeys you might suppose, but our seven routes in this section tell a more positive tale, and show how even Birmingham's edgy suburbs come to life when viewed from the top deck of the bus.

Just over 100 years ago (in July 1913), Birmingham Corporation made their debut in the bus business. It was a cunning piece of Brummie ingenuity, for the prevailing legislation was designed to preclude the city authorities from running omnibuses. Trams were the business of the corporation, but a loophole allowed Birmingham Corporation to run an omnibus in lieu of a tram service due to building work or where a tramline was being extended.

Maps in the corporation offices were embellished with many 'new' tram routes, extending the network out to the edges of the city and beyond. Most were never built, and were merely a pretext to run buses in lieu of trams on routes under construction. The ploy worked – the maps had served their purpose and were quickly forgotten, and corporation buses transformed travel on the streets of Birmingham. One of the greatest municipal bus undertakings the world has even known was in business.

The city's Outer Circle bus route features as Journey 21. For decades it had a place in the record books as the longest urban bus route in Europe and it has been a feature of the Birmingham bus map since the 1920s. Explore a little further from the major urban hubs and you'll find some wonderful countryside. Nigel Roberts' Journey 22 leads us out of Birmingham towards the Lickey Hills and Worcester, while in Journey 23 we skirt the edge of Cannock Chase, another area of open space that has long been a favourite escape for city dwellers. Peter Draper takes us through rural Oxfordshire in Journey 20 on an encounter with the ironstone hues of the Cotswolds.

Into East Anglia in Journey 25, Laurence Mitchell remarks that Lowestoft was once a town for seafarers but that they have long gone, and also guides us along the Coasthopper route beside the hauntingly beautiful north Norfolk coast in Journey 26. Anna Blair's Fenland journey takes us from Chatteris to Cambridge in Journey 24.

This region includes many remarkably long bus routes. It is possible to travel from Norwich to either Milton Keynes or Nottingham with just one change of bus. Elsewhere, the X5 leaves Cambridge every half an hour, taking over three hours for the 85-mile journey to Oxford. The route is operated by Stagecoach but, if you purchase your ticket in advance through Megabus, you can ride between the two university cities for just £1. ∎

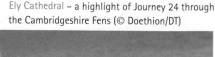

Ely Cathedral – a highlight of Journey 24 through the Cambridgeshire Fens (© Doethion/DT)

OVER THE HILLS
TO CHIPPY

Peter Draper

20 Banbury 🚐

Service no. 488 | Journey time 50mins.

OS Landranger 151, 164. Hourly, no service Sun.
Operator: Stagecoach.

Chipping Norton

T he countryside of the northern portion of Oxfordshire is surprisingly remote and unspoilt, and service 488 gives ready access to this subtle, pleasing landscape of rippling hills and copses etched with distant spires.

The towns and villages served, from Banbury via Bloxham and Hook Norton to Chipping Norton, are all full of interest, and subtle changes in the underlying geology along the way are reflected in the lie of the land and the mix of local building materials. This all adds up to a winning formula, making the 488 a route that is easy to appreciate.

BLOXHAM FOR LENGTH

We start at **Banbury**'s bus station in Bridge Street. Soon we are free of the town, climbing gently to the endearing village of **Bloxham**. The main street is lined with buildings in warm brown ironstone and dominated by the elegant 180ft-high spire of the majestic parish church of St Mary. This is one of a trio of notable local church spires, recalled in a rhyme well known to folk in the Banbury area: 'Bloxham for length, Adderbury for strength, and King's Sutton for beauty.'

Visitors to the area might like to use local buses to form their own opinion! Bloxham church, with its glowing stained glass by William Morris, Edward Burne-Jones and Philip Webb, is a fine introduction to the churches of the region.

Leaving Bloxham and passing through the rather isolated community of **Milcombe** (with a striking final view of Bloxham Church away to the left), the next few miles of the journey have a curiously remote air. Occasional passengers board or alight at isolated farms and there are sweeping views over the neatly hedged country lanes to a pastel-coloured landscape of chequerboard fields, farms and spinneys. This section is a special delight on a clear, sharp spring morning; real, unspoilt Midland England at its best.

Hooky for beer

We soon reach the large village of **Hook Norton**, known as Hooky to locals. The name 'Ironstone Hollow' on a housing development as we enter Hooky is a reminder that this part of rural Oxfordshire was once home to a flourishing iron trade with blast-furnaces and iron-ore quarries. The pillars of a disused railway viaduct built by the Banbury and Cheltenham Direct Railway in connection with

BLOXHAM AND HOOKY

You'll find no end of first-class pubs along the 488 bus route. Bloxham and Hook Norton are the two obvious spots to break your journey. With buses generally running hourly, it is easy to pause along the way. But keep an eye on the clock, for last buses on this route are quite early. Bloxham's pubs include the Joiners Arms and the Elephant & Castle.

Hook Norton Brewery has a visitor centre in the original 1849 maltings building. It is open from 09.30 daily. Brewery tours last two hours and must be pre-booked (☎ 01608 730384).

this industry form a rather eerie remnant of this period, and can be visited as part of a pleasant walk beginning in Middle Hill, a left turn off High Street near the Sun Inn (☎ 01608 737570). As well as serving good food, this inn has fascinating sepia photographs of Hook Norton's industrial past.

Most visitors to Hook Norton come to see the remarkable traditional **Victorian brewery** (see box, page 104). Hook Norton ales are familiar throughout the area and the brewery itself offers tours and has a shop and museum. On a recent journey on the 488 a group of Canadian students alighted for the brewery tour; it was entertaining to see the contrast between their quiet demeanour when alighting in the morning and their noisy chatter when rejoining the bus in the afternoon after sampling the local brew! Definitely a case where taking the bus is a big plus.

Yet another attraction in Hook Norton is the beautiful parish church of St Peter (right by the bus stop), with its striking tower and delightful setting. The 11th-century font at this church draws visitors from far and wide.

CHANGING COTSWOLD LANDSCAPES

After leaving Hook Norton on the Great Rollright road, the tenor of the landscape changes. Distant views over towards Long Compton have an unmistakably Cotswoldian feel, and we suddenly realise that we have left the brown ironstone strata behind and are now into limestone country. This whole area is indeed something of a borderland, as the boundaries of Warwickshire, Gloucestershire and Worcestershire are all close at hand.

Banbury

14 mins

Bloxham

14 mins

Hook Norton

18 mins

Chipping Norton

Connection on X8

⇌ Kingham

N

A series of steep descents through Great Rollright and Over Norton villages are a reminder that this route is certainly no sinecure for the bus driver! **Great Rollright** is an attractive village overlooked by the medieval church of St Andrew, but is not in fact particularly near the famed Rollright Stones, Oxfordshire's answer to Stonehenge. For bus passengers, access to this remarkable and mysterious stone grouping of The King's Men, The King Stone and (a personal favourite) The Whispering Knights is easier using Stagecoach service 50 (Chipping Norton to Stratford-upon-Avon), which stops on request within a few hundred yards of the Stones.

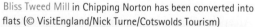

Bliss Tweed Mill in Chipping Norton has been converted into flats (© VisitEngland/Nick Turne/Cotswolds Tourism)

CHIPPY DELIGHTS

Soon we enter the grey-stone town of **Chipping Norton**, known as 'Chippy' to locals. Chipping Norton at about 700ft is the highest town in Oxfordshire – no wonder it often feels rather windswept. Take a while to get the pulse of Chippy. It has elegant 18th-century stone frontages, a lovely Neoclassical town hall and a superb row of almshouses, the last dating from 1640.

One of the most remarkable buildings in Chipping Norton owes its origins to Victorian industry: on the western side of the town is the former **Bliss Tweed Mill**, which was for many years a major employer. This monumentally impressive building, with its ornate, soaring chimney, has now been tastefully converted into luxury flats.

The imposing parish church of St Mary the Virgin is slightly tucked away from the main West Street to Horsefair axis. This church benefited from the prosperity of wool merchants in centuries past and contains many individual features of interest, including fine stained glass, well repaying detailed exploration. The building is located adjacent to the mounds of Chipping Norton's former castle, of which no trace now remains; nevertheless, the surviving earthworks are atmospheric enough. The history of the town can be more fully explored at the admirable museum (☎ 01608 641712; open Easter–end Oct).

Do try this rewarding trip to Chippy – you won't be disappointed. For those travelling onward, the X8 runs at least hourly to Kingham Station for train connections to Oxford, London and Worcester. ∎

ABOUT THE AUTHOR

PETER DRAPER is a retired lecturer, but spent the last few years of his working life with the Wilts & Dorset Bus Company. He is a lifetime public transport devotee and loves exploring.

ORBITAL DELIGHTS

Nicky Gardner

Birmingham

Service nos. 11A (anticlockwise) or 11C (clockwise) |
Journey time 2hrs 10mins to 2hrs 30mins.

OS Landranger 139. Every 8mins daytime Mon–Sat, every 20mins evenings Sun.
Operator: National Express West Midlands.
Connects with Journey 22 in Selly Oak.

circular route

This journey is a bus trip for urban explorers. It tracks a route through Birmingham's suburban web, encircling England's second city on a run that is full of cultural colour. As narrated here, it starts and ends in Bournville, but you can of course board the number 11 at any point on its orbit around Birmingham. And, if you grow to like this circular route as much as I do, you might be tempted to stay on board for ever.

Were it not for the complete absence of pubs, I might be tempted to stay in Bournville. It is a happy spot, made all the better by the gentle smell of chocolate from the nearby Cadbury factory that drifts from time to time over the park. George and Richard Cadbury – brothers, philanthropists and chocolatiers – knew the ingredients of human happiness: Tudor beams, indoor toilets, decent plumbing, education, the village green and chocolate.

Route 11, often dubbed the Outer Circle, is the boomerang of British bus routes. Climb aboard outside the **Friends' Meeting House** and it matters not if you head north or south. Whichever direction you choose, bus 11 resolutely brings you right back to Bournville. The bus route comes in two flavours: 11A (anticlockwise) or 11C (clockwise), each affording two hours or more of orbital delight as the bus circumnavigates the heart of the city known for chocolate, custard, commerce and culture. Route 11 never touches the centre of Birmingham nor the city boundary, instead maintaining a creative tension between the two as it tracks a circular trail through the suburbs.

LOST VILLAGES, NEW SUBURBS

Culture comes in many guises in modern Birmingham and route 11 touches them all. Rachmaninoff and rap, mosques and Sikh temples, halal and hijab, pawnbrokers and bingo, hair weaving and glamour nails. This is a provocative orbit through Birmingham's edgy and neglected territories, a journey that plunges through deepest Yardley and distant Handsworth before returning inexorably and inevitably to the little Utopia that is Bournville.

Birmingham's Outer Circle bus route is a veteran among urban bus routes. Brochures in the 1920s extolled the merits of the route. One Mr Baker, in those days general manager of the Birmingham Corporation Tramways and Omnibus Department, put his name to a stylish pamphlet that commanded 'see Birmingham's charming suburbs by 'bus' – if Mr Baker was as good at running buses as he was at deploying apostrophes with precision, then Brummie buses were surely a treat in those days. '25 miles for 15 pence' ran the blurb under a picture of two of the corporation's finest double-deckers processing sedately along an otherwise empty road through leafy suburbs. A distinctly rural finger-signpost pointed down a lane to Yardley and Hall Green, both nowadays dreary suburbs that have impertinently gobbled up the meadows and woodland that once fringed the Cole Valley.

The Birmingham Corporation Tramways and Omnibus Department has been consigned to transport history. It is many years since the corporation's cream and Monastral-blue double-deckers cruised the Outer Circle. Cream and that distinctive dark blue have been supplanted by garish modern buses, happily still double-deckers, but their exteriors strewn by advertisements.

Those who know their buses appreciate that these are Eclipse Gemini models, nicely astronomical names for buses destined to spend their days in orbit. They are operated by National Express West Midlands, a company that evidently has a great sense of irony, for the Outer Circle is anything but an express. These are buses that progress haltingly and often not at all. The fine men and women who are assigned to drive the buses on this route are surely among the most patient souls on the planet as they navigate their Eclipse Geminis through constellations of dense traffic.

From leafy **Bournville**, the anticlockwise bus route tracks south to Cotteridge, where it turns east towards Kings Heath. 'I'm just off to the village,' says a chatty pensioner who climbs aboard at Stirchley and politely asks if he might be permitted to share a seat on the top deck. Ex-Guards, I'd say, but don't have the courage to ask.

The village, it turns out, is **Kings Heath**: urban, choked with traffic, discount perms and not a meadow in sight. The parish church of All Saints presides over a commercial disaster zone. Where once there were the essential ingredients of village life – butchers, bakers and perhaps even candlestick makers – now there are boarded-up premises and a sad row of charity shops.

But the village is something of the mind, and no-one can persuade local residents that Kings Heath is no longer the rural idyll of their imagination. 'Here's my stop,' says the old soldier who reminds me that they do a very passable all-day breakfast at the Kitchen Garden Café in the village (☎ 0121 443 4725; open 09.00–17.00 Mon–Sat, 10.00–16.00 Sun).

Arriving in Sarehole

From Kings Heath, the bus drops gently towards the River Cole and Sarehole, a place name that is slowly disappearing from modern maps. No space for the gentle villages of yesteryear that have been gobbled up by the angry city. But **Sarehole** looks like a spot that well deserves a stop.

'Ah, you've come to Hobbiton,' says the elderly woman feeding ducks by the icy River Cole, alluding to Sarehole's illustrious place in literary history. A little improbably, it might seem, unless you know that, as young lads living just a short scamper away to the north, J R R Tolkien and his elder brother spent long summer days exploring the meadows and woods around Sarehole Mill (see box, page 112). The mill itself is just one of two remaining in a

Birmingham: a city of canals
(© Tupungato/DT)

SAREHOLE MILL

This is a delightful spot for humans and hobbits alike. The mill and its environs will appeal even to those who have never heard of Middle Earth. Yet for Tolkien fans Sarehole will evoke images of the great rebellion as Hobbits united to repel the creeping urbanisation and industrialisation of The Shire. Tolkien contributed to the restoration of Sarehole Mill in the 1960s, and today the building houses a small exhibition and an excellent tea shop (see www.birminghammuseums.org.uk/sarehole for days of tours).

city once famous for its mills and waterways. Sarehole is a good place to start exploring this little fragment of The Shire.

Kerry, not yet 21 and evidently already the mother of three children, is a resident of Springfield, just a short pram-ride from Sarehole. She is a tribute to human fertility and a discerning critic of Tolkien affairs. 'This ain't The Shire. 'Aven't you seen the film? All that stuff the council says is crap. Those 'obbits all lived in New Zealand.' Kerry's eldest is endeavouring to stick drawing pins into the back tyre of a car parked by the bus stop, but is distracted by the arrival of the Eclipse Gemini that will take us further on our urban orbit. Along the way, Kerry says that she and her flock are heading 'up the Swan'. This intelligence prompts me to reflect that, were George Cadbury on our bus today, he would surely have shared a little homily about the perils of lunchtime drinking, especially setting so poor an example to children of such tender years.

I am mightily relieved when the Swan turns out to be not a pub but a shopping centre in **Yardley**. By the time we reach it, we have seen a decent sweep of suburban Birmingham, resplendent with its tattoo studios, dental laboratories and discount stores. **The Swan**, evidently a local landmark, is not a sight to gladden the heart. Even a recent revamp (extra glass and yet more plastic) has not given this shopping centre any architectural charm.

Halal and hijab: multicultural Birmingham

From the Swan we have a clear run north, a rare few minutes of light traffic which our driver seems to relish, until we come abruptly to a standstill under the M6 at Bromford. This is container country, an eerie territory of railway sidings, canals and industrial parks where the roads are always grimy. Now there are Polish voices on the top deck of the bus as we cruise through **Erdington**, but Polish is soon eclipsed by Punjabi as we head west through **Perry Barr** towards Handsworth.

Exploring the back streets around the bus route, I could so easily conclude that this northwestern quadrant in our orbit has not made a positive contribution to the human condition. But that would be to overlook the life and work of Oscar Deutsch, the Birmingham-born son of Jewish-Hungarian parents who founded the Odeon cinema empire, which started life as a small chain of local movie houses, many of them in striking Art Deco buildings, in and around Perry Barr.

There is a disconcerting moment as we track down through **Handsworth**. Our driver, a lady this time, turns left on to Soho Road following a sign towards Birmingham city centre. I wonder if our Eclipse Gemini has somehow lost its orbital momentum. Are we being sucked inexorably into the heart of the city? There are tales told of lesser buses (not Eclipse Geminis of course) that spend their days in gruesome lines around the Bull Ring Shopping

DECODING THE ODEON

It was Harry Weedon, a Handsworth man, who designed many of Bimingham's fabulous cinemas for Oscar Deutsch. Sadly, many of Weedon's buildings are now depressingly derelict, but around Birmingham they still remember Oscar and his Odeons. 'Ah, yes... Deutsch,' said a fellow passenger as we cruised on the top deck through Perry Barr. 'Do you know what Odeon stands for? *Oscar Deutsch entertains our nation.*'

Centre and New Street Station. But after just a few yards, the driver, brimming with confidence, makes a right turn on to a minor road that more properly fits our orbital trajectory.

From hereon south, it is all 'X-Factor latest' on screaming headlines seen from the top deck. On the streets below, hair weaving and Western Union, teeth whitening 'while you wait', as we glide past mosques and Methodist chapels to Winson Green. Turbans and temples, allotments and community centres and Midland red brick sitting cheek by jowl with grey concrete. Yet there's nothing green about **Winson Green**, one of the forgotten zones west of the city centre. Once home to a large asylum, it now hosts Birmingham's most troubled prison.

'Jesus cares about Rotton Park,' proclaims a large banner, seemingly contradicting all the evidence that points to the contrary, before we move south through **Harborne**, once home to W H Auden, and back towards a more middle-class Birmingham. On past Ali Baba's fast food. Ali knows how to hedge his bets, serving both falafel and panini. But soon the Afro hair salons and discount clearance markets give way to dance studios, private nurseries and Italian delicatessens.

Birmingham's Outer Circle is a visual feast and a very fine urban kaleidoscope. The full circle is about the same length as the average feature film. As Oscar Deutsch surely appreciated, all good films can be revisited again and again, each new viewing revealing fresh layers of meaning. Just like this bus route. After a couple of circuits in one direction, hop off and orbit Birmingham in reverse, ever confident in the knowledge that the Outer Circle will always bring you back to chocolatey **Bournville**. ∎

ABOUT THE AUTHOR

NICKY GARDNER is a Berlin-based travel writer. She is co-editor of *hidden europe* magazine (www.hiddeneurope. co.uk). This journey was first published in *hidden europe*.

AUSTIN TO ELGAR:
BEYOND BRUMMAGEM

Nigel Roberts

Birmingham 🚌

Service no. 144 | Journey time 1hr 45mins.

OS Landranger 139, 150. Every 30mins Mon–Sat, hourly on Sun.
Operator: First.
Connects with Journey 21 in Selly Oak.

Worcester

It is hard to imagine two more contrasting cities than the pair which mark the start and end of this journey. Birmingham once styled itself 'the city of a thousand trades'. Today it is a vibrant representation of modern multi-cultural Britain. Worcester has never lost its archetypically English county qualities, with associations to the Middle Ages, the English Civil War, cricket, fine porcelain, Worcestershire Sauce and Edward Elgar.

This route is thus a bridge from the metropolitan bustle of Birmingham to the more sedate pace of Worcester. Every bus on this service *should* be a double-decker, but the reality is that some are singles. You don't need me to articulate the panoramic delights of the top-deck front seat, so try to be amongst the first in the queue to board the bus.

PULSE OF THE CITY

I readily acknowledge that Brummagem (as we Brummies know it) isn't everybody's cup of tea; but it's my home town so for me, it's a steaming mug with two sugars. You'll need to save its riches for another (bespoke) visit, but do return for 32 miles of canals, the Jewellery Quarter and the Balti Triangle (look that one up!).

So it's a scramble for seats and we're off, tackling the traffic and heading southwest on the **Bristol Road**. The carriageway is broad at this point (as it is most of the way to the fringes of the city), with a central reservation of grass and trees. This was formerly the line of a major tram route serving the suburbs for commuters and day trippers alike.

'That's where I used to get off the tram to visit Aunty Alice,' says the woman in the seat behind me to her husband.

We sail past the striking Art Deco apartments of Viceroy Close, and then a few minutes later glimpse Birmingham University's imposing **clock tower** – known as 'Old Joe', it is the tallest free-standing clock tower in the world. If you've made an early start and have the time, alight for a stroll through the Victorian splendour of the university campus. Selly Oak now has a bypass to ease traffic congestion, but the 144 winds its way slowly up the old high street. This is student land, and most of the Victorian terraced houses along the many roads are in multiple undergraduate occupation. Aficionados of Devon will smile fondly at the names of some of the roads off on the left.

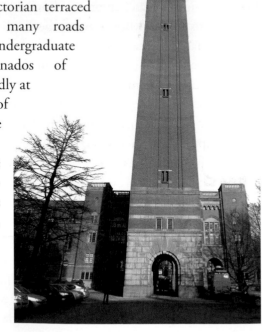

'That's where we came for our tap-dancing lessons,' says the voice behind me.

Clock tower of Birmingham University (© *hidden europe*)

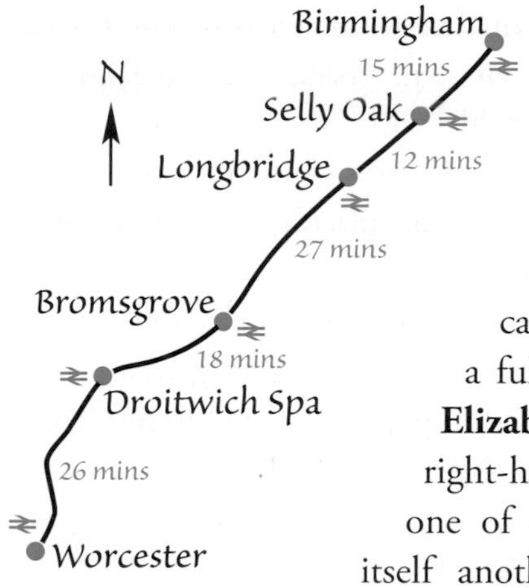

Birmingham

N

15 mins

Selly Oak

Longbridge

12 mins

27 mins

Bromsgrove

18 mins

Droitwich Spa

26 mins

Worcester

For some on board, the 144 is evidently a trip down Memory Lane.

As we climb the steepening gradient, there are more glimpses of the university campus. After the road levels out, a full view of the stunning **Queen Elizabeth Hospital** appears on the right-hand side, standing adjacent to one of the former hospital buildings, itself another beautiful example of the Art Deco style. The architecture of the new hospital is impressive on its own, but the statistics take it into new territory. It has the largest critical-care unit in the world and it runs the biggest organ-transplant programme in Europe.

The sight of the hospital evokes another memory bite from behind: 'When I was a nurse on the wards at the QE, I used to look out of the window at the university clock on night shifts and wish the time away.' This is exactly what my wife, herself a former nursing sister at the QE, says.

BOURNVILLE AND BEYOND

At the top of **Selly Oak** High Street we reach a major junction. Away to the left lies the enchanting oasis of calm that is **Bournville**, home to the Cadbury factory and the Bournville Village Trust. If you have time, it is worth a detour. The bus that heads up there is the number 11 Outer Circle – it is an extraordinary bus route, one that orbits the entire city of Birmingham, and one described in Journey 21. Hop on an Outer Circle bus at Selly Oak and just over two hours later, you'll be back where you started.

But here on the 144, we merely skirt the edge of Bournville Village Trust Estate, before climbing into the busy suburb of **Northfield**. This is mock-Tudor territory, but the woman behind me has more than architecture on her mind. 'That's where you went boozing in the war; you liked to get boozed up you did,' is her take on her husband's relationship with Northfield.

There is a sense of getting out of the city, but Birmingham is deceptive. It's a fast run downhill to **Longbridge** – not to reach sylvan glades and misty meadows, but rather to discover the forsaken heart of the Midlands motor industry. Aha, no surprise that the voice from behind has a thought on Longbridge's complex industrial legacy: 'I wonder what they'll do with the Orstin? That used to be the picture house over there.'

FAREWELL TO BRUMMAGEM

The A38 turns right at this point and it's only a short run to the edge of the Birmingham conurbation. There are glimpses left to the **Lickey Hills,** where the tram terminus used to be, disgorging Brummies in their thousands for a taste of the countryside on their day off work. Slow progress along Rubery High Street affords

THE GHOSTS OF THE CAR INDUSTRY

The British Leyland operation at Longbridge used to be a striking feature (no pun intended) of the British motor industry. The assembly lines that paused neither for breath nor sleep (except of course when silenced by the rallying cry 'all out, all out') delivered hundreds of vehicles every day; that image still lives with this Birmingham boy. Before British Leyland it was the Austin works, and most locals still refer to the entire site as 'the Austin' (actually, 'the Orstin' in Brummagem dialect). But the motor industry here is gone now, save for a modest production operation in a corner of one of the old units. The 144 bisects a vast site where once many thousands of Brummies clocked on and off daily. A few years ago, billboards foretold a glorious new age. 'A New Heart for Longbridge,' they proclaimed. It is now taking form. What say the spirits and shades of assembly-line technicians and union shop stewards of this vision I wonder? The Longbridge stage of the journey is an opportunity to reflect on the old and the new, the lost and the foretold.

more glimpses of the Lickeys in close-up. As we rejoin the bypass, the bus races out of Birmingham and we have our first fleeting glimpse of the glorious Malvern Hills in the distance.

Thus, less than an hour out of Birmingham, we reach **Bromsgrove**. The town's A E Housman connections are worthy of research and, if ever you find yourself this way again, do visit the unusual and impressive Avoncroft Museum of Historic Buildings (☎ 01527 831363; see www.avoncroft.org.uk for opening hours). Bromsgrove is roughly the halfway point on your journey and if you're ready for lunch, alight at the bus station and head to the right, along the pedestrianised high street, to the Maekong Thai restaurant (12 Worcester Rd; ☎ 01527 578888). I reckon it's the best food in town.

The A38 out of town first climbs steadily then begins to drop away as a Worcestershire vista unfolds. Look out for a small traffic island, where just right of centre is a delightful image that you won't have time to photograph, sadly. It's the escarpment of the **Malvern Hills** as a backdrop to the huge Droitwich transmitter, which will tug at the heartstrings of wireless devotees from days of yore. A mile further on, to the right, is Webb's Garden Centre, a feature in these parts for generations. The family has been trading on this spot since the middle of the 19th century. If the prospect of Thai food didn't grab you, stop here for a snack.

The small town of **Droitwich Spa** is soon reached – once famed for its brine baths opened in the 1880s, natural brine having first been mined and exported by the Romans – but look first for

GHELUVELT

Gheluvelt takes its name from the village in Flanders where in 1914 one of the early set-piece battles of World War I took place. Some 190 men of the local Worcester Regiment were killed or wounded. Many of those injured were later to be housed in this part of town. Gheluvelt is a fine example of a municipal park.

the curiosity of the Chateau Impney hotel on the left, just before you enter the town. The pace quickens after Droitwich, but keep glancing front and left for further glimpses of the Malvern Hills.

ARRIVING IN WORCESTER

At Perdiswell we cross the **Worcester** city boundary, and after a gentle downhill stretch through rows of attractive Victorian villas on either side, the road reaches a traffic light junction with a toll house to the right. This marks the start of the final mile of our journey to the bus station, and it will be time well spent to alight here and view the architectural treasures that await on foot.

The key sight in this part of town is Gheluvelt Memorial Park (see box opposite). You can wander into town through St George's Square, full of charming Regency and early Victoriana. A few hundred yards further on is the imposing Shire Hall, latterly refurbished to house the city's Crown and County courts. Immediately following is the lovely Victorian Art Gallery and Museum ('the Victoria Institute'), while ahead lies the beautiful ironmongery of the railway bridge at Foregate Street Station, immediately preceded on the right by the Odeon cinema, one of Oscar Deutsch's Art Deco finest. The bus station is to be found soon after the railway bridge and down to the right, at Crowngate.

If you have time to tarry, make your way to Friar Street to visit the delightful Tudor House Museum (☎ 01905 612309), or take a look at the National Trust's medieval Greyfriars' House and Garden (☎ 01905 23571). There are cafés and eateries aplenty nearby. Do return; many treasures await in this lovely county town. But what a contrast to Birmingham. We have swapped commercial muscle for a gentler, softer England. ∎

ABOUT THE AUTHOR

NIGEL ROBERTS lives on the 144 bus route. He works on sustainable development projects with communities in Belarus blighted by the Chernobyl catastrophe. He is the author of Bradt's guide to Belarus.

A TALE OF TWO DOCTORS: PROSE AND POISON

Richard Lakin

Stafford

Service no. 825 | Journey time 75mins.

OS Landranger 127, 128. Every 30mins Mon–Sat, hourly on Sun.
Operator: Arriva.

Lichfield

Our journey begins in Gaol Square, close to HM Prison Stafford – as it is known these days – where the murderous Doctor William Palmer met his end in June 1856. Thirty thousand people crammed the streets to watch him hanged that day, but on a chill winter morning I'm almost alone in Gaol Square. I am stamping my feet to keep a little warmth as I wait for the bus number 825.

My home town of **Stafford** doesn't shout about its heritage. It is perhaps a little shy of its better-known neighbours Chester and Shrewsbury, but there are interesting discoveries to be made. King

STAFFORD

The Ancient High House (open 10.00–16.00 Tue–Sat) is free to visit. The Shire Hall Gallery and historic courtroom (open 09.30–17.00 Mon–Wed & Sat, 10.00–17.00 Tue & 13.00–16.00 Sun) is where the replica death mask of Dr Palmer is on display. For sustenance before the bus ride try the Soup Kitchen (☎ 01785 254775; open 09.00–17.00 Mon–Sat), which dates from the 16th century and is tucked away in Church Lane close to Stafford town centre .

Charles I and Prince Rupert stayed in the Ancient High House, a wonderful Elizabethan timber-framed building towering above Greengate Street.

In the Shire Hall, a replica death mask of Dr Palmer can be seen (see box, page 121) and the former Crown Court and its treasures remain as a reminder to the poor souls sentenced to death – or transported for life for offences as pitiful as stealing a loaf of bread. One of Stafford's former MPs was the playwright Sheridan. A blue plaque stands above the entrance of his former house, but a greater literary figure awaits us on our journey through the unsung landscapes of the Trent Valley to Lichfield.

Across Cannock Chase

We leave Stafford behind and the floodplain glints in the winter sun as we make the steady climb up Radford Bank. The breaks between the houses widen as we pass tennis courts, villas and Victorian cottages hemmed in by hawthorn and privet.

At **Milford Common** mountain bikers and runners go through their stretches, heels to bums and knees to chest. For years the Common and surrounding Cannock Chase provided a welcome escape for a few short hours for factory workers and labourers who spent their lives grafting in the local industries of shoemaking and mining. A few precious hours were stolen on the fairground rides or sprawled on picnic blankets.

SHUGBOROUGH

Many visitors are drawn to the beautiful gardens and, in particular, eight monuments of national historic importance from the enormous Neoclassical arch on the hilly Shugborough skyline to the delightful Chinese House. Among the eight is the Shepherd's Monument built in 1748 and rumoured to have links to the Holy Grail story. As of 2016, it is now owned by the National Trust – see www.shugborough. org.uk for opening times and admission prices.

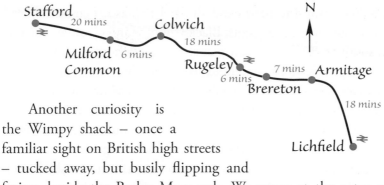

Another curiosity is the Wimpy shack – once a familiar sight on British high streets – tucked away, but busily flipping and frying, beside the Barley Mow pub. We pause at the gates of the **Shugborough Estate** (see box opposite), once home to the celebrated photographer Lord Lichfield, before passing through hills and valleys blanketed in copper bracken and swathed in mist.

Cannock Chase is a wild, open space within easy reach of millions, so perhaps it is inevitable it has attracted more than its share of stories. Thousands of soldiers trained here before going off to the trenches of the Great War and a military cemetery is tucked away amid the trees. There are lost mine shafts and abandoned quarries and even tales of UFOs.

We pull up tight to the kerb and an estate worker in green overalls steps out, cupping his hands and lighting a roll-up. The doors stutter as they slam shut, wafting in the sweet cool air of the forest before the drift of tobacco reaches us. We cross the bloated River Trent on a cobbled bridge so tight the bus can barely pass, but hardly a soul gets on or off in the villages of Colwich and Little Haywood.

COAL COUNTRY

Next stop is the former mining town of **Rugeley**, dominated by the four cooling towers of its riverside power station. An estate of new orange-brick houses has sprung up close to the bypass. A sign says, 'Yes, 95% mortgages are back' as if it's the news we've all been praying for. We leave the main road and cut through an estate of grey pebble-dash houses, picking up chatty pensioners looking forward to perms and all-day breakfasts. I crane my head for the accents: Scots, Scots, Black Country and Geordie. The pits in south Staffordshire drew plenty of miners from the north.

Rugeley's most infamous son, the previously mentioned William Palmer, trained as a doctor but his real love was for horse racing and womanising. He was accused of as many as 15 murders by poisoning, but convicted of only one murder, that of John Parsons Cook, whose grave can be found along with the Palmer vault in the town's St Augustine's churchyard. It is a short walk from the house the doctor grew up in and the pubs he frequented. The talk from my fellow passengers today is of troublesome feet and aching joints. Perhaps they should be grateful Palmer can no longer practise in their parish.

We stop in Coalpit Lane in **Brereton** and driver Mark says a few words to Reg and Albert who are getting off. The two men confide that they are heading off for their full English. We drive on and pass through **Armitage** – a name familiar to anyone who has ever drank too much (or perhaps met with Dr Palmer) and stared at the porcelain in a bathroom.

ARRIVING IN LICHFIELD

Soon the three spires of the magnificent **Lichfield Cathedral** appear, towering over the rooftops ahead. The bus empties and I head for the cathedral, which was dedicated shortly after the death of St Chad in AD700.

The St Chad Gospels are a wonderful sight and the stained Herkenrode glass in the Lady Chapel is stunningly beautiful, but, perhaps sensing scandal, my roving reporter's eye is drawn to the figure of Bishop de Langton. Once treasurer to Edward I, the bishop spent five years in prison for adultery, misappropriation and murder (and several other offences so bad I had to look the words up). He even had to visit the Pope twice to seek redress.

The need for a dictionary takes us neatly on to another doctor. The Samuel Johnson Birthplace Museum (☎ 01543 264972;

For further information on Lichfield Cathedral's treasures, history and stories, visit www.lichfield-cathedral.org. Admission is free, but donations are encouraged. The Samuel Johnson Birthplace Museum on Breadmarket Street is open every day of the week and admission is free (see page 124 and below for details).

Chapters Café (☎ 01543 306125; open Apr–Oct 09.00–17.00 daily; closes an hour earlier Nov–Mar), beside Lichfield Cathedral, has a 13th-century walled garden that is a delight in the summer. Also visit the Tudor of Lichfield tea rooms in Bore Street (☎ 01543 263951) for a delicious selection of cakes and chocolates in a wonderful building dating back to 1510. The tea rooms are just a stone's throw from the Samuel Johnson Birthplace Museum.

open Apr–Sep 10.30–16.30 daily, Oct–Mar 11.00–15.30 daily) is a great way to spend a diverting hour or so. I explore the basement kitchen where the nine-year-old Samuel read *Hamlet* and the bookshop where he worked for his father. It took Doctor Johnson ten years to complete his dictionary, a process he described with characteristic wit as 'a harmless drudge'. A copy can be viewed in the attic of the house and, yes, upon inspection it is clear the last reader has used it to look up a rude word.

The city is proud of its most famous son and Samuel Johnson frequently returned home. 'Every man has a lurking wish to appear considerable in his native place,' he said. The two Staffordshire doctors are remembered for very different reasons, but Johnson's fame is rightly far greater. Better to be a poet than a poisoner. ∎

ABOUT THE AUTHOR | **RICHARD LAKIN** trained as a reporter in Staffordshire. In 2009 he won the *Daily Telegraph*'s 'Just Back' annual travel writing prize for his essay, *The Great British Seaside*. Follow Richard on Twitter @Lakinwords.

THE MEDIEVAL AND POSTMODERN FENS

Anna Blair

Chatteris 🚌

Service no. 9 | Journey time 90mins.

OS Landranger 143, 154. 9 services daily Mon–Sat, no journeys Sun.
Operator: Stagecoach.

Cambridge ←

The question of the best mode of transport for exploring the Cambridgeshire Fens has been much discussed. John Betjeman wrote that seeing St Wendreda's Church in March justified 'cycling forty miles in a head wind', while groups leave March on foot for Cambridge each spring solely to claim they've done the March March march. There are punts and canoes in the Fens, and some towns still have train services.

Chatteris is not so blessed. Cast back half a century and diesel trains dashed from Chatteris to Cambridge in 45 minutes. The rail route from Cambridge closed in 1967. Today the number 9 bus from Chatteris to Cambridge takes 90 minutes. If one lives in Cambridge – and perhaps even if one doesn't – it's an

---

CHATTERIS

Chatteris is a town whose butchers and bus services, chandlers and cake shops have been particularly celebrated by the indie group Half Man Half Biscuit. The band has done its bit to put Chatteris on the map, commending this small Fenland community for its low crime rate. But Stagecoach don't take risks and so the bus to Cambridge starts outside the police station.

---

important journey to make, connecting a town that tends to think internationally with the landscape it actually sits beside, and making the histories and myths of the Fens tangible.

Boarding the number 9 in **Chatteris**, it is immediately obvious that this bus isn't built for sightseeing. It's a single-decker with disappointingly dirty windows. My fellow passengers are bored teenagers. But we are joined along the way by a couple of older travellers, one of whom climbs aboard carrying an old desktop computer.

These passengers rarely smile, speak or show interest in the landscape. This is not the Cotswolds, and these are not tourists. But one knows where one's going on the 9, and there's something beautiful about that: the road lies out before you as if the flat country were Borges's map – the map that is the size of the world and yet not the world itself.

In the middle distance is a paddock crowded with hundreds of swans, more than I've ever before seen together. I imagine the birds plotting, sharing secrets in this rural field before heading out to conquer Britain, their headquarters a secret linking all swans together.

Across Fenland drains

We soon cross the **Hundred Foot Drain**, a highlight of the trip. It's beneath us almost instantly, a mirror interrupted by skeletal trees. It appears as if nature has stolen and drowned the landscape, asserting itself where people dared to build houses. In actuality this waterway, like other Fenland soaks, is nature-harnessed; water's aggression has been channelled here so that the countryside itself can be habitable.

The tiny settlement of **Mepal** sits beside the Drain, dwarfed by the water. We continue along Mepal Road, raised a few metres higher than the surrounding land. These elevated roads have Roman origins, originally built up to allow for flooded fields.

We first see Ely Cathedral from **Sutton-in-the-Isle**, usually known simply as Sutton. The small hill offers beautiful views across the countryside, which can be glimpsed from the bus in the gaps between houses. There's a striking 14th-century church at the village's highest point and, like Chatteris, Sutton was mentioned in the Domesday Book of 1086.

Ely isn't far from Sutton. We enter the city, passing a large Burger King as we turn into smaller medieval streets. In some ways, this bus ride strips beauty from the Fens: they become 21st-century reality, not medieval myth.

In other ways, though, I'm reminded of how much truth there is to Cambridgeshire's medieval myth, how visible it is even when wrapped in postmodernism's less proud constructions. **Ely Cathedral** is a highlight of this bus ride as it is a highlight of this country, and Stagecoach acknowledges this crescendo with a 15-minute wait while we change drivers.

It's best, anyway, to dismount at Ely and explore. Originally named for its eel fishing, Ely is filled with antique shops, faux-independent candy shops aimed at tourists and birds circling around the cathedral. Further from the bus route, there is the River Great Ouse, where men walk dogs even in winter and Cambridge University's top rowing teams practise every morning.

The most beautiful moments on the 9 occur as the bus moves slowly between Ely Cathedral and the square before slipping along a narrow street lined with stone buildings. We stop at Tesco only a minute later, and passengers nod at one another as they settle

---

ELY CATHEDRAL

Ely Cathedral, begun in 1083, is one of England's best Gothic cathedrals. It's hard to miss, towering over the Fens, but it's possible to miss some of the surprises inside. On the upper level is the excellent Stained Glass Museum (☎ 01353 660347; open 10.30–17.00 Mon–Sat, noon–16.30 Sun), with information and examples drawn from across different periods. If you've the energy for climbing stairs, the cathedral also offers tours of the Lantern and West Towers, the latter offering magnificent views across Cambridgeshire.

into their seats. After the first minute, though, there's a return to silence, with only the regular roar and squeak of the bus as it accelerates and slows with traffic.

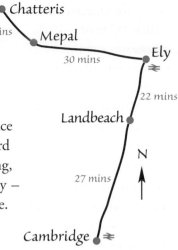

The flat landscape provides space for thinking, and the steady onward passage of the bus is comforting, ensuring thoughts are always literally – if not figuratively – going somewhere.

Cambridge in context

The bus turns into a number of industrial parks, shiny and new with no connection to the landscape. '2000 offices to let,' reads one sign, and I wonder what Cambridgeshire will look like in the future, if the damp puddles and fields will be gone completely.

As it is, the industrial parks feel like interruptions: this world belongs to seagulls and cows herded along country paths. When dark clouds speed in, one can feel the sky extending across to Holland. There are no major mountains lying between the Fens and Siberia and this, they say, is why it can be so cold in winter.

This stretch of the road puts Cambridge in context: a modern centre with its own satellite villages, not a medieval escape from London. These villages are often forlorn spots. We speed through Chittering without slowing. The last such village on the road from Ely is **Milton**, where the number 9 slips off the A10. Milton has the dramatic aura of a pioneer town, the first settlement after the stretch flatness of the Fens.

At first, it seems a dark caricature of a country village. The town's main landmark, another Tesco, is designed in a postmodern approximation of Tudor style; fans of quirky architecture will be amused by the triangular clock tower. Nearby, a pub advertises large-screen televisions ahead of ales.

Nonetheless, the bucolic is just two blocks from the bus stop at **Milton Country Park**. Fishermen wait patiently on the jetty and swans snicker amongst the reeds. This ecosystem, too, is indebted to the modern era; the creation of these lakes was facilitated by the extraction of materials for mid-century roads.

Milton is divorced from **Cambridge** proper by the A14 highway, suburbia's moat. Wider than the grandest Fenland drain, this road is a means of containing modern forces, directing cars around rather than through Cambridge. Everything feels tamer across the highway, and all the exhaustion of the Fens hits me, a sense of disbelief in the landscapes I've passed; the world behind feels instantly distant.

We pass the Cambridge Business Park, many houses, a furniture shop and a large roundabout. We cross the Cam, where genteel swans peck at boathouses painted in college colours, and the bus slips down the road between Midsummer Common and Jesus Green.

In late 2012, a bus on this route crashed off Victoria Avenue and through the fence, leaving tyre tracks and stunned passengers in the wake of its premature stop on **Jesus Green**. I want this to be always the end for this journey, bringing the wild loneliness of the hours across the Fens to a more dramatic halt than a simple turn around a corner and into the central bus station. It isn't today, though, and I step off the bus and into Cambridge, an adult Disneyland that feels like a mirage, utterly improbable after hours of England's outback. ■

ABOUT THE AUTHOR | **ANNA BLAIR** is a graduate student at the University of Cambridge.

From End of the Pier
to Under the Pier

Laurence Mitchell

Great Yarmouth

Service nos. X1s & 61 | Journey time 1hr 40mins to 2hrs.

OS Landranger 134. X1: every 15–20mins Mon–Sat, hourly Sun; 61: every 20mins Mon–Sat, every 2hrs Sun. Operator: Anglian Bus.

Southwold ←

G reat Yarmouth is not the place on most outsiders' lips when they speak of Norfolk. But, there again, nor is it Lowestoft that instantly springs to mind when Suffolk is mentioned. This bus service along England's easternmost edge crosses the county boundary to link these two workaday towns. From Lowestoft, another bus can be taken that terminates in a place that is much more a poster girl for the East Anglia coast – Southwold, a genteel resort where it can sometimes seem as if the 1960s have yet to happen. Despite a few common denominators – the North Sea, boats, beaches and piers – it is difficult to imagine two more different places than Great Yarmouth and Southwold, which is not to disparage either town but merely to note the cultural contrast that exists between the two.

Daniel Defoe once described Yarmouth as 'infinitely superior to Norwich', but he was writing in the early 18th century when the herring trade was booming. Great Yarmouth has prospered as both a thriving fishing port and busy seaside resort in the past but slowly fell into decline in the late 20th century. Holidaymakers switched their allegiance to warmer and cheaper resorts abroad. Nevertheless, enough remain faithful for it to retain two piers – Britannia and Wellington, the former having one of England's few remaining end-of-the-pier theatres.

The X1 service starts on the other side of the county in King's Lynn, but my journey begins just outside **Market Gates** in Yarmouth, next to BHS, where I find that the driver has nipped away for a coffee. When he returns I buy a day ticket and take a set upstairs at the front.

'You can use that anywhere, you know, even on Konect buses in Norwich,' he informs me helpfully, speaking as if the Norfolk capital were as distant as Samarkand. 'But not on the Park and Ride,' he adds. 'Anywhere but the Park and Ride.'

In Yarmouth, even Norwich seems distant – far more than just 20 miles along the A47. King's Lynn, also in Norfolk but more than 60 miles to the west of here, feels like another country altogether. Whilst waiting for the bus I had taken a stroll around and, venturing down **King Street**, discovered an enclave where, as well as a disproportionate number of hairdressers, trade seemed to be primarily focused on butchers' shops, tattoo parlours, tanning studios and Chinese take-aways. Polish supermarkets and a brightly painted café complete the picture, the latter with wall-mounted televisions showing Portuguese TV channels – this, a far cry from the sunny shores of the Algarve. The truth is, there's little gloss in Yarmouth

TIME AND TIDE MUSEUM

There is nowhere better for getting a feel of what Great Yarmouth was like in its fishing heyday than at the town's Time and Tide Museum in Blackfriars Road (☎ 01493 743930; open summer 10.00–16.30 daily, winter 10.00–16.00 Mon–Fri, noon–16.00 Sat–Sun). It is easily reached by taking a short walk south from the bus station along King Street and then following the signs. The museum, set in a former Victorian herring-curing works and still bearing its lingering aroma today, celebrates Great Yarmouth's maritime heritage and growth as a seaside resort, and has recreated row houses as well as newsreels and photographs of the herring trade.

these days – just the everyday needs of a working-class town and the cultural fixes of recently arrived immigrant communities.

Pulling away to drive past the Victorian town hall at the top of South Quay, we cross the River Yare by way of Harbour Bridge and turn left to travel parallel to the quay through Southtown. An industrial area of builders' yards screens most of the views beyond but a couple of ships can be seen at the quay – a trawler from Aberdeen and a black-painted vessel called *Keret* from St Petersburg. A little further on, the **Britannia Monument** can be seen rising high above the half-empty factory plots, a 144ft-high Doric column topped by six caryatids and a statue of Britannia who, counter-intuitively, gazes inland with her back to the sea.

SOUTH TO LOWESTOFT

Southtown morphs invisibly into **Gorleston-on-Sea**, where the main street has yet more hairdressers and tattooists. A handful of retired folk get on at the Gorleston High Street stop before we turn right to pass through a mock-Tudor enclave along Middleton Road *en route* to the A12. If the name Gorleston sounds unpleasantly medical then at least there is a large hospital as compensation, and the bus briefly detours into the vast car park of the James Paget Hospital. Although a few hardy souls are sitting in wheelchairs puffing away in the smoking shelter, there are no passengers to pick up today – so our detour has been in vain.

LOWESTOFT NESS

Ness Point (www.ness-point.co.uk) in Lowestoft is the easternmost point in the United Kingdom at nearly 1°46' east of Greenwich. The site is home to a directional marker known as the Euroscope and also to 'Gulliver', Britain's tallest wind turbine. A quick inspection of the distances on the Euroscope will inform that you stand 465 miles south of Dunnet Head, the British mainland's most northerly point, and 352 miles from the Lizard, the most southerly.

A minute later we plunge into farmland. The fields are dull and khaki-coloured in late winter. After a mile or two more, we cross the county boundary and turn off the main road to stop at a huge Tesco hypermarket that, somewhat pretentiously, has its very own clock tower, an unnecessary affectation considering it is open 24 hours a day. We slip past a holiday village – rather forlorn out of season – and enter the bungalow territory of **Gunton**. The enormous wind turbine at Lowestoft Ness suddenly comes into view looming over the North Sea ahead. Despite its constant proximity, this is the first time the sea has been seen on the journey so far. Another reminder of the sea comes at the stop next to **Lowestoft bus station**, where an Edwardian Catholic church is dedicated to 'Our Lady Star of the Sea' – the Virgin Mary imagined as a guiding star for seafarers. This church promotes itself as the easternmost Catholic church in Great Britain, although pretty well everything in Lowestoft is the easternmost something or other.

Like Yarmouth, Lowestoft used to be very much a town of seafarers, once home to one of the largest fishing fleets in the country. Now the boats are virtually all gone but the gulls remain – muscle-bound herring gulls that swagger nonchalantly around town as if they own the place, which, in a way, they do. But, even without its fleet, Lowestoft is still worth an hour or two of anyone's time. If you take a walk to the Ness you can delight in the knowledge that, temporarily at least, you are the easternmost person on British soil. Having bagged that windy extremity I take shelter in Poppies Tea Rooms, which advertises 'breakfasts all day.' Given its heart-warming – and heart-stopping – generosity on the saturated-fat front, this establishment's

Great
Yarmouth

16 mins

Gorleston-
on-Sea

N

29 mins

Lowestoft

33 mins

Wrentham

6 mins

13 mins

Wangford

Southwold

large breakfast would probably necessitate taking the first bus back to James Paget Hospital if it didn't stop you in your tracks there and then. Playing safe, I just plump for tea and a bun.

ALONG THE SUNRISE COAST

An hour later, take the 61 southbound. This time the bus is a single-decker and surprisingly full. We go over the swing bridge and past a monument of a sou'wester-clad fisherman gazing seaward. Leaving Lowestoft, we stop at Pakefield's Tramway pub before reaching a retail estate at the edge of town where a beleaguered-looking woman gets off at the Morrisons stop, her six children in tow. The driver knows her by name and has been patient and understanding as throughout the journey she has done her best to get her charges, awkwardly distributed along the length of the bus, to behave and not annoy the other passengers. The kind driver even magically proffers tissues to wipe the toddler's nose at one point – a real credit to his profession.

We make a brief foray into **Kessingland** before returning to the A12 to pass through **Wrentham**, which might come close to most people's idea of a typical Suffolk village were it not for the main road thundering through it. The landscape has become more undulating now, with plenty of woodland and sheep in the

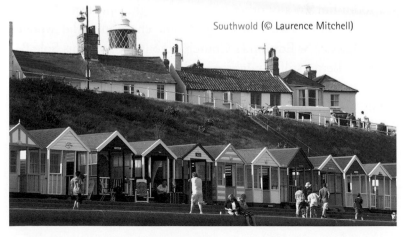

Southwold (© Laurence Mitchell)

SOUTHWOLD PIER

Southwold Pier (www.southwoldpier.com) is a good starting place to explore the town. The Southwold skyline is dominated by a lighthouse that mushrooms between the rooftops. To the south, the giant white golf ball of Sizewell B Power Station's dome can be seen in the distance. The pier is a family-run business (no entry charge). Apart from standard-fare gift shops and cafés, the pier hosts the Under the Pier Show, an arcade of hilariously eccentric Heath Robinson-style machines created by Tim Hunkin. This includes delights such as 'whack a banker', where you can wreak your revenge on the fat cats, 'my nuke', which allows you to load plutonium rods into your very own nuclear reactor, and 'pet or meat', where you get to decide the fate of an innocent lamb. Further along the pier is the infamous Water Clock, also by Hunkin, which chimes on the half-hour in an amusingly rude manner.

meadows – far more typical of the county as a whole. We leave the main road and wind down into **Wangford**, a pretty village with tidy cottages tightly bunched round a flint church. Then reed beds and marshes at the roadside signal the last stretch into **Southwold**.

Arriving at the western end of the town's high street, we pirouette around the King's Head before arcing north to arrive at the seafront right by the pier. From here it is but a short walk back into town. It's a cold day so I choose to head straight for a tea room but on any other occasion I might opt instead to visit the delightful Sailors' Reading Room, check out the wooden roof angels of St Edmund's Church or tour the Adnams Sole Bay brewery. Better still, I might even drink a pint of the selfsame ale at any one of the town's half-a-dozen or so pubs. With sufficient funds, the world is very much your oyster – or, rather, pan-fried sea bass – in Southwold, although you might struggle to find a decent tattoo parlour. ∎

ABOUT THE AUTHOR

LAURENCE MITCHELL (www.laurencemitchell.com) is a travel writer and photographer based in Norwich. He is the author of Bradt's guides to Serbia and Kyrgyzstan, as well as *Slow Travel Norfolk* and *Slow Travel Suffolk*.

With the Sea to your Right

Laurence Mitchell

26 Cromer

Coasthopper service | Journey time 2hrs 55mins.

OS Landranger 132, 133. Daily (every 30mins in summer, every 1–2hrs in winter). Route formed of Coasthopper 3 (Cromer–Wells), Coasthopper 2 (Wells–Hunstanton) & Coasthopper 1 (Hunstanton–King's Lynn). Operator: Stagecoach Norfolk.

King's Lynn ◀

The Coasthopper service that runs between Cromer and King's Lynn along the north Norfolk coast must be one of the most useful bus routes in the country – it's even free if you already have a Rover ticket for the Bittern Line rail service between Norwich and Sheringham. Few take the Coasthopper for the whole distance though: as its name suggests, it is best suited to short hops along this gorgeous stretch of Norfolk coastline. Eco-conscious (or just plain car-less) birdwatchers use it to get to the wader-rich marshes around Cley-next-the-Sea, Norfolk's birding Mecca; walkers take advantage of a one-way ride in this coastal fringe of linear footpaths that make circular walks difficult; retired locals use it for pension-day outings to King's Lynn or Cromer. Summer or winter, if you look inside the bus you'll find a microcosm of the north Norfolk community.

The Coasthopper is perfect for holidaymakers too, passing through many of north Norfolk's best-loved villages – neat, cobble-built clusters like Blakeney, Stiffkey and Brancaster. In addition to Cley-next-the-Sea for birders, there's Morston for seal fanciers, Burnham Market for fine wine and posh nosh, Holkham's beach for bathers and Brancaster for a briny round of golf. And there's

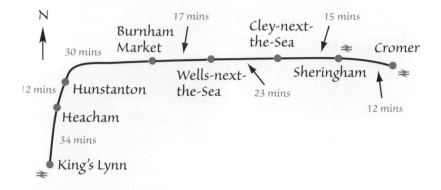

always Hunstanton, Wells or Cromer too for the simple pleasures of fish and chips and a promenade. Agenda-free passengers can simply get on and off as the fancy takes them, tempted by a cosy pub, an appealing stretch of marsh, or tea and scones in a Cley tea room.

WEST TO WELLS

I used to visit this stretch of coast a lot back in the late 1970s when I was a bit of a weekend birder. In those days there was no bus service to speak of and so I was obliged to either hitch-hike or persuade my recalcitrant Morris Traveller not to break down *en route* here. So, hats off to the Coasthopper for providing a very welcome lifeline.

Cromer is a possible starting point but coming by train from Norwich I prefer Sheringham as it is a bit more convenient – the bus stops right outside the station.

Once out of town we leave **Sheringham**'s golf course and cliff-top caravan sites behind to drop down to Kelling. Immediately, the landscape becomes rather more austere: to our right are tantalising glimpses of sea between sand dunes and pebble banks, while a green swathe of fields with ripening wheat and barley flashes by on the left. Beyond this slopes a ridge of low hills – low, perhaps, but still the loftiest in all Norfolk. At **Salthouse** – so named because of its one-time salt industry – skeins of honking geese rise from the salt marshes to punctuate the sky, a hint of what is to come at **Cley-next-the-Sea** (see box, page 140), our next port of call.

Approaching Cley, a couple of holiday birders, newly retired by the looks of it, dressed in quality camouflage gear and clutching expensive Zeiss binoculars, get off the bus. No doubt they will soon be perched on a bench in a hide trying to differentiate their godwits. It is not just birdwatchers of course: the bus is a microcosm of north Norfolk humanity – a real community bus rather than a mere tourist service. Few seem to be riding it for as far as I am though.

We pass the nature reserve's fancy new visitor centre on the left – all glass and eco-friendly pine – before skirting Cley's windmill, probably north Norfolk's most totemic building. The road twists through the village past tea rooms, art galleries and a well-appointed delicatessen to pass more marshes and ponds on the way out. In plain view of the bus, slender waders probe the mud for morsels, ignoring the stare of birdwatchers on the bank opposite who flick binoculars to eyebrows to check them out.

A pair of walkers, OS maps neatly tucked into plastic water-proof wallets, get off at the Blakeney junction beneath the imposing bulk of St Nicholas's Church – the so-called 'Cathedral

NORTH NORFOLK NOSH

Cookie's Crab Shop (Salthouse; ☎ 01263 740352; open 09.00–18.00 daily, shorter hours in winter) on the green just before the Dun Cow pub and with a nice garden facing the salt marshes is the place to enjoy all sorts of shellfish, seafood platters and smoked fish sandwiches. Cookie's is not licensed but it is fine to bring your own. At weekends it is best to book beforehand.

The White Horse (Brancaster Staithe; ☎ 01485 210262; www.whitehorsebrancaster.co.uk) has the perfect location facing out across the marshes. There's even a telescope available for birders. Good local ales and even more local seafood.

of the coast' – with its curious tiny second tower (a beacon for storm-tossed sailors some have romantically surmised). Then it's **Morston**, barely a village more just a muddy creek with seal trip boats advertising their wares. A schoolgirl gets on here and without so much as a glance out of the window texts her mates as we slip through pebble-built **Stiffkey** (see box, page 143), a curious place that for long dry decades languished without a pub despite no shortage of thirsty villagers. Thankfully, there is a pub here these days – and a handy campsite – an unpretentious base for iodine-charged walks within sniffing distance of the sea.

The girl gets off in Wells, hardly looking up from her phone, as do a few local pensioners who have come here for the shops. After Morston, Cley and Stiffkey, **Wells-next-the-Sea** seems a veritable metropolis.

BUSSING THROUGH THE BURNHAMS

We leave the main coast road for a little tour around Wells, passing in front of the harbour with its granary (now holiday flats), chippie and amusement arcade – the last a minor concession to the summer holiday trade. A gaggle of enthusiastic dads and kids suspend lines from the harbour wall angling for crabs. For fun not for food, of course – the real industry here was always whelks.

After passing the imposing gates to Holkham estate, we enter the realm of 'the Burnhams', first Burnham Overy Staithe, a haven for sailors, then a turn inland to the pristine Georgian village of **Burnham Market** or 'Chelsea on Sea' as local wags have it. A cluster of tidy allotments line the road up to the village: a breath of workaday normality in the rarefied metropolitan atmosphere of this most untypical of Norfolk villages. They come as a relief, as do the hearty Norfolk accents that board the bus here, unfazed by their village being hijacked by wealthy weekenders from 'The Smoke'. Shiny German cars now seem to be the default here, so a traverse of the village by bus is rewarded by just a hint of smugness.

Leaving Burnham Market behind, we are soon back on the coast road once more. Two more Burnhams follow in quick succession – Burnham Norton, barely a hamlet, with a round tower church but no other facilities, and then Burnham Deepdale.

Burnham Deepdale is home to Deepdale Camping (☎ 01485 210256), a delightfully green enterprise where it is possible to stay in a tipi or even a yurt if that is your heart's desire.

Marsh and windmill at Cley-next-the-Sea
(© Laurence Mitchell)

The camp reception doubles as a helpful information centre, well stocked with books, maps and goodwill.

Brancaster Staithe comes next, another charming flinty village much loved by weekend sailors that has a small staithe (quay) with a row of attractive 17th-century cottages flanking its entrance. There's a breezy golf course too, right next to the dunes. The bus stops right outside the Jolly Sailors on the main coast road but it is only a short walk from here down to the White Horse where you can gaze over the marshes as you sip your pint and delve into a bowl of mussels.

Brancaster Staithe morphs into Brancaster proper and we drive past the turn-off to Titchwell RSPB reserve, another well-respected bird Eden, to arrive in **Thornham**. If Thornham seems a little different in character from what has come before it is probably the appearance of the houses.

Here the vernacular is suddenly transformed from flint and pebble to building with blocks of chalk – a sign of things to come along The Wash. Thornham is a handsome village and the temptation to get off here is quite strong given the proximity of two fine pubs and numerous walking possibilities. If you stay on past Holme-next-the-Sea though, you'll soon arrive at the point where the Norfolk coast abruptly ends its hitherto relentless east–west orientation.

GOING ROUND THE BEND

The sea stays pretty much out of sight until **Old Hunstanton** where the road makes a sharp turn at the golf course. This marks the bend in Norfolk's coast from where you can watch the sun setting out to sea across **The Wash** – a rare experience in what is primarily an east-facing county. Like Thornham, there's plenty of chalk in the buildings here, as well as carrstone, a local red limestone. Head down to Old Hunstanton's beach; from here you'll see both *in situ* in the quite spectacular banded cliffs. The newer part of Hunstanton is quite nice too, a resort of the

STIFFKEY CONNECTIONS

As well as giving its name to a local variety of cockle ('Stewkey Blues'), Stiffkey is also known for having been the parish of Reverend Harold Davidson, the so-called 'Prostitutes' Padre' who aroused much controversy with his campaign to single-handedly save the souls of London's fallen women. The village was also the wartime hideaway of Henry 'Tarka the Otter' Williamson who had a farm here for several years before decamping to Devon.

Victorian railway age, rather like Cromer. Somehow this feels like the end of the road but the journey does not have to stop here. After a five-minute break for bus and driver to gird their loins, the Coasthopper continues south – or at least alternate services, the ones that arrive at half-past the hour, do.

BEYOND HUNSTANTON

The village of **Heacham** is next, with a stop right by the Norfolk Lavender Centre, which has a tea room and, no surprise, plenty of lavender-based souvenirs in its sweetly odorous gift shop. Then it's the final leg into **King's Lynn**, where the Coasthopper stops conveniently at the railway station before terminating at the bus station.

From here, it is just a short walk to South Quay, by far the most alluring part of the town, nicely restored and with all manner of fascinating maritime connections. ■

ABOUT THE AUTHOR **LAURENCE MITCHELL** (www.laurencemitchell.com) is a travel writer and photographer based in Norwich. He is author of Bradt's guides to both Serbia and Kyrgyzstan as well as *Slow Travel Norfolk* and *Slow Travel Suffolk*.

A FAMILY TALE

One name which has been a recurrent thread in the development of bus transport in the East Midlands is Thomas Barton. First and foremost an engineer and an early pioneer of oil-fired engines, he and his family saw the potential of public transport. The Bartons offered a pony-and-trap service along the seafront at Mablethorpe, but by 1897 had upgraded to a motorised service carrying 11 passengers. This was one of Britain's first bus services not to have horses doing the work upfront.

A similar service was launched in Weston-super-Mare in 1899. The choice of location for these early bus services shows that travel in a motor bus was, in the early days, marketed as recreation rather than as a necessity. The bus was novel and exciting – it was a treat associated with being on holiday at a seaside resort such as Mablethorpe or Weston-super-Mare.

Thomas Barton's Weston experience was not entirely positive, however. Many of the men with great influence in the affairs of Weston had vested interests in the horse trade, and the Barton family's enthusiasm for motorised wagonettes ruffled local feathers. Before long, their licence was revoked and the family returned to Lincolnshire.

In 1908, Thomas Barton and his son set off to London on the Midland Railway, intent on buying a new vehicle. Travelling south from Leicester, the two men chatted with the only other occupant in their carriage who was a director of a company that had just started making charabancs. A deal was done on the train, and the Bartons did not even proceed to London. They alighted at Luton and returned to the East Midlands, making plans along the way. The following weekend they launched their bus service from Long Eaton to Nottingham. The route still runs today.

The Bartons were ever innovative. When fuel was short during World War I, Thomas Barton devised a creative alternative of storing town gas in a balloon above the bus. Drivers were advised to avoid low bridges. The Barton family bucked convention in other ways. In summer 1913, Thomas's daughter Kate took to the wheel of a vehicle and, at age 20, became Britain's first female bus driver. 'Girl as Chauffeur of Omnibus: Sisters as Conductors', reported the *Daily Mirror*. The centenary of this moment of social progress passed with too little remark. ∎

Wales and the Borders

Wales is very palpably a different country from England, with its own language, culture and traditions. Tread gently, travel slow, take time to stop off here and there, and you will find places that are very special. The more rural areas of the principality are God's gift to the bus traveller. Explore three national parks in Snowdonia, Pembrokeshire and the Brecon Beacons, a great variety of coastal resorts and, in the hills of mid Wales, some of the most sparsely populated terrain in Britain – all very accessible by bus. Two of our six featured routes begin on the English side of the border. Sit back and savour the transition from one country to the other.

For us, part of the real delight of bus travel in Wales and the Welsh borders lies mainly in the routes operated by smaller, locally based operators, of which there are dozens. So, in addition to the big players such as Arriva or Stagecoach, our selection of Welsh journeys include travel on services run by Lloyds Coaches, Express Motors, Sargeants Brothers, GHA Coaches and Evans Coaches.

Spreading wings from Lleyn

Some Welsh local bus operators can trace their roots back to the earliest days of rural bus travel in Wales. The villages of Clynnog and Trefor on the Lleyn Peninsula of northwest Wales felt they were being bypassed by the revolution in mobility that swept Britain in the early 20th century. So in 1912, they clubbed together and purchased a bus. Their initiative was called Moto Coch (the Welsh for 'red bus'), but over time the name of the company evolved to reflect the names of the two villages where it was founded: Clynnog & Trefor. The original vehicle was a single-decker, but had a roof rack that could be used to transport small animals to market in Pwllheli.

Today Clynnog & Trefor run a web of school bus services across Gwynedd but still operate just one scheduled bus route. Fittingly, it is the service across the Lleyn Peninsula from Caernarfon to Pwllheli via Clynnog and Trefor – the very same route that the company served when it started business.

Travel passes

Holders of free concessionary bus passes in Wales can of course use their passes on the buses of any operator – large or small. The Welsh scheme long predates its English equivalent and is in some respects superior to the English initiative. Passes are available from the age of 60 and they may be used for travel at any time of the day (whereas in most areas of England travel may not commence until after the morning peak). Welsh passes also permit free travel on selected rural rail routes.

Visitors to Wales can benefit from the 'Explore Wales' pass, which offers eight consecutive days of unlimited travel by bus in Wales. The pass is accepted by many of Wales's colourful local bus operators including those mentioned in this section. On any four days of your choice (within the overall eight-day validity of the pass), you can also use train services within Wales and make cross-border rail journeys to Chester, Crewe, Shrewsbury, Hereford and Gloucester. There are also passes for south Wales and for north and mid Wales, as well as a range of day rover tickets. ∎

SEND US YOUR SNAPS!

We'd love to follow your adventures using our *Bus-Pass Britain* guide – why not send us your photos and stories via Twitter (@BradtGuides) and Instagram (@bradtguides) using the #BradtBus.

Les Lumsdon

27 Ludlow

Service nos. 738 or 740 | Journey time 60mins.

OS Landranger 137. 4 services daily Mon–Sat, no service Sun.
Operator: Arriva.

Knighton

A driver once mentioned to me that he loved doing the runs through the Marches as there are so many beautiful chimneys to admire. I know what he means. In **Ludlow** for example, the streets are rich with Georgian town houses, almost every one possessing an ornate brick flue, standing tall above the roofline. But Ludlow is essentially a Norman town wrapped within the old walls; witness the narrow streets that the bus has to negotiate. That's where you'll catch a glimpse of fine examples of half-timbered houses, many of which lie between the ruins of Ludlow Castle and the parish church dedicated to St Laurence.

The half-timbered façade of the
Feathers Hotel in Ludlow
(© Visitor Economy Team, Shropshire
Council)

These are remarkable survivors of the Middle Ages and much loved by the locals.

There have been changes, of course. I overhear two older men on board talking about a cinema that once stood in Old Street, which they refer to as the 'flea pit'. It was evidently the place to be in their youth. Lamentably, it has gone now the way of many small-town cinemas. The bus eases up to the lights at the Bull Ring, a traditional crossroads where bulls might well have been tethered in previous decades – but not now. Well not today at any rate. There are more passengers to be picked up in Corve Street but the bus soon leaves Ludlow bound for Wales.

The first stop on our cross-border journey is at **Bromfield**, where the Ludlow Food Centre makes and sells fresh produce, most of it grown on local farms. Now begins the climb, gently at first, but then in a determined manner towards the wooded scarp slope known as **Mocktree**. If you're lucky you'll spot fallow deer to the right where pockets of woodland give way to pasture. There's often a change of mood on the bus at the summit. The bus falls quiet. People stop conversing in order to concentrate on the view – and what a view it is! Look over the hedgerow to the Wigmore Rolls, a succession of low-lying hills that surround the village and castle of **Wigmore**. But it is the higher and more foreboding Radnor Forest ahead that catches the eye, miles of rough moorland plateaux where hardy sheep graze in all weathers on the highest terrain for miles around. In winter, snow lies on the exposed tops when everywhere else remains green.

CORACLE COUNTRY

The bus arrives at the ancient Roman settlement of **Leintwardine** (Bravonium), a strategic bridging point over the River Teme. There's no evidence of the Roman camp above ground but it is a good place to stop off awhile. The village is known for its coracle making and a local man, known as the Oracle of the Coracle, still practises the ancient skills using locally grown willows, hazel

THE SUN INN, LEINTWARDINE

You'll find the Sun Inn on Rosemary Lane (where the bus pulls in). This is one of the few remaining Victorian parlour pubs in Britain, a pub where people used to sit in the parlour and be served beer from jugs directly tapped from the cask! The pub was for decades in the hands of Flossie Lane, the oldest landlady in England at the age of 94, until her death in 2009. The greatest tribute to her, however, is that a local brewer, Nick Davis of Hobsons, has brought new life to the pub, while at the same time maintaining the character of the two 19th-century rooms. They have done this with panache and it is a fitting place to take refreshment. Open every day from 11.00 except Monday when the pub opens at 17.30 (☎ 01547 540705).

rods and cow hides from Griffiths, the village butcher. He even runs courses for those who want to make their own under the supervision of his expert eye. The parish church of St Mary Magdalene stands at the very centre of the village and is two minutes' walk from the bus stop.

The bus route in Leintwardine can be confusing to the uninitiated. The 738 continues ahead across the stone bridge to **Brampton Bryan**, where the ruins of its ancient castle are open to the public but once a year – during the Scarecrow Sunday event in early August.

Anyway, back in Leintwardine, the other service (the 740) sweeps round to set down passengers underneath the tall shady oak opposite the Lion Hotel, then runs back on itself through the village before branching off to **Clungunford**. This was one of A E Houseman's 'quietest places under the sun'. Next stop is **Hopton Heath**, which is where you can alight for a one-mile walk to Hopton Castle, recently restored by local residents. The castle harbours the story of one of the worst atrocities of the English Civil War. But those planning to explore this area might also consult the train timetable as there's a railway station at Hopton Heath – very useful in case return bus times don't suit.

Whichever route is taken, all buses end up in the sprawling village of **Bucknell**; it has grown up around the sparkling waters of the River Redlake. Bucknell has, in recent times, become a mini Mecca for walkers and the 'Walking with Offa' project encourages walks from here, including a route through to Knighton, about six to seven miles by way of woods and sheep pastures. Fortunately, there are also two pubs in the village: the Baron at Bucknell (☎ 01547 530549) and the Sitwell Arms (☎ 01547 530213), so it is a good place to enjoy refreshment.

The bus crosses the track of the **Heart of Wales railway**, a stubborn survivor if ever there was one. With a number of stations on or close to this bus route, there's a lot of scope for creating fine bus–rail itineraries (more on www.heart-of-wales.co.uk).

Approaching the border

The bus begins to complete the last leg of the route into Wales. The changing landscape hints of the border. Suddenly there is a sense of wilderness. The gentle familiarity of Shropshire is being challenged by something different. The Teme Valley narrows and the high hills hold a greater presence now than hitherto. They are, in part, shrouded with dense woodland which in some respects makes them look more striking, most particularly in autumn.

Between these beckoning hills sits the classic gap town of **Knighton** where England meets Wales. It is with some irony that the railway station is actually in Shropshire but the remainder of the town lies well and truly in Wales. Its Welsh name is Tref-y-Clawdd, meaning 'town on the dyke,' and this refers to its significance as a trading post on Offa's Dyke, said to have been built by the Mercian King Offa to hold back Welsh tribes.

The situation was far more complex than can be told here and it is not unreasonable to conclude that this border dyke allowed multi-directional trade between communities. Visit the Offa's Dyke Centre (☎ 01547 528753; open summer 10.00–17.00 daily, winter 10.00–16.00 daily, with a short break over lunch), about a ten-minute walk from Knighton bus station, for the full story. Entrance is free and the friendly staff have stacks of

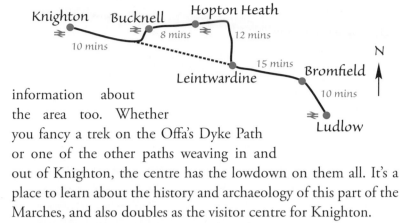

information about the area too. Whether you fancy a trek on the Offa's Dyke Path or one of the other paths weaving in and out of Knighton, the centre has the lowdown on them all. It's a place to learn about the history and archaeology of this part of the Marches, and also doubles as the visitor centre for Knighton.

Knighton bus station is somewhat of an exaggeration in terms. It comprises one draconian shelter and a raised kerb, sandwiched between recycling bins and the cattle market. It is not surprising then that it rarely gets nominated for any bus awards. Yet there are some redeeming features, such as a public toilet nearby and, for those with an interest in farming, an almost ringside view of the livestock in the auction pens. You'll certainly hear and smell them!

Probably the best way into town is to walk along Bowling Green Lane, past the market, towards the small supermarket and then to turn right for the centre. This is marked with a Victorian clock tower, a landmark that cannot be missed. Leading up from here are the 'Narrows', a network of narrow streets, distinctly medieval in layout, which rise to the top of the town, where there's an old castle mound (not open to the public).

If you are out to discover Knighton and the Offa's Dyke Centre then the time available between buses is about right before returning through a part of the borderland that too few visit. ∎

ABOUT THE AUTHOR

LES LUMSDON lives near Ludlow and spends much of his time exploring the Welsh Marches on foot, by cycle or by bus. He is author of *A Guide to Slow Travel in the Marches* (Logaston Press).

BORDER CROSSING

Tim Locke

28 Hereford 🚌

Service nos. 461 or 462 | Journey time 1hr 50mins.

OS Landranger 149, 148, 147. Hourly Mon–Sat.
Operator: Sargeants Brothers.
Connects with Journey 32 in Llandrindod Wells.

Llandrindod Wells ←

The two-hour ride by bus from Hereford to Llandrindod is a perfect cross-section of some of my favourite countryside, giving a most satisfying sense of crossing a national border. Here England metamorphoses into Wales spectacularly abruptly: one moment you are in a gently pastoral, rolling, quintessentially English landscape.

Then comes the 'Welcome to Wales' sign and the landscape changes dramatically as moors, bracken, gorse and crags appear. Herefordshire's half-timbered villages give way to scattered sheep-farming communities and grey-stone hamlets. Accents also change along the way.

This is an easy route to access, with rail stations at either end of the journey. There are also several places along the journey that make good stopping-off points. I have known this area for many years, and have a second home on the Welsh side of the border. But until recently I had never ventured on the little red bus that takes a meandering, utterly rural route from Hereford to Llandrindod Wells. It was a rewarding way to appreciate how the area might look to a newcomer. I sat at the back – the rear three rows on the 31-seater bus are raised enough to get grandstand views over the ubiquitous hedgerows. The convoluted route isn't one I had ever followed in its entirety before.

Cider Country

Hereford is a big place compared with everything else on this route. Don't be deterred by its nasty inner ring road, too often clogged with serious traffic. From the bus you get little idea of Hereford's many charms. The city has many gracious partly Georgian brick streets around the cathedral, which is home to the medieval Mappa Mundi. This is a quite remarkable 13th-century map that plots the world as seen through the eyes of scholars of those times. Just outside the cathedral stands a life-size statue of the composer Sir Edward Elgar, on whom this region's landscape made such a profound impression. The statue depicts Elgar about to mount his beloved bicycle, known as Mr Phoebus.

The starting point for the bus journey to Wales is Hereford's exuberantly Gothic railway station, and there are glimpses of Herefordiana as you travel – a chunk of the medieval city wall, then, opposite the Bulmer's Heineken depot, a retired cider press poses as street sculpture. After Victorian suburbs give way to semis, the whole urban scene evaporates and is replaced by the most gorgeously rural Herefordshire scenery. Lush greenness, deep-red

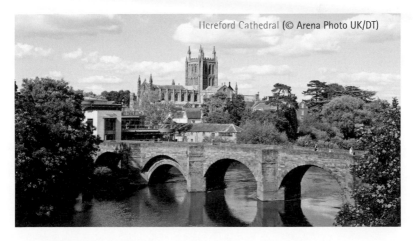
Hereford Cathedral (© Arena Photo UK/DT)

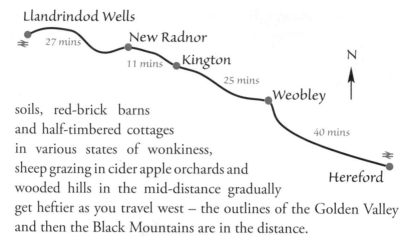

soils, red-brick barns
and half-timbered cottages
in various states of wonkiness,
sheep grazing in cider apple orchards and
wooded hills in the mid-distance gradually
get heftier as you travel west – the outlines of the Golden Valley
and then the Black Mountains are in the distance.

My bus edges along sleepy back roads with cow-parsley
verges; at **Mansell Lacy** the 461 meets us coming the other way.
I spot an oast house to the south, a reminder of the hop industry,
though the cider orchards are nowadays much more in evidence
than hop gardens.

Weobley looks like a film set for some idyllic chronicle of
rural life, with an extraordinarily rich array of half-timbered houses
gathered around a knot of streets, centred on a long triangular
space and still real village shops, including a butcher's whose
signboard of a Hereford bull promises the famously wonderful

HERGEST RIDGE

Entry signs announce Kington as 'the centre for walking', and even
though that might sound like marketing speak the town has some
vintage walks leading from it – notably on the Offa's Dyke Path. This
cuts through the town: in a couple of gentle, miles for example, you
could stroll along it up the road signposted to Hergest Croft (itself
a wonderful garden open to the public) and on to Hergest Ridge for
a sublime stroll on carpet-like turf up to a strangely incongruous
group of monkey-puzzle trees, looking out over the Black Mountains
and the twin peaks of the Brecon Beacons – the highest land in
Wales outside Snowdonia.

local beef which in itself is a reason for venturing to this county. Aptly for such a riot of black and white, the magpie is the village's symbol, hence the magpie sculpture erected in 2001 on the tiny green.

Beyond Lyonshall, the bus drops down the A44 to Kington, with a hint in the distant hills of the drama to unfold shortly. **Kington** itself looks handsomely urban, in the nicest retro way (see also the box on page 154). You may want to check out the free volunteer-run Kington museum in Mill Street (☎ 01544 231748; open 10.30–16.00 Tue–Sat) with its entertaining miscellany of bits and pieces, including the remains of a circus elephant buried here and later exhumed.

ACROSS THE BORDER

At **Stanner Rocks**, the hills loom up suddenly and sternly as Radnorshire, the central part of Powys, begins. Our bus slips across the border and now the bare moorland tops contrast completely with the mellowness that ushered us gently through Herefordshire. The bus deviates past **Hindwell Farm** – where William Wordsworth frequently stayed with his relations – and

NEW RADNOR WALK

Water-break-its-neck, a couple of miles out of the village and a level mile's walk from the A44, might be one of the most memorably named waterfalls anywhere. A century or so ago, this was a popular charabanc excursion from Llandrindod, and I can remember finding it in the 1970s when I stumbled on a Victorian finger-signpost saying simply 'To the falls'. Its signposting is now more prosaic but the atmosphere still quite magical: you walk for a quarter of a mile along the stream at the foot of a mossy precipice, with ferns and trees clinging to near vertical slopes. It has the scale of a cathedral aisle, with the high altar, invisible until the last moment, being the waterfall which sprays down impressively after prolonged rain.

round a back road that skirts the southern side of Radnor Forest, an austere, bleak, exposed upland that often gets snow when everywhere else around remains green. **New Radnor** (Maesyfed in Welsh) has nothing much 'new' about it – it's a rare medieval planned town laid out on a grid plan within walls that are now reduced to sheep-nibbled grassy humps; the castle mound above the church provides the best views over it all. Now shrunken to village size and recently minus shop and post office, it's amiably sleepy, and beautifully placed among the hills; a preposterously grandiose Gothic memorial to the Victorian statesman and local politician George Cornewall Lewis soars at the southern approach.

West from New Radnor the road contours round the western flanks of Radnor Forest, with a grand bus-seat view of mid-Wales as you drop to Llandegley, where **Llandegley Rocks** loom impressively along a wild-looking ridge – actually they're much smaller than they look and you can climb up in a matter of minutes from Llandegley Church.

Just past Penybont Station on the north side of the road is one of Wales's great visual jokes – an official-looking sign that solemnly advertises 'Llandegley International Airport Terminals 1 & 3' a few miles up the road. There's nothing there except sheep pasture, of course, but this spoof sign has somehow survived official

FOOD ALONG THE ROUTE

You'll hardly starve on the bus ride to Llandrindod. The Herefordshire villages bristle with pubs and cafés, though things are a little sparser once in Wales. Here is a trio of cafés on this route that I like. In Hereford, Café@Allsaints (All Saints Church, High St; ☎ 01432 370415; open 08.00–17.00 Mon–Sat) is in a converted church. It's a nicely unpretentious, bright and airy place for a light lunch or coffee. On the far east side of Kington, the Olde Tavern (22 Victoria Rd; ☎ 01544 230122) is a gloriously unsophisticated alehouse where nothing much has changed for well over a century; let's hope it stays that way. No food. Closed weekday lunchtimes. Finally, in Llandrindod head for Powell's Bistro (Spa Rd; ☎ 01597 824737) where you'll find decent-value light lunches and snacks in a spotless Victorian house opposite the National Cycle Collection.

attempts to get it removed. Were there really airport terminals in these remote hills, I wouldn't be surprised if they were subject to closure during the lambing season.

Finally, the ultimate visual surprise: **Llandrindod Wells** itself (invariably shortened to Llandrindod, or even Llandod). I know of no other quite such richly late-Victorian and Edwardian streetscape in Britain, even though it's hardly a bustling resort nowadays: Art Nouveau shop fronts, frilly iron canopies, lavishly built spa hotels of railway-age brick all jut out unexpectedly into the green pastures of mid-Wales. Llandrindod's railway station still has some of its original signage, and an ancient signalbox that is open to the public on some days. A wander around town brings you to Rock Park, where you can sample the rusty-tasting chalybeate spring water that brought the health-seekers here in those halcyon spa days. It doesn't taste too great, which is why I take it people thought it is good for you. ∎

ABOUT THE AUTHOR | Travel writer **TIM LOCKE** lives in Lewes in Sussex and has a long-standing affection for the Welsh borderland. He is author of *Slow Travel Sussex*, published by Bradt.

Through Snowdonia: Wild Wales

Julie Brominicks

Bangor

Service no. T2 | Journey time 3hrs 12mins to 4hrs 7mins.

OS Landranger 115, 124, 135. 5 Mon–Sat, 2 on Sun.
Operators: Lloyds Coaches & Express Motors.
Connects with Journey 30 in Aberystwyth & Journey 31 in Dolgellau.

Aberystwyth ◄

B angor is a town on the edge – scruffy, bitten by wind and the Menai Straits. As the last spot on the mainland, only Anglesey beyond, it's a transient place for students, for those heading for Ireland via Holyhead and for Bardsey-bound pilgrims.

To me **Bangor** is exciting, as edgy places often are – rough and rich in music and poets. I like to head down Garth Pier before the bus leaves to see the oystercatchers race the Straits and read the sweet-sad tributes on the memorial benches – 'he loved to sail, we loved to see him smile'. The bus depot is a shifting mix of vehicles vying for space outside Debenhams but is so close to the museum and cathedral you can visit them both in a 20-minute wait.

I used this bus many times when my work in Machynlleth took me to schools on Anglesey or the north Wales coast. On the way I'd be deep in teaching thoughts but the return journeys south were an indulgent ramble through Snowdonia, ruled by clouds and mountains.

The bus climbs south from Bangor and before long you see across the Straits to Anglesey and Newborough Sands stretching soft into the sea. **Caernarfon** is the first major stop. Do not be fooled as I was by the undignified entrance through back streets where the bus comes to sulk a few moments between Argos and a multi-storey car park – Caernarfon is a pretty, cobbled town with a continental feel when the sun shines on the great castle by the sea.

MOUNTAINS AND SHADOWS

From here to Porthmadog the landscape is wide: west to the sea over wild fields dashed with bent hawthorns and lichen-scored walls, and east to the Snowdon range – snow-stricken, brooding in cloud, or dissolving into blue distances. The sky dominates this highland, chasing shadows across peanut-butter hills and rusted heather, wind ravaging the Welsh dragon flags around Penygroes – and then we descend.

At sea level **Tremadog** is quiet and stately in slate, a genteel introduction to Porthmadog a minute along and more gregarious – 'Darren pays more for your gold!' writ large by the harbour. **Porthmadog** is a steam town, home to both the Ffestiniog and Welsh Highland narrow-gauge railways.

There are gentle beaches nearby at Borth-y-Gest and Morfa Bychan but I love to walk along the Cob, an embankment built to form a deep harbour from where slate was shipped round the world, now carrying the A487, the **Ffestiniog Railway**, and

Porthmadog – home of the Ffestiniog Railway (© Gail Johnson/DT)

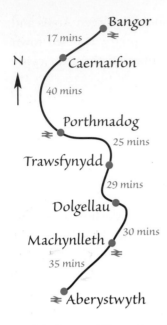

N

Bangor
17 mins
Caernarfon
40 mins
Porthmadog
25 mins
Trawsfynydd
29 mins
Dolgellau
30 mins
Machynlleth
35 mins
Aberystwyth

the Wales Coast Path across the Glaslyn Estuary. The best views are from here. The estuary flutes with birds, the sand flats are riven serpentine with silver water and framed by mountains, and you can watch curlews from behind the buddleia.

The lady behind me is also excited by the views, and we begin sharing them. She has come especially for the scenery. 'A bus ride is the best way to forget your troubles,' she says. Passenger chat flows in Welsh and English and the bus is busy. We call at green bus shelters in Penrhyndeudraeth, Gellilydan and Trawsfynydd, the green paint bright like the scarlet phone boxes in dark slate streets.

In **Penrhyndeudraeth** – where the mighty pylons stand serene in Afon Dwyryd before marching up the creek – Rob and I spent a rose-gold night at the end of summer. We were in need of a beer and drawn to Y Dderwen ('The Oak') (☎ 01766 770652; open from 13.00 daily), a lively pub with a good spirit. Penrhyndeudraeth just seemed the right place to be.

Welsh black cattle shelter, and sheep graze the marshy fields. The landscape changes towards **Trawsfynydd** where the nuclear power station sits square and peculiar in the pewter lake – the hills are closing in and the brisk windscape is replaced by woodland and slate. Trees, stone walls and dripping rocks by the road are all moistly resplendent in moss and the air is wet and silver. Across the wilds to the west are the craggy blue Rhinogs – sometimes Rob and I get off at Ganllwyd to walk across them to the coast.

There are woodlands in this damper climate, and from Ganllwyd you can also visit Coed-y-Brenin (Kings Woodland)

Forest Park (☎ 01341 440747). It has bike tracks and a café, but for me it's the waterfalls Pistyll Cain and Pistyll Mawddach on the Waterfall and Goldmine Walking Trail that make it special, particularly in autumn when beech leaves whirl copper over the spray. These falls and rivers once powered wheels for the gold mines of which you can still see the relics – John the Rock, a friend of ours, once found a nugget on a rock after heavy rain.

SAUSAGES AND SLATE

The bus waits in **Dolgellau** for a few minutes, so there's time to walk round Eldon Square or buy sausages perhaps from the Roberts Bros butchers by the bus stop – pork and leek, sage and red onion, or pork and black pepper chalked up on the board, and maybe homemade faggots, too. Dolgellau dwells beneath Cadair Idris glowering craggy to the south and is at the mercy of its weather.

Cadair Idris backdrops the T2 for some distance yet and walkers alight at Minffordd at Talyllyn. The landscape here has a ragged glacial beauty. I like to get off at the gates where sheep are herded across the road to hike left up to Crach Fynydd Pass with

---

EATING AND DRINKING

This route is rich in good food and drink. Try the Tap and Spile at Garth Pier in Bangor (☎ 01248 370835) – it is full of character and characters. In Porthmadog the Station Inn (☎ 01766 806517), otherwise known as 'the pub on the platform', is home to locals guffawing at old British sitcoms. Steam fans head for Spooner's bar and café (☎ 01766 516032; open daily) at the Ffestiniog Railway Harbour Station.

Y Sospan (☎ 01341 423174) in Dolgellau was a court house in 1606 and is now a café – head through the old jail door to cosier tables upstairs. In Machynlleth, The White Lion Hotel (☎ 01654 703455), a rambling old coaching inn with a log fire and a snug, has good pub food, real ales and a choice of wine.

---

views back over the Rhinogs and south to the Cambrians. I've picked gluts of whinberries there and lain in yellow grasses under the great sky bowl.

But not everyone comes here for quietude – across the moor that faces Cadair Idris and down on to the ribbon of A487, men from the Midlands gather to spot fighter jets from Anglesey screaming down the valley.

Perhaps my favourite view on this route is at the top of the Talyllyn Pass when the bus crests the final peak before plummeting down, the waters of Talyllyn shining below. 'Oh how I do wish an artist would get off here and paint that,' says a woman sitting behind me.

Now we roll through slate country: Upper Corris, Lower Corris, the Centre for Alternative Technology (☎ 01654 705950) – the eco-centre developed on a derelict slate quarry – and into **Machynlleth**, the small market town where I live and where the bus pauses a moment by the clock tower.

THE DYFI BIOSPHERE

UNESCO has awarded International Biosphere Reserve status to the Dyfi Valley in recognition of its biodiversity. It is the rich coastal waters, salt marsh and peat bogs which make the valley special. But biosphere reserves are about more than wildlife – they are places where people care for and cultivate language, culture and sustainable development.

Three nature reserves at the heart of the biosphere are within easy reach of the T2 – ask the driver to stop at Morben Isaf caravan park to visit the Dyfi Osprey Project (☎ 01654 781414; open 10.00–18.00 daily), run by Montgomeryshire Wildlife Trust, at Cors Dyfi Nature Reserve, or at Eglwys Fach to visit the RSPB Ynys-hir Reserve (☎ 01654 700222) – this will be familiar to BBC *Springwatch* fans.

Get off at Bow Street and take a Mid Wales 512 connection to Ynyslas to visit the Dyfi National Nature Reserve (☎ 01970 872901), managed by Natural Resources Wales and home to spectacular sand dune, estuary and peat-bog habitats. You can read more about the Dyfi Biosphere at www.dyfibiosphere.org.uk.

THE DYFI VALLEY

The route beyond Machynlleth is another chapter in my history. We are now in the Dyfi Valley, indeed the **Dyfi Biosphere** (see box, page 162), and heading for Aberystwyth where I spent my student years. The bus here is always busy despite the route being well served by frequent buses and trains, and we are joined by students, shoppers, men going to watch the rugby and Rob for the final stretch. Still on the A487, the route kisses the river and is gentler than in the highlands but just as beautiful. It is the Tarren Mountains that backdrop the Dyfi, often glowing in a richer light than reaches the road – keep watch for ospreys and in summer water buffalo that graze Cors Dyfi.

At **Taliesin** you glimpse the sea and Aberystwyth with Pen Dinas hill fort on the skyline, and the glorious peat bog which is Cors Fochno, a raised bog rich in sundews, raft spiders, and rosy marsh moths. And suddenly we're on the edge of Bow Street (where you would be unlucky not to see red kites wheeling above the road), the start of the final descent into **Aberystwyth**, where the mountains meet the sea.

It's a lively town, lovely at the castle and the old college, dignified at the National Library of Wales, quiet and wild towards South Beach and the Ceredigion coast. It's where we come to hide in coffee shops or the cinema, or watch the starlings whirl over the pier. And sometimes, like today, we come to find a pub and watch the rugby. The Ship and Castle (☎ 07773 778785) is still my favourite, as good for cider and folk music as it is for real ale. Ultracomida (☎ 01970 630686) on Pier Street is a great deli and tapas restaurant. ■

ABOUT THE AUTHOR | **JULIE BROMINICKS** recently left her career in sustainability education to become a writer. She lives in mid-Wales and loves to travel – slowly!

A Taste of
Wild Wales

Nicky Gardner

Aberystwyth 🚌

Service no. T21 | Journey time 55–70mins.

OS Landranger 135, 146. 3 to 4 times daily (not Sun) as far as Pontrhydfendi-
gaid; 2 journeys per day continue to Tregaron.
Operator: Evans Coaches.
Connects with Journey 29 in Aberystwyth.

Tregaron ⬅

The average British bus station is an uninspiring spot and the list of bus operators often as dull and repetitive as the architecturally monotonous bus stations that their vehicles serve. Big players like Arriva, Stagecoach and First have extended their networks across the country. So it is always a refreshing change to come to Aberystwyth where local players still hold a little sway.

Richard Brothers (three of them – Marteine, Malcolm and Nigel – and the third generation of Richards in the bus business) still run the bus service down the coast to Aberteifi, though English visitors often still insist that the market town and port on the River Teifi is called Cardigan. Lloyds Coaches operate the hourly X28 north to Machynlleth. They organise these things well in Aberystwyth. Most buses very sensibly depart from just by the train station, and it is there that I find service T21 run by Evans Coaches bound for Tregaron.

The traveller heading for the Teifi Valley towns of Tregaron and Llanbedr Pont Steffan can choose between a number of services from Aberystwyth ('Aber' for short), but the T21 is a local institution, created in a moment of adversity. Just a fortnight before Christmas in 1964, heavy rainfall over the Cambrian

Mountains raised the level of the normally placid River Ystwyth. A railway bridge over the river at Llanilar was washed away in the flood. No trains ever ran south from Aber after that fateful day, but the locals at least took heart that the railway had succumbed to Welsh weather rather than the terrible axe wielded by the very English Dr Beeching.

If it's Tuesday

The T21 is the lineal descendant of the rail-replacement bus service created in December 1964 to link Aberystwyth with the upper Teifi Valley. J Alwyn Evans is the man behind Evans Coaches, a company which has its modest headquarters in the old station yard at Tregaron. Alwyn and his crews are nothing if not flexible. The T21 to Tregaron takes a different route according to the day of the week, sometimes preferring the road via Pontrhydygroes and sometimes not. 'On Tuesdays and Thursdays, I always go through Ystrad Meurig,' explains the driver. 'And on other days, if someone asks then I'll go up to Ystrad. Of course we like them to phone in the day before, but sometimes they forget.'

Aberystwyth Castle
(© Wqsomeone/DT)

We have hardly left the bus stand in **Aber** when the driver's mobile phone rings. Our driver carefully pulls in at an Arriva bus stop, a little impertinence that creates a flurry of expectation among the small crowd of students waiting for the local bus up to the university. Our driver answers the phone, speaks briefly and then announces that we will be diverting via Morrison's supermarket to collect Mrs Lewis. 'A late request for a Morrison's pick-up,' he says. 'She really should have called in yesterday afternoon.'

Mrs Lewis, it turns out, takes her shopping seriously and has evidently purchased sufficient supplies to last for many weeks. 'You know, what with the shortages and all,' she explains as the driver helps her stack three boxes of tangerines on to an empty seat. This is the first I hear of a national shortage of tangerines.

Murder in Llanafan

Before long we and Mrs Lewis's tangerines are bouncing at some speed along a B road, right beside the River Ystwyth, with the long-abandoned railway line on the opposite bank of the river. All around are patterned meadows, hedgerows that even in late autumn are lush and green, and stone walls. Each of the surrounding hills is capped with an old Roman fort or ancient earthwork. We pull into **Llanafan** two minutes early and stop outside the church. The village is a spick-and-span place on a little shoulder of land overlooking the River Ystwyth. The church is high Victoriana, a little out of place in this remote Welsh valley, yet the graveyard tells the tales of country life and death in rural Ceredigion. There lies poor Joseph Butler, a gamekeeper on the nearby Trawsgoed estate, who was shot dead by a poacher in 1868.

My musings on Butler's fate are interrupted by a toot of the bus horn so I hop back on board and Mrs Lewis recounts the story of Mr Butler's assassin, who is evidently something of a hero in these parts. William Richards stood up to the local bigwigs and his potshot at Lord Lisburne's gamekeeper was judged as being no bad thing. 'It was about time,' says Mrs Lewis, 'that someone stood up for the rights of the ordinary people of Ceredigion.' I hardly expected to run across such revolutionary zeal on the T21. Richards slipped from one cottage to another, protected by publicans and preachers, well looked after by the locals, until one day someone hit on the inspired idea of dressing Richards as a woman and shipping him off to America in disguise. Richards's girlfriend was smuggled out the following year and evidently the two lived happily ever after.

Aberystwyth

N

27 mins

Llanafan

27 mins

Pontrhydfendigaid

15 mins

Tregaron

Druids and Dutch connections

Much as I like the Ystwyth Valley, its charms are in my mind greatly eclipsed by those of the Teifi – a valley that for some years was the area I called home. On the T21 it is just a short hop over the watershed that divides the two valleys.

First stop in the Teifi Valley, no matter what route the bus takes, is **Pontrhydfendigaid** – a village that while rooted in Welsh Wales has an other-worldly dimension. Mrs Lewis mentions that nowadays it is inordinately popular with Druids and Dutch people, the latter on account of the village having played a bit-part role in a Dutch novel that acquired cult popularity in the mid 1990s. The novel, I subsequently discovered, is called *De Ontdekking van de Hemel*, which means *The Discovery of Heaven*. This seems just right for Pontrhydfendigaid, for if there is a stairway to Heaven from this Earth, I have a hunch that it might well start in the Teifi Valley.

Mrs Lewis and her tangerines decant in Pontrhydfendigaid and from there it is an easy run south to Tregaron, skirting the edge of **Cors Caron** – Tregaron Bog to English-speakers. This is

POETS AND PRINCES AT STRATA FLORIDA

There is a gem of a walk from Pontrhydfendigaid east to Strata Florida Abbey (Abaty Ystrad Fflur in Welsh). With almost four hours between southbound buses from Pontrhydfendigaid, you'll have plenty of time to reach the abbey, which is 1.2 miles east of the village. Just follow Abbey Road, a lovely lane with little traffic that runs up the Teifi Valley towards the abbey. Amid the lonely ruins of this former Cistercian abbey you will find the graves of a dozen Welsh princes and poets.

Pontrhydfendigaid has the Black Lion Hotel (Llew Du in Welsh), an amiable little inn on Mill Street with very comfortable rooms (☎ 01974 831624; sometimes closed between lunch & dinner, so check ahead).

a fabulous piece of peaty wetland, home to otters and red kites. A Welsh drizzle has set in and today is not good for spotting birds, yet we are rewarded as a lone hen harrier glides slowly over the road in front of the bus. And then, as we approach Tregaron, the sky clears to reveal a rainbow dancing over the hills away to the east. That upland is known as **Elenydd**, a remote and desolate range of hills that is the backdrop to all Tregaron life.

TREGARON CONNECTIONS

Tregaron is the principal market town of the upper Teifi, a laid-back sort of place where buses gather for a chat in the main square. End of the route for the T21 which arrives in good time for a connection onto the 585, operated by Lewis Coaches – a gem of a route.

The bus follows the B road down through Llanddewi Brefi on the east bank of the Teifi. That road runs close to the hills and it is a chance to ride through the village where once I lived. Wales is like that. Once it gets a grip on you, it lures you back. And happily there is still a plethora of small independent bus operators that will ferry you to even the remotest corners of the principality. ∎

ABOUT THE AUTHOR

NICKY GARDNER lived for some years on the banks of Afon Teifi in Ceredigion. She now lives and works in Berlin, where she is co-editor of *hidden europe* magazine (www.hiddeneurope.co.uk).

East to West Across NORTH WALES

Tony Hopkins

31 Wrexham

Service no. T3 | Journey time 2hrs 30mins.

OS Landranger 117, 125, 124. Every 2hrs Mon–Sat, 4 journeys Sun.
Operator: GHA Coaches.

Barmouth

Wales boasts some of Europe's most spectacular scenery and a great network of bus services. This 60-mile journey is one of the longer-distance routes branded as TrawsCambria or TrawsCymru. From Wrexham, the largest town in north Wales, our journey tracks south and west, following the delightful valleys of the Rivers Dee, Wnion and Mawddach until it reaches the coast at Barmouth. The railway used to come this way, until, like so many other rural lines in Britain, it fell victim to Dr Beeching's sharp axe. Happily public transport survives in the form of the bus, so take a seat and enjoy!

LEAVING WREXHAM BEHIND

The first leg of the journey is unremarkable as the T3 leaves urban **Wrexham** and runs via Ruabon to the village of **Trevor**. If time allows, do break your journey here, because, although you cannot see it from the bus, you are within a five-minute walk of Thomas Telford's famous **Pontcysyllte Aqueduct**. Constructed between 1795 and 1808, it is the highest navigable aqueduct ever built and carries the Llangollen Canal over the River Dee. There is a towpath

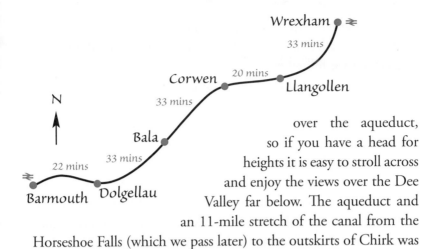

over the aqueduct, so if you have a head for heights it is easy to stroll across and enjoy the views over the Dee Valley far below. The aqueduct and an 11-mile stretch of the canal from the Horseshoe Falls (which we pass later) to the outskirts of Chirk was granted UNESCO World Heritage status in 2009.

FOLLOWING THE DEE

From Trevor, we follow the canal into the Vale of Llangollen and join the River Dee for the first time. Look up to your right on the approach to **Llangollen** to see the ruins of the 13th-century **Dinas Brân Castle** perched high above the town. Llangollen clusters around the river, which at this point is very fast flowing. For a closer look at the river, visit the former corn mill in Dee Lane. It is now a very comfy riverside pub serving good food (☎ 01978 869555; open from noon daily).

West from Llangollen, the surrounding hills close in, and at Berwyn we pass the Horseshoe Falls mentioned above. This is not a natural waterfall at all, but a semi-circular weir designed by Thomas Telford to feed into the Llangollen Canal. This is the western end of the World Heritage Site.

On reaching the small market town of **Corwen**, look out for the dramatic life-size statue of Owain Glyndwr, the last Welshman to hold the title Prince of Wales. Owain's ancestral homeland was in these parts and he has left an indelible imprint on local history. Beyond Corwen our bus forsakes the main road to take quieter lanes through the pretty villages of Cynwyd, Llandrillo and Llandderfel. After **Cynwyd** we lose sight of the river for a while as the valley opens out, but soon we are reunited with the Dee which we follow upstream to **Bala**, a town blessed with an enviable location at the northern end of Llyn Tegid (Bala Lake). The town is very much the gateway to **Snowdonia National Park**, (Parc Cenedlaethol Eryri), established 60 years ago as Wales's first national park.

Now past Bala, our bus skirts the shores of the lake, with extensive views southwards to the Cambrian Mountains beyond. At the end of the lake we detour to serve Llanuwchllyn, the home of the **Bala Lake Railway** (www.bala-lake-railway.co.uk), which runs seasonal narrow-gauge trains along the lakeshore to Bala. A mile and a half further, we make a final crossing of the Dee; here, in the heartland of Welsh-speaking Wales, it is more commonly known by its Welsh name of Afon Dyfrdwy. Soon we lose it altogether – its source is on the slopes of Dduallt, behind the wooded hills to our right. However, it is not long before we have picked up the course of another river – the Wnion – which is no less scenic and which leads us down its verdant valley to Dolgellau.

From a tiny village, **Dolgellau** grew steadily on the back of the wool trade in the 18th century. Later a blossoming print industry and nearby gold deposits added to Dolgellau's prosperity. Today

WREXHAM

It is easy to dismiss Wrexham as a grimy place shaped around a trio of industries: coal, iron and brewing. But Wrexham has reinvented itself. The modern university town has a lively buzz. There are three covered markets and a good museum (☎ 01978 297460; open 10.00–17.00 Mon–Fri, 11.00–16.00 Sat), where you can learn of Wrexham's earliest-known resident – Brymbo Man. At Bersham, two miles west of Wrexham and easily reached by local bus (no. 6), a heritage centre and ironworks explores Wrexham's industrial past (☎ 01978 318970; open Apr–Oct 10.00–17.00 Mon–Fri, noon–17.00 Sat–Sun; admission free).

BARMOUTH

Barmouth is called Abermaw in Welsh, literally 'mouth of the Maw', referring to the nearby river. But this is a place where, curiously, the English name has greater currency than its Welsh equivalent. Barmouth is a traditional seaside holiday town, with fine beaches backed by pleasing hills. The Panorama Walk, created in Victorian times, is a must. Barmouth Bridge was built for the railway, and still carries trains, but there is also a footway over the bridge (small toll payable) which links into the Mawddach Trail on the far side. This is a superb nine-mile-long footpath along a now-abandoned railway back to Dolgellau (www.mawddachtrail.co.uk).

the town has over 200 listed buildings, making it an attractive destination in its own right, its location also ensuring popularity as a great base for exploring the exceptional scenery of southern Snowdonia.

Our bus stops briefly at Eldon Square in the centre of Dolgellau. West from Dolgellau is what many would judge to be one of the finest stretches of bus route anywhere in Britain. The road hugs the north bank of the tidal **Mawddach**. It is beautiful in any weather, but if you ride this route at low tide on a summer evening, you will be rewarded by stunning views of golden sands with **Barmouth Bridge** silhouetted against a setting sun. The bus pauses at Bontddu, a place that in the late 19th century was the scene of a modest gold rush. There are superb views across the Mawddach to the heights of Cadair Idris as the bus cruises along the north side of the estuary to its final destination in **Barmouth** (see box above). Journey's end is near the railway station, with the tourist office just nearby. ∎

ABOUT THE AUTHOR | **TONY HOPKINS**, a retired engineer, moved to north Wales 20 years ago, originally to work for the Snowdon Mountain Railway. A public transport enthusiast, he organises regular outings for his local U3A's 'Explore by Bus' group.

Tudor Thomas

Newtown

Service no. T4 | Journey time 3hrs 45mins.

OS Landranger 136, 147, 161, 160, 170, 171. 6 journeys daily Mon–Sat.
Operators: Stagecoach for TrawsCymru.
Connects with Journey 28 in Llandrindod Wells.

Cardiff ◄────────────

With a route length of over 100 miles, this is no ordinary bus journey. This is a trip on a local bus with an express feel, and a ride comparable to a magic carpet with an ever-changing vista. It covers a great swathe of countryside – sometimes revealing quiet pastoral beauty, sometimes dramatically wild – before ending at the capital city of Wales. Along the way we take in rivers, reservoirs and rich industrial heritage. Today's buses on the TrawsCymru T4 are easy access, have leather seats, and Wi-Fi – so you could in theory update your Facebook profile or tweet your way through Wales. But only the most unromantic of travellers would miss the opportunity of gazing at the landscapes that slip by beyond the window of the bus.

We start at the Back Lane bus station in **Newtown** (Y Drenewydd in Welsh) in the county of Powys. So we're off, and almost immediately we have a sense of the journey to come. Although the route south follows a trunk road (the A483), it is formidably twisty and has a switchback quality. Soon we are looking down onto the rooftops of Newtown.

There are views that hint of a wilder Wales that lies away to the west. Plynlimon in the Cambrian mountain range is discernible as a modest pimple on the horizon. But Powys is wild enough for now and we should be grateful that our driver evidently knows the dangers that might lurk in every dip and bend of the road ahead.

A WELSH SPA ROUTE

Talk of spas today and most folk think of five-star chic. But the spa towns of central Wales are from another era – one that was less cosseted, not so relentless in the pursuit of luxury. And, less than an hour out of Newtown, we are cruising into our first spa stop: **Llandrindod Wells**.

Time for a five-minute break, and a handful of passengers hop off to stretch their legs. Across the way stands the bright-red Sargeants Brothers bus, ready to set off on its run to Hereford. That cross-border route is described as Journey 28 in this book.

Llandrindod's annual Victorian Festival in August recalls the town's heyday when the supposed healing qualities of the local waters pulled visitors from far and wide. Back on board the bus, we pass the Metropole Hotel – once the largest in the country. It is a mark of how Llandrindod's reputation has waned.

Leaving Llandrindod, we run parallel to the Heart of Wales rail route which was so important in building Llandrindod's trade. We sweep south through rolling countryside, the rugged ridge of Carneddau edging up towards us on the left and suddenly we reach the River Wye. Close by the road is the Royal Welsh showground. Here is **Builth Wells**, a town that draws the crowds for its four-day agricultural show each July.

Newtown

50 mins

N

Llandrindod Wells

19 mins

Builth Wells

24 mins

Llyswen

9 mins

13 mins / Felinfach

Brecon

16 mins

Storey Arms

19 mins

Merthyr Tydfil

60 mins

Cardiff

Heading south from Builth on the A470, we follow the partly wooded Wye Valley downstream. Every now and again, the hills open out to give a glimpse of the Black Mountains ahead. For the most part this is a stretch of route where the focus is close to the bus with riverside scenes of rare beauty in the right light. Unexpectedly, the landscape opens out and we stop at the village of **Llyswen**, where the bus stop is by the 17th-century Griffin Inn, which has accommodation (☎ 01874 754241). It is a good spot to just stop for a day and take in the tempo of Welsh life. This is not a country to rush through.

Just a few minutes later we stop at another pub with a similar name, the Felin Fach Griffin (☎ 01874 620111), which also has rooms available. It has garnered accolades from national media for its high-quality restaurant and was acclaimed as one of the top ten pubs in the 2015 *Good Pub Guide*. The last time I was there it had a large roaring fire which set the tone for a very good lunch. Don't get the two Griffins confused! Both are equally deserving of a visit, and each attracts many well-heeled visitors from across the border.

It is a fast run south to **Brecon** (Aberhonddu in Welsh). The town is the midway point on our journey, and I'm not the only one to give thanks for the fact that there's a brief toilet stop at the bus station. If you follow the call, just let the bus driver know and he'll

BRECON BEACONS NATIONAL PARK

Webwise travellers can start exploring the national park before leaving home by going to www.breconbeacons.org. 'One of Britain's breathing spaces,' reads the tagline on that website and it's a good reminder that there is fresh air aplenty in this gorgeous sweep of mountains and moorland. For accommodation options, check with the tourist information centre in Brecon (☎ 01874 622485).

If heading to the summits or into remote valleys, dress for the conditions. Weather can change suddenly. Mobile phones may not always have any reception, so always tell someone where you are going and when you'll be back.

wait for you. If you are tempted to stop off, Giglios Coffee Shop on Bethel Square (☎ 01874 625062) is much to be recommended. Leaving Brecon, we cross the River Usk and head determinedly south with the dark summits of the Brecon Beacons rising up in front of us. From the bus stop at Libanus, it is a stiff half-hour walk up to the Brecon Beacons Mountain Centre (☎ 01874 623366; open Mar–Oct 09.30–17.00 daily, Nov–Feb 09.30–16.00 daily), where there is a café and viewing interpretation area.

The Beacons and beyond

Gathering pace on an empty and well-graded road, we move into wilder territory. The road clings to the edge of the hillside, passing waterfalls on the right, and here and there giving glimpses of the old drovers' route which nowadays is part of the **Taff Trail** – a route that takes walkers and cyclists to no great heights but gives wonderful views of the national park.

We have already seen the potential for confusion over those two Griffins. Now comes another puzzle in a similar vein. 'Next stop, Storey Arms,' calls out the driver to two young women with rucksacks who are clearly bound for the summits. It sounds for all the world like a pub. But the old **Storey Arms** was demolished in the 1920s, and nowadays there is an outdoor education centre on the site. So it's not a place to stop for a pint. And be warned: it is a wild spot and there is not even a bus shelter.

Into industrial Wales

Over the summit at Storey Arms, our driver shifts down a gear as we roll south towards Merthyr. The road dips and dives, taking its cue from the surrounding hills. We pass three reservoirs in quick succession: Beacons, Cantref and Llwyn-on. It's good to be on board the T4 on a bright day. Drivers on this route tell tales of fearsome winter storms and the snow fences above the road lend credence to those accounts.

MERTHYR'S INDUSTRIAL LEGACY

Cyfarthfa Castle Museum & Art Gallery (☎ 01685 727371; open Apr–Sep 10.00–17.30 daily, Oct–Mar 10.00–16.30 Tue–Fri & noon–16.30 Sat & Sun) is well worth a visit. This area at the heads of the Welsh valleys has a rich heritage. Dowlais Iron Company started in 1759 and, over the following 50 years, pioneered many new techniques in iron working. In 1802 a tramway was built. Two years later, Cornishman Richard Trevithick invented the first working steam engine to run on rails.

There is a palpable sense of a change in the landscape as we return to more settled terrain. On the left there is a glimpse of Cyfarthfa Castle (see box above) and a minute or two later we are in **Merthyr Tydfil**. This is a town that was shaped by industry, growing by the mid 19th century to become the largest community in Wales. It was eventually betrayed by the very industries that it had nurtured – with the coal seams worked out, the iron and steel industry moved towards the coast. From here we follow the Taff Valley down to **Cardiff**.

If you are staying on board, keep a lookout on the right-hand side as you travel south down the valley. You'll see the village of **Aberfan**, scene of the awful disaster in 1966 when a hillside spoil heap collapsed, engulfing the village school. One hundred and forty four people perished in the tragedy, robbing this part of the Taff Valley of an entire younger generation. A trip on this route should be planned in advance, so consider staying overnight to take full advantage of the national park and this extraordinary cross-country service. The Brecon Tourist Information Centre (☎ 01874 622485) operates a Book-a-Bed-Ahead scheme. ∎

ABOUT THE AUTHOR | **TUDOR THOMAS** is a marketing and transport specialist currently working for Stagecoach in south Wales. He lives near Cardiff and is a regular user of the T4 TrawsCymru bus service.

COMMUNITY BUS SERVICES

Brits may be prone to complain about their bus services, but the truth is that we benefit from a dense network that would be the envy of many of our European neighbours. Britain is unusual in having an exceptionally good network of inter-urban routes. Using Journeys 41 and 42 in this book, one might travel from Carlisle to Berwick-upon-Tweed with just one change of bus – a journey of 150 miles.

But no bus network can perfectly serve everyone, and that's where community bus services come in. We praise the merits of locally owned and operated bus services in rural Northumberland, yet there are some folk for whom regular scheduled bus services are not a credible option. Nicola Crane is transport manager for Upper Coquetdale Community Transport (UCCT; ☎ 01669 621855). She is a volunteer, as indeed are all who work with UCCT. The group's 17-seat white minibus is a regular sight on the lanes around Rothbury. 'We work with local ramblers who need transport up to Alwinton and beyond,' she says. Every Friday, UCCT runs a shoppers' special, collecting elderly residents of Upper Coquetdale at their front doors and taking them to local shops in Rothbury. 'For some of those on board, the ride to Rothbury might well be the social highlight of their week. These are folk who don't get out a lot,' says Nicola, who explains how UCCT passengers shop together and visit cafés in Rothbury.

UCCT caters very much for locals, and the terms of their operating licence do not permit Nicola and her team to operate regular scheduled services for the general public. But at the other end of England, the Cuckmere Community Bus does just that. Since 1976, the bus has been ferrying residents of the Cuckmere Valley in East Sussex to nearby towns for shopping, hospital appointments or just for fun. But now they also run a weekend bus service for visitors to the area – which is part of the South Downs National Park. Hourly bus services meet trains at local railway stations. Some on board are bound for the spectacular chalk-cliff scenery at Seven Sisters Country Park, while others look for nothing more demanding than cream tea in Alfriston. We are grateful to John Bishop of Hailsham (East Sussex), a volunteer driver with the Cuckmere Community Bus, for drawing our attention to this bus service. ■

THE PENNINES

The Pennine region includes the big cities that nudge up against the hills, and it's an area which offers some of the most varied bus experiences in Britain. The Wilmslow Road in Manchester is Britain's busiest bus corridor, with around 100 buses an hour. At the other extreme is a weekly service along the B6276, a secondary road which sweeps over bleak and windswept moorland on its way from the headwaters of the River Eden to the Tees Valley. The treeless Lune Forest is to the north, Stainmore Common to the south, and it was across this latter wilderness that we walked on a Wednesday morning in late October intent on getting the 572 bus to Barnard Castle. We missed the bus by a matter of moments.

Briefly, very briefly, we yearned for the Wilmslow Road bus corridor. Another bus in a minute perhaps? A farmer driving an old Land Rover offered us a ride. 'I'll take you down to Middleton,' he said. 'We'll overtake the bus on the way,' he added. As indeed we did, and what a good thing that was for the next 572 was not scheduled until a week later.

Journey 35 passes spectacular Peveril Castle on its way to Mam Tor (© VisitEngland/Alex Hare)

Well, you'll not find the Wilmslow Road bus corridor nor the 572 to Teesdale in our medley of routes in this section. But you will find five journeys that capture the variety of bus travel in the region. This is a part of England where great conurbations rub shoulders with wild terrain. It makes for a beguiling mix of communities and scenery, and presents special challenges for planners keen to facilitate cheap access by public transport for city dwellers wanting to visit their local national parks. The Peak District really is on the doorsteps of both Sheffield and Manchester and the Yorkshire Dales are but a stone's throw from Leeds and Bradford.

For a real dose of bus nostalgia, you might like to try the summer Tuesdays only 127 service from Ripon to Garsdale, which uses beautifully restored vintage vehicles and is run by Vintage Omnibus Services. Concessionary passes are accepted, and this most civilised of journeys takes 4½ hours, but that includes a two-hour stop in Hawes: time enough for lunch and a look round a lovely Pennine village that also features on Journeys 36 and 37 in this book. ∎

MILLS ALONG THE
DERWENT VALLEY

Helen Moat

Derby 🚌

Service no. 6.1 | Journey time 1hr 40mins.

OS Landranger 128, 119. Hourly Mon–Sat, every 2hrs Sun.
Operator: Trent Barton Sixes.

Bakewell ←

I am standing at **Derby** bus station, waiting to travel back through time. This is the departure point for a journey that takes in the Derwent Valley Mills (a UNESCO World Heritage Site) and continues to the picturesque Peak town of Bakewell.

My bus arrives and I climb aboard with city workers, shoppers and other day trippers.

'Eeh up, m' ducks.'

'How ye bin?'

'Fair to middlin', aye.'

'Get on wi' thee.'

The flat Derbyshire voices bounce around the bus. The route is well used by locals and there is a lively atmosphere on the bus as the travellers chatter and joke together.

The Sixes are a family of services run by Trent Barton. The buses are clean and bright with large picture windows. 'Fancy a road trip?' reads the advert for the company's 'Zigzag' ticket. It's a pass that costs £6 and gives unlimited bus travel across Trent Barton land after the morning peak.

Soon we are leaving the leafy suburbs of Derby behind and heading up the Derwent Valley on the A6. At first the landscape is expansive, but slowly the hills close in. At **Milford** we catch a glimpse of a water-powered cotton mill built by Jedediah Strutt. The Strutt family pop up here and there along this trip. We pass over a low-built stone bridge and continue, with the River Derwent now on our left, before long reaching **Belper**. At first sight it's a down-to-earth place but you see its mills soaring heavenward like industrial cathedrals. We find Jedediah here too. He built the North Mill which nowadays hosts a homely museum exhibiting a wide range of factory paraphernalia including spinning machinery.

Trent Barton likes to tease passengers. I am warming to the mill theme, but now we leave the Derwent Valley, detouring west through undulating farmland to serve **Wirksworth**. It's worth stopping off at this pretty market town popular with artists. Beyond Wirksworth the countryside begins to change. Here the land is higher, the hillsides steeper with rock faces rising dramatically from the valley. The bus driver, foot hard on the brake, inches down to the village of **Cromford**. The bus squeaks past impossibly narrow three-storeyed terraced homes with tiny, tiny windows.

HIDDEN TREASURES

The bus stops outside the market square beside the handsome Greyhound Hotel. If you look carefully, there's a narrow lane hidden away in the corner of the square that leads up to Scarthin Books (☎ 01629 823272; open 09.00–18.00 Mon–Sat, 10.00–18.00 Sun). The bookshop sits opposite the village pond, home to mallards and a swan. This is a fine place to while away an hour or two. Scarthin's is an eccentric, higgledy-piggledy establishment composed of a series of connecting rooms that are filled with an odd assortment of objects and furniture (and books, of course). Need freshening up? The toilet has an ancient roll-top bath in it! Require refreshments? Uncover the secret organic café hidden behind a curved bookcase. But best of all are the weight-bent shelves of new and secondhand books. You need look no further if you want to learn more about the Derwent Valley Mills.

Of all the mills on the trail, **Cromford Mills** is surely the most significant. It was the first successful water-powered cotton-spinning mill in the world, built by Richard Arkwright (initially in partnership with Strutt) who lived in Rock House across the road from the factory – a constant reminder to Arkwright's employees that they were being watched. Cromford Mills, an excellent example of industrial history, have been carefully restored and are well worth a visit.

To Matlock and beyond

Now back on the A6, the bus heads towards Matlock Bath. Not far out of Cromford is Arkwright's **Masson Mills**. It is mainly a shopping complex nowadays, but there's also a sprawling working textile museum in its bowels (☎ 01629 581001; open Jan–Nov 10.00–16.00 Mon–Sat, 11.00–16.00 Sun). Between the retail clothing, you'll find bobbins of all shapes and sizes, baskets of cotton and a clocking-in machine for the workers. A tour of the tucked-away museum will give you the chance to see the spinning machines at work.

The bus continues on through **Matlock Bath**. The Victorians called this part of the valley 'Little Switzerland' but Matlock Bath is more of a 'Little Blackpool' with its rows of souvenir shops, slot machines and fish-and-chip shops. It even has its own illuminations. Unlike Blackpool, there is, of course, no sea at Matlock Bath, but the promenade that runs alongside the river gives the landlocked town a seaside feel.

The bus now squeezes through the narrow valley with its soaring rocks and passes under the cable cars that rise up to the cave system on the **Heights of Abraham**. Soon the bus reaches the town of Matlock.

Slightly off the Derwent trail on the outskirts of Matlock is Lumsdale, a forgotten wooded gorge. Hidden off a narrow country lane and obscured by thick undergrowth, few venture here, yet it's a place of strange decaying beauty. The first mill was built here in the 1600s. By the height of the Industrial Revolution, there were at least seven mills crammed into this narrow dale.

Masson Mills (© Adrian Farmer/DT)

It's worth making your way out there to climb the steep-sided ravine (knees permitting) to the ruins of the old mills. If you close your eyes, you can almost smell the ground minerals, the crunched bone of animal, the chaff of the wheat and the

DARLEY ABBEY MILL

Darley Abbey Mill was built in the early 1700s by the Evans family. The mill owners provided their employees with houses, subsidised coal, blankets in cold weather, and the old and infirm with hot meals, as well as a convalescence home in Wales. They even took care of their employees' burial arrangements and costs. But all this came at a price: the villagers were required to work exceedingly long and arduous hours.

woven cotton and imagine the millstone grinding and the voices of mill workers hanging in the heavy, dust-filled air. High above the dale, a waterfall spills 100ft. At the top, there is one surviving mill pond of three.

Back on the bus, we wind our way through Darley Dale and on to **Rowsley**. There's one last mill here: Caudwell, a flour mill with a riverside café, craft shop and museum. The bus now enters the **Peak District National Park**, fittingly signed with a millstone, then makes its way through woodland, dale and hill, past the stately home of Haddon Hall and on into the picture-postcard town of **Bakewell**. Here you can grab yourself a Bakewell tart and a coffee and reflect on the Derwent Valley Mills that line the gateway to the beautiful Peak Park. It's a fine finishing point on a magnificent bus route rich in history. ■

ABOUT THE AUTHOR | **HELEN MOAT** is happiest when travelling and writing about her experiences. She is the author of Bradt's *Slow Travel Peak District.*

Hey Diddle Diddle, the Cat and the Fiddle

Ann Clark

Buxton

Service no. 58 | Journey time 35mins.

OS Landranger 119, 118. Runs hourly Mon–Sat, 5 journeys on Sun.
Operator: High Peak.

Macclesfield

The spa town of Buxton isn't a big place. Small enough for folk to recognise each other. Whenever I get on a local bus, the chances are that I might well know one or more of the other passengers on board. So friendly are Buxtonians that complete strangers are invited to join in the gossip. Virgin Trains gave a boost to the 58 when, about a dozen years ago, they had the good idea of using Macclesfield Station as a gateway to the Peak District. Passengers hopped off the train at Macclesfield, transferring there on to the bus for Buxton, Bakewell and Chatsworth House. Nowadays, it is only on Sundays that two buses extend east beyond Buxton, and for most of the week the route is thus essentially a shuttle between Buxton and Macclesfield. It is therefore one of the shortest routes in this book. Short and sweet.

Leaving Buxton

Buxton may be located at some altitude – 'the highest market town in England', we claim – but you often have to go uphill to leave Buxton. Cyclists always moan at this fact of Buxton life. Climbing up from the bowl that shelters Buxton on the bus to

Macclesfield, the first port of call is **Burbage** where the bus makes a short diversion to drop off shoppers. Why not take the bus rather than lug heavy shopping for a mile and a half up a hill? Once clear of the last houses of Burbage, the vista opens up. I see for miles over the moors and feel my lungs fill with fresh air and my heart swell with the immensity of the sky.

The chocolate-coloured moors spread out on both sides of the road; to my right are ravines where in the past coal was mined for the Duke of Devonshire's limekilns. Today, very little remains of the tracks and

Victorian pavilion gardens in Buxton capture the grace and elegance of this Peak District spa town (© VisitEngland/ VisitPeakDistrict)

tunnels that carried the coal but just now and then vestiges can be picked out. Lime production is still a major industry here but hidden from view. On my left I can make out the deep peat that covers most of the ground. It's no longer dug for fuel but, even as recently as ten years ago, it was common to see summer turfs being stacked to dry for the upcoming winter.

Our bus driver needs to watch the road carefully as marauding sheep stray from the grazing of heather and bilberry plants to lick the salt from the road surface. Salt is spread over our winter roads to help keep them clear of snow and ice, and the canny sheep have realised that dark road surfaces warm up quickly, even in winter sunshine, and make a more appealing place to lie than rough heather or snowy moors. Sleeping sheep are potentially a big hazard to motorists in these parts, so perhaps it's no bad thing that the last bus on this route is off the high moors by early evening.

OVER THE TOP

Soon the **Cat and Fiddle Inn** (see box, page 190) comes into view. I have often wondered how the pub got its name. Although the road is shown on maps as the A537, we locals know it as the 'Cat and Fiddle road'. And it is certainly notorious. It was at one stage dubbed 'the most dangerous road in Britain' by local police because of the number of accidents, mostly caused by motorcyclists racing too fast around the sharp bends and steep inclines.

Beyond the Cat and Fiddle there are fine views across open country that I know well from many rambles. The sun glints on

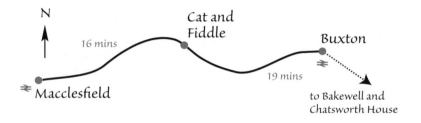

CAT AND FIDDLE INN

Set on the highest point on the A537, this is the second-highest pub in England at 1,690ft. The name is interesting, perhaps a corruption of the French *le chat fidèle* ('the faithful cat'). Others suggest it recalls Catherine of Aragon, first wife of Henry VIII, who was often called Catherine la Fidèle. I stopped at the Cat and Fiddle (☎ 01298 78366; open 09.00–17.00 Mon–Fri, 09.00–19.00 Sat–Sun) one winter day to find the publican keeping warm by shovelling 10ft of snow from his door. There was no electric power and no beer either, but the welcome was sincere and I made it back in better weather to enjoy a drink.

Lamaload Reservoir away to the northwest. The next landmark on our bus journey is **Shining Tor**, the culminating point of a fine sandstone ridge. Then, as we drop down slowly into Cheshire, the scenery changes. The mood on the bus changes too. No longer are there just Buxtonians on board, for we stop here and there to pick up other passengers heading for Macclesfield. There are views of **Shutlingsloe**, a fierce spine of rock resembling more the fin of an attacking shark than a hill. But these are the last of the hills. The view ahead is dominated by the lush Cheshire plain.

One distinctive landmark, pointing skyward, is the **Jodrell Bank telescope**. It looks like a huge soup bowl angled towards the heavens. Now, as we near **Macclesfield**, in contrast to the stone houses of Buxton, I see that bricks are king. This manner in which vernacular architecture echoes the underlying geology is endlessly fascinating in England. And the bus gives one the time to take things in. ■

ABOUT THE AUTHOR | **ANN CLARK** has lived in Buxton for over 35 years and is a keen rambler and sometime paraglider pilot. A non-driver and over 60, she now uses her bus pass enthusiastically.

A Peek at the Peaks:
Off to Mam Tor

Ian M Packham

Sheffield

Service no. 272 | Journey time 50–70mins.

OS Landranger 110. Daily, once an hour.
Operators: First South Yorkshire, TM Travel, Hulleys of Baslow.

Castleton ◀

I have a choice of three bus operators on this short route. There is something contrary about taking the off-white First South Yorkshire double-decker into the Peak District. It gives a definite sense of energetic Sheffield washing over the city boundary into a rural hinterland. I prefer the double-deckers for that very contrariness, though the other two companies playing the route, TM Travel and Hulleys, use single-deckers that are perhaps a little more luxurious, relaxed and friendly; country buses entering the city rather than a city bus in the country.

The centre of Sheffield lies just five miles from the border with Britain's first national park, and only 16 miles from my destination of Castleton. Yet every year the majority of the ten million plus visitors use their cars, creating increasing problems with congestion and pollution for the National Park Authority and Peak District inhabitants. It's unusual to see more than a handful of tourists on the 272. The bus is used primarily by residents of the scatter of Derbyshire villages that lie on the route.

The journey starts at **Sheffield Transport Interchange**, positioned between the train station and the city centre's galleries, winter garden and shopping district. This is the heart of Sheffield and one of the city's most diverse areas. Gallery-goers mingle with

HIGH, LOW, WHITE OR DARK PEAK?

The term White Peak comes from the colour of the area's limestone bedrock. The area is also called the Low Peak to distinguish it from the High Peak region of the national park. The High Peak area is formed from a high moorland plateau of dark stone. It is recognised as the highest and wildest part of the Peak District. In contrast to the White Peak, the limestone beneath the heather of the High Peak is covered by a cap of millstone grit, a coarse-grained sandstone. This ensures the soil above it is continuously wet through the winter months, creating a dark soil that gives the High Peak its alternative name of the Dark Peak.

after-school skateboarders; and busy shoppers with cloth-capped elderly gentlemen. The Interchange gives no sense of the feeling of freedom to come, the uninspiring glazed structures trapping the diesel fumes of waiting buses.

INTO SUBURBIA

From the heart of the city, the 272 tracks southwest towards the leafy, green parks and ancient woodlands that dot the commuter belt of suburban housing along Ecclesall Road. A key artery for the city's inhabitants, the road is an excellent area in which to get a sense of Sheffield's welcoming atmosphere. Despite being Britain's fifth-largest city, Sheffield is proud of its reputation as a friendly place and of having the highest proportion of trees to people of any city in Europe. I'm frequently told the city 'is the largest village in England' – it certainly feels like it.

My bus continues along Ecclesall Road for more than three miles. The change from side roads of suburban housing and narrow shop-fronts to larger industrial premises records my departure from the city centre.

The route kisses ancient woodlands before edging past **Dore**, one of the wealthiest suburbs of the city. Now part of Sheffield,

Dore was once a town of neighbouring Derbyshire. Before that, it was the boundary between Anglo-Saxon Northumbria and Mercia, and the site where Wessex's King Ecgbert became the first 'Overlord of all England' in AD829. Following a twist in the road to face west on passing Dore, a small cluster of fields becomes visible. The bus cuts a stolid figure between the farmland that separates the Sheffield conurbation from the wilds of the moorland.

The route continues with few true turns though the road it follows changes name several times, marking its progress from village to village. Now Hathersage Road, it loses its pavements to verdant verges and hedgerows outside settlements. The cream stones of Sheffield are swapped for the greens, browns and purples of the Peak District.

The simplicity of the bus route allows me to examine the open landscapes that surround the vehicle. My seat on the top deck gives a unique, even unusual, perspective on rolling heathlands and the limestone outcrops of **Hope Valley**. It's a name that lingers in my thoughts like the aromas of a warm pint of ale washing over my tongue. On the road verge is a simple round stone on a rectangular plinth that marks our entry into the national park. Farms and woodland continue on the left, moorland of a mysterious almost sinister purple in the spring light to my right.

After the Fox House Inn in **Longshaw**, the bus follows the road's tight twists first right then left, passing over Padley Gorge. The farmland disappears, the untamed wilderness mixing with woods before the stone buildings of **Hathersage** come into view and the bus enters Derbyshire.

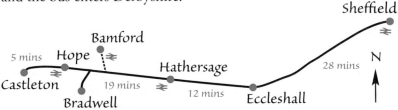

The dotted line indicates that the route is used only on certain journeys.
Bradwell to Castleton takes 10mins.

The route beyond Hathersage sees the fields return, their boundaries dotted with deciduous trees. The road straightens out as it continues its passage further westward, now paralleling the Hope Valley railway line. Crossing the Pennines to link Sheffield and Manchester, the line was completed in 1894.

Near Bamford railway station, the next stop along the Hope Valley line, the buses operated by Hulley's make a short detour from the main road, turning north to serve **Bamford**, a village of 1,400 residents. The village, less than a mile off the main road, is home to the Touchstone Sculpture Trail, created to commemorate the millennium. The five-mile trail is a good place to stretch stiffening legs. The modern monolithic sculptures were designed by local families and created by resident artist Jenny Mather. They depict the four elements of earth, wind, fire and water, and are also combined in a fifth sculpture in the centre of Bamford.

From green pastures to white quarries

A second diversion, made by most buses on this route, takes us down to **Bradwell**, a village of stone-built cottages. It seems a traditional sort of place, but the view is not quite the rural idyll one might expect. A cement factory and adjoining quarry give a bold splash of grey-white, offsetting the rich green of surrounding farmland.

The cement factory at Bradwell is a foretaste of what is to come. **Hope** has an even larger cement works, a strange cuboid structure beside an even taller, slender round smokestack. Mercifully, this eyesore is largely hidden from the village, which has a fine location at the point where **Peakshole Water** joins the River Noe.

It is just a few minutes to the final stop. **Castleton** is an easy village to navigate. **Peveril Castle** (see box, page 195) stands proudly on a vantage point to the south of the town centre; the four limestone show caverns of Treak Cliff, Blue John, Peak and Speedwell are all a short walk to the west. It was in these caves that minerals like the semi-precious Blue John used to be mined.

THE CASTLE THAT NAMED A TOWN

The English Heritage-owned Peveril Castle (☎ 01433 620613; open Apr–Oct 10.00–16.00 daily, Nov–Feb 10.00–16.00 Sat–Sun), right in the heart of Castleton is an excellent place to get to grips with the history of the High Peak. With a keep occupying the southern corner dating back to 1176 and the reign of Henry II, the ruined castle has a great position overlooking the town from a steep hillside. Already recorded in the Domesday Book, the roughly triangular Norman fortress has sheer drops on all but one side. A breathy winding path leads up the remaining side, giving superb views across Hope Valley. It's possible to enter several rooms in the keep, including a Norman-era toilet.

Mam Tor threatens the village with shade to the northwest, a great rounded mound looking like a benign green boil on the skin of the earth. It is threatened in return by the sheer number of visitors that wrestle with its steep flanks each high season in the High Peak.

At 1,696ft, **Mam Tor** is the spiritual focus not only of Castleton, but also of my whole journey on the 272 from Sheffield. For much of the route I have followed Hope Valley, which ends in the shadow of Mam Tor. The source of Peaceshole Water lies below the hill too, before running beside cottages and paths so narrow it is difficult to pass the postman and his large red shoulder bag.

Mam Tor's summit provides views of the castle, and the cement works at Hope. For me the contrasting vertical structures, old and new, demonstrate the enduring struggle we have in this crowded country between maintaining our open spaces and providing the jobs and materials we need for our cities. It's this very clash between the countryside around Castleton and the city of Sheffield that the 272 helps to highlight. ▪

ABOUT THE AUTHOR | **IAN M PACKHAM** is an adventurer, writer and speaker. He enjoys off-beat, off-season travel, preferably by public transport.

Colin Speakman

 Morecambe

Service nos. 832 or 830 | Journey time 3hrs 35mins.

OS Landranger 97, 98, 92, 99. Once on Sun & bank hols (seasonal).
Connects with Journey 37 in Hawes.
Operator: DalesBus.

Richmond

The Northern Dalesman is a different kind of bus service. It runs not because of the wishes of a local council or a national park, nor even a bus or coach operator. It is, rather, a genuine community initiative, created because a group of individuals who love the Dales felt so passionately about the loss of many Sunday bus services to and within the Yorkshire Dales National Park, they set up their own not-for-profit social enterprise, the Dales & Bowland Community Interest Company.

Over the past decade, this company has taken responsibility for the funding, management and promotion of the Sunday and bank holiday network serving the national park. This network is now firmly branded DalesBus, and there are comprehensive rover tickets and excellent connections with train and other bus services, designed *by* users *for* users.

The jewel in the crown of the DalesBus network is the Northern Dalesman. This is a route that operates every Sunday and public holiday from early May to late September. It crosses the Pennines to link the historic county town of Lancaster with the market town of Richmond, along the way taking in some fabulous mountain and moorland scenery. The greater part of the route lies within the boundaries of the Yorkshire Dales National Park.

Keld

7 mins

Thwaite

Reeth

Richmond

25 mins

N

20 mins

28 mins

Hawes

25 mins

Ribblehead

20 mins

Ingleton

50 mins

25 mins Lancaster

Morecambe

This three-hour journey is really a one-off. Perhaps no other regular scheduled bus service in England allows the traveller to enjoy such a remarkable range of landscapes. More's the pity – it runs little more than two-dozen times each year. But those with an appetite for bus timetables will find year-round services that cover some parts of the same route. But not all: this is the only bus route that takes in the spectacular Buttertubs Pass – the 'up and over' mountain road that links Wensleydale with Swaledale.

The 832 bus leaves **Morecambe**, travelling on through **Lancaster**, morphing at Ingleton into the 830. But passengers making the entire journey can stay on the same bus throughout.

INTO THE DALES

Sunday morning, at an hour when most folk are either at church or asleep, there's an eager gaggle of outdoor types waiting for the run into the Dales. The first part of the journey is happily undemanding, as we follow a pleasant-enough route along the Lune Valley, picking up more passengers in villages along the way.

Ingleton is the first real visitor destination. The village with its winding main street is dominated by a great railway viaduct, long bereft of any trains, crossing the narrow gorge of the River Greta. Beyond Ingleton, the mood of the landscape changes, becoming strikingly dramatic. We slip past White Scar Caves – one of the finest show caverns in the north, rich in stalactites and stalagmites – with the B6255 road climbing between two of Yorkshire's mighty **Three Peaks**. The great flat-topped summit to our right, above some of the most impressive limestone pavements in the British Isles, is Ingleborough. To our left is the long, whaleback shape of Whernside, the highest of the Three Peaks, and reached via an impressive ridge walk from Ingleton.

At Chapel-le-Dale with the Old Hill Inn (☎ 01524 241256), a popular walkers' pub, we cross the route of the Three Peaks Walk. Soon the great 24-arch stone **viaduct of Ribblehead** comes into sight. Once under the viaduct, the Northern Dalesman turns up the bumpy drive to Ribblehead Station (which has a small visitor centre) to await the arrival of the train.

For many people this is the easiest and best way of experiencing the Northern Dalesman, by taking the celebrated Settle and Carlisle rail route. Through trains from Leeds connect conveniently with the bus. Most of those who climb aboard here have rucksacks or walking poles (or both). This is real integrated transport – something that Britain could and should do so much better.

Once past the Station Inn the bus begins the climb out of Ribblesdale up to Newby Head, through an area of wild and desolate countryside crossed by the **Pennine Bridleway**. We breach the watershed between the Ribble and the Ure, then drop gently through Widdale into Upper Wensleydale, and the little market town of Hawes.

THE WATERFALL TRAIL

Ingleton's lovely waterfall walk starts a quarter of a mile below the village (an admission fee applies as the paths and estate are private), then follows a series of carefully engineered footpaths and footbridges up the valley of the River Twiss past the swirling white waters of Pecca Falls to majestic Thornton Force, returning along the valley of the Doe past Beazley and Snow falls. Not only are the waterfalls spectacular, but the trail is also one of the most fascinating geological walks in England, with ancient Silurian and Cambrian rocks superbly exposed underneath the dominant Carboniferous limestone.

> ## SWALEDALE
>
> For many people Swaledale is the most beautiful of the entire Yorkshire Dales: green, intimate, and beguilingly lovely. This is a valley famous for its drystone walls and scattered barns. The latter recall a sustainable farming practice followed between the 17th and 20th centuries, storing hay above the cattle for insulation during the winter months to provide both warmth and sustenance. Sadly it was very labour intensive, which has meant that the barns, walls and wonderful, herb- and flower-rich meadows, are now very much at risk. Thanks to various conservation projects, many of these iconic features of this delicate rural landscape are now being preserved.

Hawes (see also the box on page 205) is a town with character. Its busy main street boasts a Tuesday market – sadly not the day the Northern Dalesman calls. As well as the usual choice of cafés, pubs and shops, there are many other reasons to visit the town – the Wensleydale Creamery (see box, page 205), five minutes' walk from the centre. It is here that the famous Wensleydale cheese is made, so memorably promoted by Wallace and Gromit whose mention of 'Not even Wensleydale?' in *A Close Shave* helped initiate a spectacular revival in the creamery's fortunes. Visitors can watch the cheesemakers at work.

The Northern Dalesman calls at the old railway station, which is now the Dales Countryside Museum (see box, page 205) – if you are making the entire run from Lancaster to Richmond, you'll cherish this chance of a toilet stop. There is still a stationary tank engine and coach behind the station buildings as an evocative reminder of the town's railway heritage. But now our bus takes to terrain where no railway has ever ventured.

Up and over

The Northern Dalesman heads north out of town, crossing the River Ure over an ancient stone bridge before heading up to the hamlet of Simonstone. To the left, a paved path crosses the fields towards **Hardraw**, where England's highest waterfall, behind the Green Dragon Inn, thrusts down a rocky ravine.

Now comes a real test of driving skills and engineering. The gradient on the narrow mountain road suddenly gets noticeably steeper. Low gears are needed. The engine growls and rumbles. Pity the poor cyclists who in July 2014 tackled these formidable gradients in the opening stage of the Tour de France.

We quickly emerge from tame country hemmed in by white stone walls into the more expansive landscape of **Abbotside Common**. Here the line of the road is marked by posts which in times of snowfall are sometimes the only indication of where the route lies. The bus, now well laden with passengers, climbs nearly 1,000ft to the summit of **Buttertubs Pass**. At 1,726ft, this is one of the highest roads in the Pennines.

The views are breathtaking. To our left is the massive whaleback of **Great Shunner Fell**, one of the highest points of the Pennine Way. Away to our right is Lovely Seat. 'Last time I was up there, it was anything but lovely,' quips a voice from the back of the bus. 'So darn windy, I lost my hat.' But his voice is drowned out by the many expressions of surprise at the scenery around. Over the top, we see the celebrated butter tubs that give the pass its name. These are water-carved pot-holes and limestone columns said to look

Swaledale is often said to be the prettiest of the dales (© Stephenmeese/DT)

.like wooden tubs. Then on down around quite terrifying bends, with views along the whole length of Swaledale. It is the contrasts that make these landscapes. Here we are atop a wild moor, but Swaledale below seems like a green paradise.

Down in the dale, we serve a medley of Swaledale villages. We stop in **Thwaite** (birthplace of the famous wildlife photographers Richard and Cherry Kearton), then head up to the hamlet of **Keld**. It is on both the Pennine Way and Coast to Coast Path, so is the starting point for some very special walks in Swaledale. The bus reverses in the lane that leads up to **Tan Hill Inn** (☎ 01833 628246), England's highest pub, before returning to Thwaite and continuing along the narrow road down the dale, often squeezing over bridges and passing cars or tractors with only inches to spare.

The next village, **Muker**, with coffee shops, the Farmers Arms and the Swaledale Woollen Shop, is the starting point for many walks over Kisdon or up Swinner Gill. Then follows Gunnerside, a village with many remnants of the great lead-mining industry of the dales. Next are the linear villages of Low Row, Featham and Healaugh, bringing us to **Reeth**, with its huge village green. This is the unofficial capital of Swaledale, with a lively tourist office and a good museum on Swaledale life (☎ 01748 884118; open 10.00–17.00 daily).

From Reeth the dale is less dramatic, but equally impressive. The road curves through Fremington to Grinton, then on through thickly wooded countryside, below Marrick – with its medieval priory (now an outdoor centre) – and Marske, before finally crossing the River Swale to ascend to the market town of **Richmond**, dominated by its Norman castle on a high cliff above the river, its huge marketplace and unique Georgian theatre.

For most people Richmond is the natural terminus of the Northern Dalesman. It's hardly a conurbation, so most travellers will continue northeast on the Arriva bus to Darlington. ∎

ABOUT THE AUTHOR | **COLIN SPEAKMAN** is a writer and environmentalist from Ilkley, west Yorkshire. He is Chairman of the Yorkshire Dales Society, campaigning to protect the Dales and to promote its green travel networks.

A WENSLEYDALE
DOUBLE DELIGHT

Richard Kingsbury

Leyburn

Service no. 156 | Journey time 40mins.

OS Landranger 99, 98. 6 journeys Mon–Sat only.
Operator: Little White Bus.
Connects with Journey 36 in Hawes.

Gayle

Wensleydale lies at the heart of the Yorkshire Dales National Park. It is a generous, green, glacial valley, enclosed by Addleborough and Wether Fell. This gentle sweep of territory is best explored on a magical bus route which, with Yorkshire cunning, splits into two, offering magnificent views from each side of the dale.

Diverting from the main A684, one route takes in villages on the south side while the other covers the dale's northern hamlets. Picture the legendary Rod of Aaron, in this case the main road, with its entwined serpent: though there is nothing venomous about these scenic bus routes. Go up the dale one side, come down the other.

Although buses on these routes do not run on Sundays, there is a limited Sunday service between April and October. It is branded the Wensleydale Flyer, running as service number 856, and gives a useful link from the railway station at Northallerton to Hawes. But it sticks in the main to the A684. The Wensleydale Flyer is fast, unadventurous, the Rod of Aaron option, and not a patch on its weekday equivalents.

Up-valley on the 156

In terms of maximising the good views, I recommend timing your journey so that you see both variants on the theme from the outward and return legs: the first bus of the day takes the northern route via Preston-under-Scar, Redmire, Castle Bolton and Caperby, while the southern route traces a course past West Burton, Thoralby, Aysgarth, Thornton Rust and Worton.

From **Leyburn**, we start to appreciate the sweeping majesty of **Wensleydale**. On the left is the town's hillside cemetery, surely one of the most desirable sites in England in which to be laid to rest, with mighty Pen Hill (1,790ft) brooding over the dale and the River Ure. Like the other Yorkshire dales, Wensleydale was originally named after its river. Thus it was Uredale, or on some maps Yoredale. But, in the early 18th century, the valley adopted the name Wensley after what was then a significant market town. Nowadays Wensley is just a pleasant dales village – and the spot where the northern variant turns right, climbing above Bolton Hall to **Preston-under-Scar**, giving panoramic views of the dale. We might see a train of the **Wensleydale Railway**, run by volunteers, chugging up the dale from Bedale to Redmire. You can learn more about this train service at www.wensleydalerail.com.

After Redmire village we climb to **Castle Bolton**, where Mary Queen of Scots was imprisoned 1568–69. Dominating this northern flank of Wensleydale, the castle, dating from 1399, was built by Sir Richard le Scrope, Lord Chancellor to Richard II. Focal point for Royalists, Bolton Castle suffered a six-month siege by Parliamentarian forces in 1645. It remains an impressive bastion,

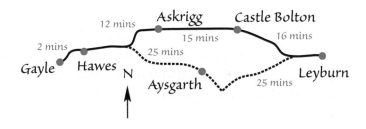

worth a visit, and it's a good starting point to venture out for walks on the surrounding moors.

Still on the northern side of the dale, we come to **Carperby**, stone-built and slate-roofed, where we pick up villagers heading for the shops in Hawes. With the Ure winding through hay meadows below, we call at **Askrigg**, a favourite spot for walkers. If you like the television series *All Creatures Great and Small* you'll quickly see that Askrigg is the fictional Darrowby of the series. Now the bus drops down to the A684 at **Bainbridge**, a broad, open village below Addleborough's 1,560ft peak. Bainbridge is a popular starting point for a walk in the footsteps of the Romans (who had a fort at Bainbridge) to Semer Water, two miles south, the second-largest natural lake in Yorkshire. It is a haven for birds, the surrounding meadows a profusion of colour in summer.

For the final lap (four miles) to Hawes on the narrowing A684, we climb towards the head of the dale. We've now left hedgerows a long way behind. This is drystone-wall country. Sheep wander over rough fell pastures. In 2001 this was a desolate scene. The tragic spread of foot-and-mouth disease through this part of England meant wholesale slaughter of flocks, bringing despair to already poor hill farmers. It left the countryside bare of livestock, access barred to tracks and paths. The dale was shrouded in eerie silence. If the bus is suddenly halted by wandering sheep or a flock being driven, breathe a prayer for their well-being, daft-eyed and feckless though they may seem.

HEAD OF THE DALE

Hawes welcomes us with its narrow one-way streets. The bus squeezes over the cobbles between country stores, pubs and tea shops. It has not been a long ride, but the marketplace here feels a long way from its equivalent at Leyburn. The bus carries on for a couple of minutes before terminating at the virtually conjoined village of **Gayle**.

For the run home from Gayle or Hawes, I prefer the alternative route (left-side seats are again best for views). Beyond Bainbridge, the bus leaves the A684 to serve **Thornton Rust**, with sweeping views of the dale's northern flank, along which we travelled on the outward route. We briefly rejoin the main road at Aysgarth village, from where you can visit the impressive **Aysgarth Falls**. After Aysgarth, it makes a little foray south to Thoralby and West Burton, before continuing east along the main valley to West Witton, Wensley and **Leyburn**. ∎

AYSGARTH FALLS

Justifiably popular, Aysgarth Falls are not visible from the main road, so ask the driver when to alight. Buses on the southern route stop near the falls; to avoid an unduly long wait till the next bus, it currently works better to take the southern route out, stop off at Aysgarth for a couple of hours, then carry on, returning from Gayle or Hawes by one of the two afternoon buses on the northern route. It is free and open daily, but be generous at the 'honesty box' by the gate to the upper falls. The artist J M W Turner visited the falls in 1816, and William and Mary Wordsworth came here on the day after their marriage in 1802.

ABOUT THE AUTHOR | **RICHARD KINGSBURY** is a retired Anglican priest, now living in Bedale in the fair North Riding of Yorkshire.

BENDY OR BORIS?

The bus business has always been innovative. In another Bus Stop in this book (see page 144), we saw how Thomas Henry Barton brought much ingenuity to bus operations in the late Victorian and Edwardian period. Buses are so much a part of the fabric of our cities, so woven into the texture of everyday life, that meddling with buses is a sure way of exciting public opinion. Remember the outcry when bendy buses first appeared on the streets of London? These articulated buses had proved very successful in many cities across the world, but their arrival in London was judged by many of a more conservative disposition to herald the demise of civilised life in the capital.

Outraged citizens saw the bendy buses, introduced while Ken Livingstone was still Mayor of London in 2001, as part of a left-wing conspiracy to challenge the reign of the traditional double-decker on London streets. When one of the new buses had a minor fire in 2003 (which was quickly extinguished), the incident fuelled the imagination of headline writers. 'Fire-breathing buses threaten the capital,' screamed one tabloid. Media images suggested scrums of tourists fleeing self-combusting buses. Londoners succumbed to waves of nostalgia about the Routemaster buses of yesteryear.

Bendy buses were the political downfall of Ken Livingstone and his successor. Boris Johnson seized the moment. In his bid to become mayor, Boris promised to ban Ken's chariots of fire from the streets of London. And that's just what he did. Not since the first decade of the last century, when motorised buses suddenly pushed aside horse-drawn vehicles, has a capital city so dramatically changed its policy on buses. The new Boris bus programme has brought back double-deckers, but with a new design that has echoes of the much-loved Routemaster. Sadly, the vehicles do not comply with the latest carbon-emission standards, but that's the price that Londoners must pay for a slice of political vanity.

The bendy buses were sold off cheap, many ending up on Malta's roads. Back in London, residents and tourists all seem to like the Boris bus. Politicians across the world look in awe at the prowess in building the entire Boris brand on the back of a bus. ∎

Cumbria and Northumberland

England's northernmost counties are a bus traveller's paradise, and our challenge in this section of *Bus-Pass Britain* has been to select just five routes out of the dozens that begged to be included. We opted for two in the Lake District National Park, two in the North East, and one which links Carlisle with Newcastle upon Tyne.

Rural Northumberland benefits from many locally owned and operated bus services that provide a year-round service to out-of-the-way villages. One of our favourites is the 880 from Hexham to Kielder, the last village in England before the Scottish border – no easy journey on snowy winter days. Howard Snaith Coaches operate this route, which runs on Tuesdays, Fridays and Saturdays. At the other end of Northumberland, on the North Sea coast, is one of Britain's most extraordinary bus services: the 477 to Holy Island. We have included a short account of this route across a tidal causeway as an optional diversion from Journey 42.

Cuts in local authority funding by the Conservative government have taken their toll on local bus services in the region, but difficult times have fostered innovation. Some deeply rural areas in the region are now served by demand-responsive services, rather than having buses sticking to fixed routes and timetables. Some communities have even set up their own bus services, a good example of which is Spirit Buses, based in Rothbury, Northumberland. ∎

UPDATES WEBSITE

You can post your comments and recommendations, and read the latest feedback and updates from other readers online at www.bradtupdates. com/buspassbritain.

Escape From
PENRITH

Ruth Kershaw and Paul Heels

(38) Penrith

Service no. 508 | Journey time 1hr 25mins.

OS Landranger 97, 90. 3 buses daily (route over Kirkstone Pass
is seasonal (Apr–Oct daily, school holidays Mon–Fri),
goes only as far as Patterdale in winter).
Operator: Stagecoach.

Windermere

Tourist literature often plugs the Lake District as the most beautiful corner of England. Few will be inclined to dispute this claim as they ride this bus route through the heart of one of the country's first generation of national parks. For those with a head for heights, Helvellyn via Striding Edge beckons. Those with less energy might opt to cruise Ullswater by boat. Happily this service runs year-round. As appealing in deep midwinter as it is on a sunny spring day, it is a route for all seasons. You have a choice of two buses in the morning to take you into the Lake District, so there's only limited scope for breaking the journey on the way out, but there's plenty to occupy you before the late-afternoon bus returns you to Penrith. This route starts and ends at rail stations (between April and October), giving useful alternative return options.

The starting point for our exploration of the northeast part of the Lake District is **Penrith Railway Station**, good for direct train connections via the main West Coast route from London, Manchester and Scotland. Travellers from afar are thus already on board when a few minutes later the service stops briefly at Penrith's rather spartan bus station.

THE FELLS BECKON

Penrith ⚏
24 mins

Pooley
Bridge

N ↑

26 mins

Patterdale

20 mins

Kirkstone
Pass Inn

21 mins

Windermere

Most of those aboard are bound for a day in the hills. One or two passengers are really just there for the ride, travelling out and back on the same bus. There is a relaxed atmosphere, as the bus navigates streets with their hallmark red sandstone buildings. Dates prominently inscribed over door lintels attest to the fact that Penrith is no upstart new town. Many buildings date from the 17th century, and settlement in the area dates back far longer. As the bus to Windermere heads south out of town there is a good view on the right, just before the M6 is crossed, of **Mayburgh Henge**, a well-preserved Neolithic henge.

Soon after the M6, we have a sense of really being in the country, and the scenery becomes ever better as we follow a B road southwest towards the hills. Soft Cumbrian farmland area around Tirril gives way to hillier terrain at **Pooley Bridge** , although sadly due to floods in the region in late 2015, the 300-year-old bridge was washed away. Plans are in place for the construction of a new one, however.

LINGERING AROUND ULLSWATER

You don't need to be an accomplished mountaineer to enjoy the fells. Ullswater 'Steamers' (The Pier House; ☎ 01768 482229; see www.ullswater-steamers.co.uk for times & fares) cruise the length of Ullswater from Glenridding to Pooley Bridge. Walkers can take the boat from Glenridding across to Howtown and follow a delightful lakeside path at the foot of Place Fell back to Glenridding via Patterdale (7 miles). A short cruise on Ullswater is tempting: you can board the boat at Glenridding, from where it is a 60- to 70-minute journey to Pooley Bridge, where you can rejoin the afternoon bus to return to Penrith.

Much of the next section of the route, some eight miles in all, clings to the west bank of **Ullswater**, a serpentine ribbon of a lake that has three reaches with two dog-legs. By now passengers who just a half-hour earlier were strangers are chatting amiably with each other, pointing out landmarks and sharing their plans for the hours ahead.

At the first dog-leg the scenery becomes more wooded and picturesque with a great vista east to Howtown framed by Hallin Fell. At just 1,271ft, **Hallin Fell** is no great mountain, but for one or two of those aboard the bus it has a special meaning. 'That was the first Lakeland fell I ever climbed,' says one lady who reveals that she was only four years old when she made her first ascent of mighty Hallin. Her revelation prompts a man two rows behind to interject: 'And that's where I want my ashes scattered.'

REACHING AIRA FORCE

Now **Helvellyn** is heaving into view, little wisps of cloud lacing the summit that towers high above the west side of Ullswater. We skirt Dobbin Wood and stop near **Aira Force**, where a number of passengers alight and in 2015 the Aira Force landing stage came into being. This is a place for all the family. Children can paddle in the stony beck, gentle walks in Gowbarrow Park afford stunning views and the force itself, falling 70ft, is a textbook piece of Romantic scenery.

A pier at Ullswater
(© Atgimages/DT)

SOMNAMBULISTS BEWARE!

Aira Force is the scene of a tragedy, recorded by Wordsworth in his poem 'The Somnambulist'. The legend is of Emma, betrothed to Sir Eglamore, becoming so disturbed by his absence in the Crusades that she took to walking in her sleep by the banks of the torrent. It was there that Sir Eglamore found her on his return. He touched her and she suddenly awoke, so surprised by the appearance of her lover that she fell over a precipice into a deep ravine. The knight tried in vain to rescue her. And Sir Eglamore? Well, he is said to have then led a lonely life as a recluse in a cave near the great waterfall.

Beyond Aira Force comes **Glencoyne Bay**, the shores of which inspired Wordsworth to pen 'I wandered lonely as a cloud', also known as 'Daffodils'. It is still a fine spot on an April day when the daffs are in bloom. Now the lake makes its second dog-leg into the final reach. The scenery becomes markedly more rugged and, on a wild day, even forbidding. Over to the left Place Fell drops steeply into the water, while on the right the cliffed slopes of St Sunday Crag look like a landscape of the Gothic imagination. The booted brigade shuffles gear in preparation to leave the bus at Glenridding or **Patterdale** to climb Helvellyn.

Glenridding is an old mining village with excellent facilities. Try the Inn on the Lake (☎ 01768 482444) for real ale and traditional bar food – a hotel with lovely gardens running down to the lake. Fellbites Café (☎ 01768 482781; open 11.00–20.30, until 17.00 Wed), centrally located, also offers a good range of sandwiches, light meals and temptingly delicious cakes.

Beyond **Patterdale** the characteristic stone walls make a patchwork of the valley floor. Yet more walls climb up hillsides populated by the ubiquitous and infinitely agile Lakeland sheep. On the left are the slate roofs of the hamlet of Hartsop nestling below the fells, then on the right is **Brothers Water**, named after two brothers who died in it while skating. Soon we start to climb

AN INN WITH ALTITUDE

No kudos to the writer for the snappy title, for actually it is Kirkstone Pass Inn which styles itself 'an inn with altitude' (☎ 01539 433888; www.kirkstonepassinn.com). And surely true, for this is the highest inhabited building in Cumbria and the third-highest inn in England. Meals are generally available both lunchtime and evenings, but opening times vary by season – so check in advance. Good en-suite rooms are ideal for those seeking a comfortable mountain retreat. Keen fell walkers can scramble up the rocky slopes of Red Screes (2,545ft) or take a gentler climb up to the oddly named High Street (2,718ft).

steadily, and our driver deftly shifts down through the gears as the vehicle growls up **Kirkstone Pass**. Just beyond the summit of the pass, **Kirkstone Pass Inn**, a traditional coaching inn, makes a fine stop (see box above). There are glimpses of shimmering Windermere away to the right, and a dauntingly steep minor road – aptly named 'The Struggle' – joins us from the right. It takes skill to drive these mountain roads and our driver today is clearly very adept at coping with all that comes his way. We edge down the steep road, stopping briefly to allow a tourist coach labouring up the pass to go by, followed by a line of frustrated car drivers. To the east the terrain is severe and forbidding, and includes the fells that mark the Kentmere Horseshoe. Then gradually the scenery becomes tamer as the gentle valley carved by the Trout Beck appears to the left. The A592 drops down into the valley to pass Troutbeck Church before ending at Windermere Station. ■

ABOUT THE AUTHORS

RUTH KERSHAW is a former walks leader for CHA, East Cumbria Countryside Project and U3A.
PAUL HEELS, a retired business studies teacher living in Cumbria, has had a lifelong passion for bus travel.

THE HONISTER RAMBLER

Michael Holmes

 Lake District

39

Service nos. 77 or 77A | Journey time 1hr 45mins.

OS Landranger 90. Runs 5 times daily in both directions
from mid Apr–late Oct.
Operator: Stagecoach.

circular route

This journey is a fine circuit through some of Lakeland's best scenery, starting and ending in Keswick, and including along the way two mountain passes (Whinlatter and Honister) and a ride along the shores of three beautiful lakes (Crummock Water, Buttermere and Derwent Water).

Keswick makes an excellent base for exploring the Lake District. Open-top buses run down the east side of Derwent Water. The double-decker bus to Windermere is also a popular choice, but my favourite is the Honister Rambler, a seasonal circular bus service that is a real delight, and you don't have to be a bus-pass holder to enjoy this route at a reasonable price. A Keswick and Honister Dayrider ticket allows unlimited travel on the Honister Rambler as well as services to Bassenthwaite Lake, Threlkeld and Thirlmere.

ROUND TRIP THROUGH A NATIONAL PARK

So let's join the steady stream of ramblers boarding the first anticlockwise service of the day, the number 77. That's a detail you need to note with the Honister Rambler. A bus with an 'A'

WHINLATTER VISITOR CENTRE

The centre is open from 10.00 daily, and closes at 17.00 in summer, 16.00 in winter (☎ 017687 78469). Siskins Café (inside the centre) is a safe bet for coffee, with very tempting cakes (even lemon with parsnip!) and home-cooked meals. There are well-signed walks through the forest, cycle trails, and – for the truly adventurous – a Go Ape route, where you can explore your primal instincts on rope bridges and Tarzan swings.

makes the circuit clockwise, while one without an 'A' travels the route anticlockwise. No doubt there's some logic tucked away in there somewhere, but it's certainly confusing to many first-time users of this bus service.

Once on board, all the chat is of plans for the day. Some travellers are bound for the fells. There is talk of Lakeland landmarks like **High Stile** and **Haystacks**. One couple, dog-eared Wainwright and old OS map in their hands, have lofty Grasmoor in their sights. Some are making the journey for the first time, others are revisiting old haunts, and a few are clearly here just for the ride, waiting to see how the day unfolds.

We leave Keswick to the northwest with imposing **Skiddaw** to our right. At Braithwaite the first serious climb of the day begins. We are soon into Forestry Commission territory, with dense plantations on both sides of the road. There are inviting gaps in the trees, giving sight lines to distant fells and, at one point, a fine view down to Bassenthwaite Lake far below.

The road climbs to Whinlatter Visitor Centre (see box above) at the top of the pass, just 15 minutes out of Keswick, and a good spot to learn about Forestry Commission work in the area.

The area is exceptionally rich in wildlife. The combination of forests, open heathland habitats and the nearby waters of **Bassenthwaite Lake** encourages variety – so there are crossbills, siskins, merlins and even ospreys. The last-named had not been seen in England since 1842, so when a pair was spotted at

Bassenthwaite in 1997, it created huge interest. With support from the RSPB, nest platforms were provided and to great excitement the first chick was reared in 2001. Red squirrels are a common sight around the visitor centre at Whinlatter, and the surrounding forests are home to many roe deer.

Whinlatter is a fine introduction to the area, but now the hills beckon, so travellers are back at the bus stop to continue their Lakeland circuit on the next Honister Rambler. The 77 bus comes into view, and we climb aboard to a cheery greeting from the driver. We head west down into Lorton Vale, all eyes on a buzzard that lazily circles in the sky ahead. With the farming communities of High and Low Lorton behind us, we turn south to follow the rugged shoreline of **Crummock Water**. Across the water, in a cleft in the fells, we see one of the most spectacular waterfalls in the Lake District. This is Scale Force which can be reached on foot from **Buttermere** village. The road skirts Hause Point, a wild headland that juts impertinently into Crummock Water, and suddenly there is a complete change of scenery. Here is gentle woodland and sheep pasture as Buttermere is approached.

BUTTERMERE

Buttermere is a Cumbrian idyll, judged by many who visit to be the perfect Lakeland village. You'll find no shortage of cafés and there are two good hotels. With its clean whitewashed walls and neat slate roof, The Fish Inn (☎ 017687 70253) blends perfectly into this happy pastoral scene. But there is a darker side to Buttermere history. In 1802 the landlord's daughter, a celebrated local beauty, was tricked into marrying one John Hatfield, who claimed to be a man of means with aristocratic connections. A nationwide hue and cry ensued when it almost immediately emerged that Hatfield was by no means all he purported to be, but rather a bigamist and forger. He met his end at Carlisle the following year, not for his abuse of Mary, but a long catalogue of other crimes. The story did have a happy ending, however, as Mary subsequently married a local farmer.

Buttermere's lovely village church is worth a visit. Here you will find a memorial to **Alfred Wainwright**, whose classic walking guides did so much to bring the Lake District to wider public popularity. The memorial tablet is situated by a window, from which there is a clear view to Haystacks,

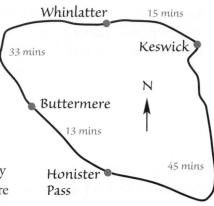

Wainwright's own favourite fell, and where his ashes were scattered. The circuit of the lake is a most rewarding low-level walk; alternatively stroll along the southwest side and rejoin the bus route at Gatesgarth Farm.

Beyond Gatesgarth, the road climbs steeply to the top of **Honister Pass** (1,167ft) – the highest spot on this journey. The slate mine has become a popular tourist attraction, and gives some insight into the difficult conditions in which the miners toiled. But the star attraction at Honister is the panorama, taking in many of the major Lakeland summits. The eastern side of Honister is even steeper than the climb up from Buttermere, culminating in a heady 1 in 4 gradient on the road that drops down into Seatoller. 'Stay in low gear,' implore the road signs. Our driver obliges.

We have now reached **Borrowdale**, singled out by Wainwright as 'the finest dale in England'. I just sit back and enjoy the view. At Grange Bridge, there is the chance to change on to the open-top bus that skirts the east bank of Derwent Water. I take the easy option, keeping my front seat on the Honister Rambler, as we cruise the west shore of the lake back to Keswick. ∎

ABOUT THE AUTHOR | **MICHAEL HOLMES** and his wife have been visiting the Lake District for over 40 years, and they eagerly anticipate the next visit.

Brian Robson

40 Middlesbrough

Service no. X9 | Journey time 80mins.

OS Landranger 93, 88. Hourly Mon–Sat, no service Sun.
Operator: Go North East.
Connects with Journeys 41 & 42 in Newcastle upon Tyne.

Newcastle upon Tyne←

Years ago, 'Tyne Tees' was the name of our local commercial TV station. Friendly faces with local accents brought us news, weather and even birthday greetings from their studios in Newcastle. Nowadays, the brand has been swept away in favour of a stronger national identity for ITV, and that little bit of local colour is no more. Sad, perhaps, but the name lives on – not least as the Tyne Tees moniker is still applied to the fleet of buses which ply the express route between Middlesbrough and Newcastle.

BRIDGING THE TEES

The plum-coloured Tyne Tees Express double-decker which awaits me at **Middlesbrough**'s central bus station leaves me in no doubt that I've found the right departure stand. 'Newcastle Middlesbrough – every 30 minutes' scream the slogans on the side, also advising that our bus is equipped with Wi-Fi internet and electric sockets. This is a thoroughly modern bus route.

So I'm upstairs for the view as, on the stroke of the hour, we pull away on the run north to Newcastle. Middlesbrough is red-brick country, but the view is more than just Victorian terraces. There's a glimpse of the **Tees Transporter Bridge** to the east. An ingenious solution to the challenge of crossing the Tees whilst not affecting navigation on the busy river, the Transporter is a rare breed of bridge. Motorists drive gingerly onto a gondola suspended by cables from a blue ironwork super-structure, and are hauled across the river in just 90 seconds. Sadly, our bus takes the less exotic but more practical option of the modern **Tees Flyover**, which does have the advantage of offering us further views of the Transporter.

We are not long on our way when we stop at **Billingham**. It's recently been regenerated – one of those modern planning euphemisms – so I was keen to pay a visit to the town's shopping centre to see the results.

Billingham's town centre was built as part of a planned expansion of the area in the 1950s. It was intended to provide facilities for the growing workforce at the nearby ICI plant. An unusual circular tower block which resembles Birmingham's more famous Rotunda dominates the skyline.

As Billingham's chemical works have declined, so too has the town centre. The deserted precinct reminds me of town centres in the former eastern bloc. There's a sculpture – entitled *Family group* – which would surely have been at home in Belgrade or Bratislava 30 years ago, the shirtless father bending to lift his son aloft. All that's missing is a 'workers of the world unite' inscription.

The art gallery is forlorn, a hastily printed sign announcing Stockton Council's decision to close it permanently. I'm beginning to wonder where everyone is, so I walk further into the precinct where posters outside the Forum Theatre proclaim that the Grand Opera of Belarus is appearing soon. Perhaps the X9 has delivered me into an alternative socialist universe? The Forum is pretty dead but a lone member of staff in the foyer tells me that Billingham is more a spot for sport than Belarusian opera. She suggests I take a look at the nearby leisure centre.

Here, indeed, there is life aplenty with a gym, swimming pool and ice rink. Youthful shrieks fill the air, and the café is packed with anxious-looking parents waiting for children to emerge from the rink, hopefully with limbs intact.

I settle down with a tankard-size cup of tea and read about how the upcoming regeneration will transform Billingham life, whiling away time before the next X9 arrives to whisk me onwards.

WIND AND WEAR

Once on board, the bus rejoins the A19 dual carriageway at Wynyard, and we cruise northwards. Windmills fill the air, with some particularly huge turbines to the east as signs welcome us to **County Durham**. It's not just windmills of the modern variety, either. Soon we pass a pub called the Windmill, and to the left emerges its namesake – a slender red-brick windmill of the traditional variety, its sails sadly no more. Clearly the winds which are buffeting our tall double-decker as it makes its way north have been put to productive use for many years.

Signs by the A19 invite us to 'locate, invest, succeed' in **Peterlee**. On cue, our bus sweeps into the town, built to provide homes for the Bevin Boys who had toiled in the Durham coalfields during and after World War II. My top-deck seat affords views over terraces of hexahedron houses, most of which have had their cube-like quality destroyed by the addition of a pitched roof.

They owe their design to abstract artist Victor Pasmore. East Durham's new Jerusalem attracted the finest creative minds, and Pasmore was enlisted to provide a 'synthesis of architecture, painting and sculpture' in the town's Sunny Blunts estate.

Pasmore's efforts proved controversial. One complaint – perhaps apocryphal – is that his penchant for floor-to-ceiling windows left no room for curtain rails, much to the disgust of east Durham housewives, some of whom are perhaps on our bus now, taking a jaunt to Newcastle for its shops and market. At the time the *Northern Echo* wrote that the houses were 'brave and imaginative in their general design' but 'wretched and shabby in their details and practical execution'. A fair assessment.

Now bereft of the mines it was built to serve, Peterlee is experiencing hard times, but lying halfway along the route, it makes a useful stop to stretch your legs. The bus station has limited facilities, but toilets are available in the Asda supermarket and the Five Quarter pub offers good-value food (Hailsham Pl; ☎ 0191 578 5880; open 08.00–23.00 daily).

Moving on from Peterlee, we catch glimpses of the North Sea, but as we enter **Sunderland**, further windmills give way to a more unexpected sight – what appears to be a Greek temple set atop a steep hill. **Penshaw Monument** is a folly, modelled on the Temple of Hephaestus in Athens. Erected in 1844 in memory of the Earl of Durham, the monument's Doric columns are now in the care of the National Trust.

Soon, we're crossing the third of the North East's major rivers, the Wear. You may glimpse to your right a concrete barge, which marks the site of the proposed New Sunderland Bridge. When constructed this will soar more than 100m in the air, and – in a

PASMORE'S PAVILION

Pasmore's houses weren't his only contribution to Peterlee. Even more infamous is his Apollo Pavilion. Slabs of concrete float above a lake, an anonymous monument which Pasmore intended to 'lift the activity and psychology of an urban housing community onto a universal plane'. It didn't work out as he intended. So despised was Pasmore's structure that in the 1980s local residents invited the Territorial Army to blow it up as an exercise. Fortunately it was saved this ignominious end, and has enjoyed a reappraisal in recent years. The Pavilion has been restored, and now enjoys listed status. Find out more at www.apollopavilion.info.

region where local rivalries matter – give the Wear a crossing to rival Middlesbrough's Transporter or Newcastle's Tyne Bridge.

For now, though, Sunderland's most famous sight remains Penshaw Monument, and the city's most famous export the Nissan car. A cluster of ten more windmills tower above the ugly Nissan plant. The dirty chemical and coal industries of the North East's past are giving way to the clean electric cars of Europe's most productive car factory. The 'Leaf', as the latest model is known, is now reckoned to be the best-selling all-electric vehicle ever.

ACROSS THE TYNE

Heading into the Tyneside conurbation, the X9 halts briefly at **Heworth** metro station, one of 60 stations on the UK's first modern light-rail system. Box-like yellow metro trains have shuttled around Tyne and Wear for over 30 years now, with the drivers' plea to 'stand clear of the doors please' being as much part of Geordie life as the London tube's more famous instruction to 'mind the gap'.

Next stop is **Gateshead**, where many of my fellow passengers rush to alight for buses to the Metro Centre – Europe's largest shopping centre, built on the site of a former ash dump. Hit by the success of the Metro Centre, Gateshead's town centre has been modernised – an ugly 1960s shopping complex has been replaced by an equally ugly modern complex, anchored by a huge Tesco

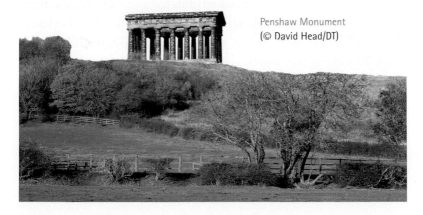

Penshaw Monument
(© David Head/DT)

A VERY SOCIAL SERVICE

With free Wi-Fi on board, it's no surprise that the X9 figures in social media. It even has its own Twitter hashtag: #TyneTeesXpress. And regular X9 users meet not just on the bus but in a dedicated Facebook group. That's where I first ran across Colin Dunn who often uses early-morning buses to Newcastle. He explained: 'We're a close-knit family on the X9. Some of us have been getting this bus for 20 years, and we make the hour-long journey more interesting by talking, doing crosswords and having quizzes.' Colin is now the group's self-appointed communications tsar and was keen to share the group's exploits with me. 'Hey, I must tell you about my 50th birthday party. I decided I didn't want a party at work, but I did want a party with my friends from the bus. We all get on well with the very friendly drivers, so I invited them too. The bus company made a special cake for me, the drivers got me a bottle of very nice whisky and we had a great night. For me, it was surreal!'

store. At least the 1960s version was graced by the Owen Luder car park made famous in the film *Get Carter* – its raw concrete now a thing of the past as one form of progress is replaced by another.

Crossing the River Tyne into **Newcastle**, the 'blinking eye' Millennium Bridge arcs into the sky and the shell-like Sage Gateshead music and arts venue shimmers in the sun. On the quayside beneath the **Tyne Bridge**, lawyers and art lovers mingle, distinguishable from each other by the degree of purpose with which they walk. When our bus terminates, some of the passengers sitting alongside me will take the walk down what Betjeman described as the 'descending, subtle curve' of Gray Street to join those already in the courts, coffee shops and barristers' chambers. From chemicals and coal mines to electric cars and contemporary art, my journey through England's North East has concluded. ■

ABOUT THE AUTHOR

BRIAN ROBSON is originally from Sunderland, but now lives further down the A19 at Northallerton. He has driven along the A19 more times than he'd care to remember, but prefers the journey by bus – especially when accompanied by his son Barney.

COAST TO COAST

Carol Purves

Carlisle 🚐

Service nos. 85 or 685 | Journey time 2hrs 15mins.

OS Landranger 85, 86, 87, 88. Runs hourly Mon–Sat, 5 journeys on Sun.
Operators: Arriva & Stagecoach.
Connects with Journeys 40 & 42 in Newcastle upon Tyne.

Newcastle upon Tyne ←

I love this journey for it has the makings of a very relaxing day out, more often than not taking me from my Cumbrian home to meet my Newcastle cousin. These excursions are a chance for tea and cream cake at the Tyneside city's posh Fenwick department store. The journey is a vehicular coast to coast, linking the River Eden which decants into the Irish Sea with the great industrial River Tyne which flows into the North Sea. The route generally keeps well south of Hadrian's Wall, but from time to time along the way the Carlisle to Newcastle bus does afford glimpses of the Wall. A parallel seasonal bus route, the AD122 from Hexham to Haltwhistle, follows Hadrian's Wall more closely.

We leave behind **Carlisle**, a Cumbrian city that is famous for its castle, citadel and cathedral, as we journey east through lush farmland. The sun highlights the northern Pennine hills on our right, and away to the southwest is a fine vista of the heights of the Lake District. Most of the route from Carlisle to Newcastle is in beautiful open landscape with some really spectacular views.

As bus journeys go, this is one of the friendliest. Passengers chat happily to each other, often about inconsequential matters,

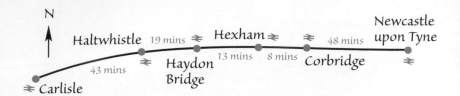

but occasionally veering on to more controversial topics – and that's when the 685 bus becomes a debating society on wheels. The bus always attracts a nice cast of local characters: Betty is carrying newly laid eggs to a friend in the next village, Gavin is travelling to his part-time job in Newcastle, while lonely Moira rides the route each day. As the journey east along the A69 progresses I notice how the accents shift from Cumbrian to Geordie.

INTO NORTHUMBERLAND

Before long we are in **Brampton**, little more than a village, but a place that once boasted 63 pubs. Then on across the border into Northumberland.

We follow the main road, the railway to Newcastle immediately on our left and a fast-flowing burn beyond, and soon we are approaching **Haltwhistle**. This market town makes an extraordinary claim, namely that it is located at the very centre of Britain. I have my doubts, for surely other spots make similar boasts. But the lady in the town's tourist office assertively backs up Haltwhistle's geographical claim to fame with a postcard that shows Haltwhistle perfectly positioned on a straight line linking Portland Bill in Dorset with the Orkney Isles.

I punctuate my regular journeys to Newcastle with stops here and there at villages or towns along the way. **Haydon Bridge**, really a halfway house between Carlisle and Hexham, caught my attention on one journey. It is a place that in 2009 regained its status as a quiet and peaceful village when a bypass was opened. 'Thirty years too late,' says a man in the public library, referring to the bypass. 'But better late than never.'

The village library alone justifies the stop in Haydon Bridge. The library, run by volunteers, bristles with community spirit. Books are lent and sold, there are paintings by local artists on sale, and the building (known as 'The Bridge') also serves as tourist information centre and internet café.

THE TYNE VALLEY

The journey continues past fallow fields, ploughed fields and sown fields, all seasons rolling into one. However, the area is noted mostly for cattle and sheep. As the bus doors open at each stop we can hear the lowing of cows and the bleating of sheep. This is a happy symphony, a welcome contrast to the deathly silence in 2001 when the area was devastated by foot-and-mouth disease. I still shudder when I recall those awful days.

By far the largest spot along the route to Newcastle is **Hexham**, a market town of some 11,000 inhabitants, and the place where the two Tyne streams, North and South, combine to create the much larger River Tyne. Hexham bustles, for it's the obvious shopping centre for those living in a great swathe of Northumbrian hill country.

The next stop is **Corbridge**, where our bus pulls up outside the Angel Inn. This thriving town, just 18 miles from Newcastle, grew up around the site of Roman Corstopitum. The town was burnt to the ground several times by the cross-border raiders known as Reivers. These agile horsemen created mayhem for three centuries, but particularly in Tudor times, as they swept down from the hills. So bad were these raids that at one time Tyne Valley communities like Corbridge called for Hadrian's Wall to be reinforced as a defensive barrier against raiders from the north. But today Corbridge is a peaceful spot, no longer harried by wild horsemen, and happily the village's Saxon stone church has survived.

East of Corbridge, the demeanour of the Tyne Valley slowly changes as we approach Newcastle upon Tyne. But Northumbrian history still makes an appearance. The place shown as Heddon on the bus timetable is more properly **Heddon-on-the-Wall**. Hadrian's Wall of course. The *vallum* is on either side of the village, where a preserved section of the Wall can be seen. The village of Throckley is also situated on the Wall with splendid views of the distant Pennines. Before long, the city has eclipsed the country and we are travelling along crowded roads through urban **Tyneside**. We pass Newcastle's Royal Victoria Infirmary, the General Hospital and the Freeman Hospital and then there is a glimpse of St James' Park, the football stadium where Newcastle United weave a little sporting magic. Eldon Square is the end of the line. Time for tea and cake. ∎

ABOUT THE AUTHOR | **CAROL PURVES** is a freelance writer. She lives in Carlisle and loves exploring her home region – whether by bus, on foot, or even occasionally in a car.

David Beilby

Newcastle upon Tyne

Service no. X18 | Journey time 3hrs 15mins.

OS Landranger 88, 81, 75. Hourly, limited Sun service.
Operator: Arriva.
Connects with Journeys 40 & 41 in Newcastle & 44 in Berwick.

Berwick-upon-Tweed ←

Journey 42 offers a splendid panorama of coastal Northumberland – made possible by the Arriva X18 bus service. Travellers in a rush to get to Scotland can trim an hour off the journey with the X15 from Newcastle to Berwick, but the X18, albeit slower, is much the more adventurous route. It takes in castles galore: Alnwick, well preserved and with a flourishing garden, lonely ruined Dunstanburgh, and Bamburgh, rebuilt in Victorian times.

The first part of the run from **Newcastle** is urban England, then leafy suburbs, until the bus is eventually clear of the Tyneside conurbation. Here is a bus with attitude, speeding north along the A1, but leaving the main highway here and there to serve communities like **Morpeth** and Felton that are bypassed by the dual carriageway.

This is undemanding country, with views that stretch for ever, and the first half of the journey north is a chance to relax. There are good things to come. At **Alnwick** the fun begins, as the X18 takes to the coast. It loops down by **Alnmouth Station**, a reminder of how the speed of modern trains contrasts with the leisurely pace of Britain's local bus services. The fastest direct trains will whisk you from London to lonely Alnmouth in just 3½ hours. Most buses on this route then head directly for Longhoughton, passing the RAF base at Boulmer, which, for 37 years until October 2015, was home to a fleet of air–sea search and rescue helicopters.

Northumberland's coastal path is a superb walk and **Longhoughton** is one place you can easily join it from the bus. The path threads along the coast a mile east of the village but it is well worth the effort. At the north end of Longhoughton you can also alight to walk through woodlands to **Howick Hall**, a tranquil place with large gardens and a historical association with Earl Grey. He was the man who used bergamot to improve the flavour of tea made using local water with a high lime content, so inventing the trademark blend that made Earl Grey a household name.

Berwick-upon-Tweed

Holy Island

44 mins

Bamburgh
10 mins

N

Seahouses
32 mins

11 mins   Craster
23 mins
Alnmouth
Alnwick

37 mins

Morpeth

30 mins

Newcastle upon Tyne

I CAN SEE THE SEA!

You finally get a close encounter with the sea at **Craster** (see box, page 229), as the X18 makes a tour of the village, passing the harbour twice. Quarrying was once a major industry, and whinstone for London's kerbs was shipped from Craster harbour, but there is little sign of that now and it is a pleasant place to enjoy the oystercatchers and eider ducks. Crab pots, flower beds and a lifeboat house make it hard to resist the temptation to linger.

After back-tracking to the main road, the bus heads north to Embleton. From the village centre, where there are several pubs and a shop, you can take a short walk down to **Embleton Bay** and discover another thing that Northumberland has in quantity:

CRASTER

Craster harbour is still used by local fishermen. It is a delightful stop-off point, not just for the harbour and village facilities, but also for coastal walks. A favourite is the amble north through meadows for a mile to what was once the largest castle in Northumberland. Dunstanburgh Castle is long-ruined and perched on a rocky promontory. The romance of the location was not lost on Turner, who did several paintings of it.

Craster is famous for its kippers. As you pass on the bus, you may well see smoke rising from the roof vents of Robson's smoke house, where they have been produced for over 150 years using traditional methods. You will find crab and kippers aplenty at the Jolly Fisherman (☎ 01665 576461; open 11.00–23.00 daily).

superb beaches. It is indeed a blessing that the North Sea is so cold as otherwise this coast would have been developed and spoilt.

Further north the bus makes another detour to the coast to visit **High Newton-by-the-Sea**. If you get off here and it's the right time of year, look out for swallows nesting in the bus shelter. It is a short walk south along a quiet lane to Low Newton-by-the-Sea, a slip of a place with the 18th-century Ship Inn and cottages set round a village green. Adjacent is Newton Pool which is a nature reserve with hides for birdwatching.

In contrast, **High Newton beach** has nothing at all which makes it one of the best spots to sit and enjoy this coast as it is so utterly peaceful. The walk to the beach is super with plenty of flowers along the verges of the country lane, the long grass in the adjacent fields shimmering in the wind and – if you are lucky – larks singing high above. To my mind this is what Northumberland is all about and just being there lifts the spirits.

It is five miles to **Beadnell**, where the bus dives down a narrow lane to go through the village centre. Look out for St Ebba's Parish Church, named after the sister of Oswald, the 7th-century Northumbrian king. Near the church is the Craster Arms

THE FARNE ISLANDS

Seahouses is still a busy port, not just for fishing, but for boat excursions to the Farne Islands. A trip can last from two to six hours (☎ 01665 720308; www.farne-islands.com). You can visit the islands year-round and every season offers something different. An early summer journey might lead to close encounters with nesting terns which are very aggressive – it's Alfred Hitchcock's *Birds* in real life!

Hotel. This building started life as a pele tower, a place of refuge in small settlements where folk feared the raids of the Border Reivers and other marauding incomers from Scotland.

A short hop from Beadnell takes you across a golf course to Seahouses which has the feel of a real seaside resort.

CASTLE IN THE AIR

The bus heads through **North Sunderland**, an oddly named place far distant from Sunderland, prior to a dash along the dunes to Bamburgh. On the other side of the dunes is a particularly fine beach and beyond there are fine views out to the Farne Islands. But **Bamburgh** boasts something special, a castle that is truly one of the highlights of this route. The basalt outcrop at Bamburgh acts as a natural fortress. The castle which you see today is a Victorian creation, restored and reconstructed by the first Lord Armstrong. From the castle there are splendid views all round.

In the village is the Grace Darling Museum (☎ 01668 214910; open Oct–Apr 10.00–16.00 Tue–Sun, May–Sep 10.00–17.00 daily), run by the RNLI Heritage Trust. It tells the story of lifeboats with particular emphasis on the rescue by Grace Darling who is buried at St Aidan's Church across the road. Well worth a visit, the church is central to the history of Christianity in this corner of England.

Route X18 has one last close encounter with the sea as the bus skirts Budle Bay. However, unless you catch high tide you are more likely to see waders feeding on the sands than any serious water. Then the bus turns inland to Belford, an old market town which is an important interchange point for local buses.

The rest of the journey to Berwick is back on the A1. However, you are rewarded by the sight of **Holy Island** on the right. At Beal, there is on certain days a connection by bus to the island (see box below). **Berwick-upon-Tweed** is journey's end. Much of this historic town is perched on a fragment of land on the north side of the Tweed. It is an oddity of geography, and of course a rare spot north of the River Tweed that can be reached with an English bus pass. ■

| ABOUT THE AUTHOR | **DAVID BEILBY** has long experience as an engineer working in the rail industry and local transport. He has enjoyed many relaxing visits to the Northumberland coast. |

BY BUS TO HOLY ISLAND

Perhaps the quirkiest bus route in Northumberland, though certainly not the most frequent, is service 477 from Berwick-upon-Tweed via Beal to Holy Island. There are connections at Beal with buses to and from Newcastle upon Tyne. Holy Island relies on a tidal causeway for a link to the mainland.

During the brief summer season, the bus to Holy Island operates daily except Sundays. For the rest of the year, it is generally Saturdays only with sometimes Wednesday journeys thrown in too. Because the causeway is flooded at high water, the timetable for this bus service is necessarily complicated, varying as required to catch low tide. On days when buses do run, there are two journeys out to Holy Island, allowing anything from three to eight hours on the island. Details at www.lindisfarne.org.uk, where you will find the current bus schedules under 'general'.

The bus to Holy Island is not the only bus route in Britain with a timetable governed by the tides. Another example is on the Hebridean island of Barra, where services to the island airport are governed by the pattern of arriving and departing flights. As the planes land on the beach the flight timetable is dictated by the tides, the buses which serve the airport following suit. ■

TRAMS AND TROLLEYBUSES

Some British bus routes today still follow long-forgotten tram lines. The bus eclipsed the tram in the years after World War II. Although the cable tramway at Llandudno survived, Blackpool is the sole municipality that has shown uninterrupted loyalty to its trams. The Seaton Tramway, a tourist attraction mentioned on page 75, is newer – it opened only in 1970.

Yet trams are enjoying an English renaissance with new networks developed in recent years in Nottingham, Sheffield and Manchester. Even within Greater London, there are now trams again in the shape of Croydon Tramlink. The West Midlands has a single tram route that links Wolverhampton with Birmingham.

Trams are returning to grace in Scotland too, with Edinburgh trams running from the city centre to the airport since 2014; the scheme was not without controversy, though, and went way over budget. Wales, which in 1807 introduced the world's very first public tram service – horse-drawn in those days – nowadays has no urban tram networks. The Great Orme Tramway at Llandudno is the principality's sole homage to a form of transport that has deep Welsh roots.

Britain's ambiguous relationship with trams reflects a broader issue in the history of urban road transport in Britain. Those of a generous disposition may be inclined to read that history as a creative web of innovation as municipal authorities experimented with successive modes of transport. More critical commentators will see it as a story of vacillation, reflecting the lack of purpose and endemic amateurism that has characterised the country's whole engagement with transport issues for 150 years or more. Sir Benjamin Hall – the civil engineer, MP and Commissioner of Works, a man most noted for presiding over the installation of Big Ben at the Palace of Westminster in 1858 – fiercely opposed trams in London, worrying that tram lines might impede the passage of his own horse and carriage. Almost a century later, it was a generation of first-time car owners who led the rallying cries for trams to be banned from Britain's streets.

The trolleybus first made its debut on Britain's streets in 1911, much later than the tram. The centenary of its birth went almost entirely unnoticed. The trolleybus outlived the great municipal tram networks. But not for long. The last surviving trolleybuses ran in Bradford in 1972. ■

Scotland

When Laurence Sterne first set foot on French soil, he was impressed with what he found. In *A Sentimental Journey through France and Italy* (1768) he remarked how some matters are better ordered in countries beyond England. The English bus traveller venturing north of the border into Scotland might be similarly impressed.

Of course, an English concessionary bus pass finds little recognition in Scotland – but there are exceptions. Travel on the afternoon bus from Newcastle upon Tyne to Jedburgh (service 131) and the driver will gladly accept an English bus pass for a journey right through to Jedburgh. It's one of those oddball exceptions – and conversely holders of a Scottish National Entitlement Card (NEC) can ride the 131 from Jedburgh down to Newcastle. The NEC can also be used for cross-border journeys to Berwick-upon-Tweed and Carlisle. Residents of England nearing retirement age can only look with envy across the border where their Scottish counterparts can get a free NEC on their 60th birthday, a pass that is in many respects far better than the English counterpart. The distinction between local bus services and long-distance coach services in Scotland is less cut and dried than south of the border, meaning that the Scottish NEC can be used on many express and limited stop bus services in Scotland, of which there is a remarkable network. That benefits not just NEC holders of course, and it is possible to make long hops in Scotland. If you are chasing records, look to the 915 Citylink service from Glasgow to the Isle of Skye. You can check out that 233-mile route and other Citylink services at www.citylink.co.uk.

Traveline Scotland (www.travelinescotland.com) is a great resource for planning journeys by bus across Scotland. It has a comprehensive library of timetables for all Scottish bus services,

Inverness – the starting point of Journey 48 to the far north (© Sa83lim/DT)

where you'll find the times of buses that vary with the tides on Barra, and details of the rare journeys to Britain's northernmost bus stop on the island of Unst in the Shetlands.

In this edition, we have some journeys that venture to the very extremities of Scotland's bus network, heading to the far north of the mainland to Thurso, as well as exploring the Borders and Scotland's southwest, and venturing from Glasgow to the Kintyre Peninsula. Four of the eight Scottish routes that we present here are on islands: Arran, Jura and two journeys on the Western Isles.

In a perfect world, we would have included more Scottish routes. We'd have loved to cover one of the new breed of demand-responsive services, such as the Rannoch Dial-a-Bus. The 95, running south from St Andrews around the Fife coast, is a very fine excursion, but pressure of space squeezed it out. Lothian Buses 26 through the heart of Edinburgh, which links the beach at Portobello with Edinburgh Zoo, taking in graceful Princes Street along the way, suffered the same fate. ∎

By Bus with the Bard: A Burns Encounter

Richard West

43 Dumfries

Service no. 102 | Journey time 3hrs.

OS Landranger 84, 78, 72, 65, 66. Twice daily Mon–Sat, once on Sun.
Operator: Stagecoach.

Edinburgh

This is a journey that can start and end with Burns. In and around **Dumfries** he lived, drank, farmed (with mixed results) and at nearby Brow Well tried to cure his final illness by immersion in icy waters. Of the monuments to him in Dumfries itself, the most appealing must be the Globe Inn (☎ 01387 252335; open from 10.00 Mon–Sat, from 11.30 Sun), his regular howff. It is a cosy, welcoming pub where the literary connection is recognised but not overdone. Dumfries plays the Burns card, but not overwhelmingly so and still feels like a working town with a pretty high street – a little scarred by the effect of recession and competition from out-of-town supermarkets.

Scotland's Southern Uplands

Waiting for the bus at **Whitesands**, you can contemplate the fine river frontage, the sweep of the River Nith and the crumbling stone steps down to the racing weir. It is sad that the pedestrian-friendly development hereabouts is for now rather let down by riverside buildings that await renovation.

Once clear of the town, the bus makes steady progress along the A76, the main route towards Kilmarnock. **Hollywood** is the first village, but you will be lucky indeed to spot any stars here-abouts. Ellisland Farm, where Burns tried his hand at agriculture, is a little further along the way.

Auldgirth and **Closeburn** both still boast eating options (a picturesque inn and a functional snack bar respectively), village stores and working rural post offices, but alas no longer railway stations. The station at the small town of **Thornhill** is also long gone, but, if you are minded to do the journey in stages, this elegant spot with its broad high street, unspoilt townscape and selection of eateries makes a good first stopping-off point.

Thus far, the countryside has been hilly and wooded, but at **Carronbridge** the bus turns off onto a narrowing road and suddenly the hills close in. The climb to Dalveen Pass has begun. Under a graceful railway viaduct, round a bend, and bulky mountains immediately loom in front. The trees fall away and the route ahead appears barred by the great bulk of the Lowther Hills and its outliers. Now we have all the scenic grandeur of the Highlands transposed into the Southern Uplands of Scotland. Yet despite the sense of remoteness, there are still working sheep farms, and the route is long established, as part of the valley once carried a Roman road.

The scattered settlement of **Elvanfoot**, announced by its tiny kirk and large cemetery, is a slightly surreal spot, sitting in an upland

BUS WARS

The journey described here is one of a family of bus services linking Dumfries with Edinburgh. There are additional journeys, such as the 101 that serves the small town of Moffat along the way, rejoining the main route described at Crawford, just before Abington.

These services have been the subject of mighty tussles between operators over the last year, with the various councils that subsidise them piling into the fray. For many years, MacEwans Coaches ran the routes, winning local approval for their service. In November 2012, the contract for the service was suddenly awarded to Stagecoach, the change being effected with just a very few days' notice. Recriminations, threats of legal action and an inquiry followed.

Edinburgh

22 mins

Morningside

26 mins

N

Penicuik

15 mins

18 mins West
Linton

Biggar

30 mins

Abington

13 mins

Elvanfoot

20 mins

Thornhill

25 mins

Dumfries

mountain bowl that is traversed by the M74 motorway and the main-line railway from London to Glasgow. The 102 sticks firmly to the old road – although the notion of a local bus in the Scottish hills slipping onto a motorway is an engaging one. The next stop is **Crawford**. A handful of mock-Tudor houses seem to have migrated here from suburban Surrey. The long-derelict Post Horn Hotel, surely a pit stop in the days when a drive from Glasgow to London was much slower and more adventurous than today, is well past renovation.

At **Abington** we make a bizarre detour into the M74 service area, amid a sea of trucks and the inevitable strong smell of burgers. Soon we are back in more rural surroundings, following the valley of the infant Clyde. At Roberton a church on a rocky bluff marks the site of a much more ancient place of settlement. At Lamington, the viaduct for the West Coast Main Line was closed due to flood damage on my last visit – even 19th-century builders, with their penchant for over-engineering, could not anticipate the full force of nature at what is still a wild place.

Biggar is the first community of any size since we left Dumfries. The town has an air of prosperity, its long central square well tended and lined with a wide range of independent shops. It is also home to a puppet theatre and a gasworks museum, an oddball combination of tourist attractions surely not replicated anywhere in Britain. Burns is not far away, for hereabouts lived one Archibald Prentice, a well-to-do farmer and significant subscriber to Burns's 'Edinburgh Edition'. Now the bus turns away from the Clyde and runs through sheep country once more at the foot of the Pentland Hills.

You can soon begin to sense the commuter pull of Edinburgh. **West Linton** is a very pretty, if slightly over-egged, conservation village of the sort that often appeals to middle-class commuters. But then, just as you think it's all going to be an increasingly suburban landscape into Edinburgh, the bus makes a sharp turn down an improbably narrow road and diverts via **Penicuik** to reveal an altogether different face of what is now Midlothian.

You are suddenly in ex-mining country; the Shottstown Miners Social Club proves it, even if coal is no longer extracted hereabouts. The houses are more modest, and although Penicuik is still a lot more vibrant than many ex-mining towns, there are the inevitable empty shops. The local building material is a warm, gold stone which lifts the atmosphere, even on a dreich day.

Shortly afterwards, as the bus drops towards Edinburgh, you see on the right the first views across the city, including the growing piers of the new Queensferry Crossing road bridge, and in good weather the Firth of Forth and the hills of Fife beyond. Although the long-distance view is grand, the initial approach to the city close-up is less inspiring. The bus picks its way across the city bypass, and, after the elegant sweep of Braidlaw Park, is suddenly in a world of upmarket urban bustle.

The citizens of **Morningside** can clearly sustain a wide range of independent retail services. You may soon lose count of the number of interior design shops, delicatessens, complementary therapy practitioners, coffee shops and wine bars that line the route. Morningside gradually merges into Bruntsfield, a more bohemian student district. The same warm sandstone tenements; the shops are still varied, but geared to more modest pockets.

After the homely suburbs and on passing the Usher Hall, a sharp right turn at the end of Princes Street brings you suddenly to the pure theatre that is tourist **Edinburgh**. You are immersed in the landscape of a million tourist photos. Nothing here needs much introduction: Princes Street Gardens, the castle, the former

North British Hotel, Arthur's Seat and the Old Town ranging up the hill across the railway tracks.

But the link with Burns is not forgotten. He came to live in the city in 1786, and was, for a time, feted by wealthy Edinburgh society. Although the novelty value of the Bard later wore off for the Edinburgh glitterati, he himself foresaw this. He did not allow this relatively short-lived social and intellectual whirlwind to change the underlying principles of his work. Today, walking tours will show you the numerous addresses that figured in the poet's all-too-brief period of fame.

Most folk will get off in **Princes Street**, and this may be just as well since the very end of the trip is rather an anticlimax as the bus picks its way to the cavernous St Andrew Square bus station.

So there you have route 102. Warm urban streetscapes, verdant valleys, an upland vastness, from Roman history to all the paraphernalia of 21st-century communications. From workaday towns with lost industry to urban chic and tourist superstar city. Not bad for three hours and under a tenner! ∎

ABOUT THE AUTHOR	**RICHARD WEST** is a retired civil servant looking forward to getting his bus pass soon and revisiting routes like the 102.

EXPLORING THE
TWEED VALLEY

Richard West

Berwick-upon-Tweed

Service no. 67 | Journey time 1hr 45mins.

OS Landranger 75, 74, 73. Every 2hrs Mon–Sat,
5 journeys Sun.
Operator: Perryman's Buses.
Connects with Journey 42 in Berwick-upon-Tweed.

Galashiels

I have a long-standing interest in railways, a mode of transport that was for a long time virtually unknown in the Scottish Borders. The Tweed Valley rail route from Berwick to Galashiels closed in 1964, and the main line from Carlisle to Edinburgh succumbed five years later. Happily, the Borders Railway, which follows the Waverley Line from Edinburgh to Galashiels that was subject to the Beeching cuts in 1969, reopened in 2015; but the rest of the region remains something of a rail desert.

So us Border folk have learnt to use buses, and the information boards at Berwick-upon-Tweed railway station have adapted to the new order by even including some bus departures in their listings. They show, for example, the number 60 service to Galashiels via Duns. It is a tame route, operated by Perryman's, and nowhere near as interesting as the 67 which follows the Tweed Valley upstream all the way to Galashiels. The latter is not deemed worthy of a mention on the information boards, which is a pity, for it has the edge over the other route via Duns. The 67 is well run by a respected local operator called Perryman's, a family business worth supporting. Companies like this add colour and variety to the increasingly uniform British bus transport scene, and, like other routes commended in this book (eg: Journeys 30 and 31), the service is essentially a rail-replacement bus link, in this case closely following the route of the erstwhile railway to Galashiels, although the railway north from Galashiels to Edinburgh reopened as the Borders Railway in 2015. All that besides, the 67 stops right outside my house.

Perryman's drivers are a friendly bunch, and the 67 is a convivial excursion through splendid Borders scenery. There's always a lively conversation on board – much better, surely, than the tinny rattle of leaking headphones.

Leaving **Berwick** we have fine views of the magnificent Royal Border Bridge and, looking in the opposite direction, the mouth of the Tweed and the North Sea. Berwick is hard to place: this notionally English town has a mainly Scottish hinterland. Its football and rugby teams play in Scottish leagues.

The disused railway along the Tweed Valley haunts this route, and you'll catch many shadows of the old line. Looking out towards the silvery, and here very languid, Tweed, you will see isolated sections of embankment and soon, as our bus passes the hamlet of Velvet Hall, the first set of broken bridge abutments. The 1963 Scottish Region timetable shows that while only two daily trains travelled this section of the route towards the end of its life (such was British Railways' keenness to discourage use and make the case for closure), the slowest was still 25 minutes quicker than the current bus service. This rail route, like so many others across Britain, was swept away by the unlamented Doctor Beeching in the name of progress.

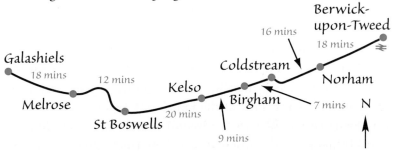

We leave the main road to serve **Norham**, a sizeable village that still boasts a handful of real shops. The town's most striking monument is Norham Castle. Besieged 13 times, including once for a year by Robert the Bruce, the castle fell to James IV in 1513 just before he himself was defeated at Flodden Field. The present structure, largely rebuilt in the 16th century, is in the care of English Heritage. All in all, Norham is a good point to stop off for a pub lunch or a picnic.

CROSSING THE TWEED

Continuing up the valley, and still on the English side of the border, the bus crosses the River Till – a watercourse with a bad local reputation for drownings – and soon reaches Cornhill. Here, at last, our bus plucks up the courage to cross the frontier. And it's done in style, using Smeaton's elegant seven-arched bridge over the Tweed. Robert Burns crossed the bridge in 1787, the first time in his life that he left Scottish soil. A plaque on the bridge recalls the moment.

Across the Tweed, we arrive in **Coldstream**. 'The First True Border Toon' is home of the regiment of the same name. It has a pleasantly old-fashioned small shopping centre. Just northwest of the town is the **Hirsel Estate**, ancestral home of the Home family who readers of a certain age will recall for Sir Alec Douglas-Home. A remarkably lifelike statue of the former Conservative Prime Minister adorns the entrance to the estate. The Hirsel also offers an excellent tea shop, delightful walks and a herd of instantly loveable Highland cattle. Beyond Coldstream, there are excellent views of the River Tweed on the left. The village of **Birgham** makes a pleasant lunch stop (see box, page 243).

Kelso, the midpoint of the route, has the best-preserved historic townscape in the Borders, a cobbled square and a fine range of tea rooms. Pick of the bunch is Caroline's Coffee Shop on Horsemarket (☎ 01573 226996), which offers light lunches, and all things Scottish from home baking (including Millionaire's

Shortbread and Rocky Roads) to black pudding rolls. Kelso has a fine riverside location (of which, it must be said, more could be made), and a ruined abbey. This recalls past monastic wealth and the time when nearby Roxburgh was the seat of King David's power in Scotland. Roxburgh Castle is now but a huge grassy hump crowned by a few stone fragments, while the adjacent meadow lands, once occupied by a thriving community, surely still have many archaeological secrets to reveal.

The jewel in Kelso's crown is undoubtedly **Floors Castle**, home of the Duke of Roxburghe's family since 1721. The fine riverside pile boasts magnificent gardens and, this being Scotland, the Terrace Café offers lunches and Scottish home baking by the duke's own chef (check opening times for the house and café on www.roxburghe.net). The estate can be reached on foot from the town or ask the bus driver to drop you off at the lodge.

We pass the distant, somehow slightly sinister, tower at Smailholm and, after another crossing of the Tweed, the bus reaches **St Boswells**. The penultimate town served is **Melrose**, with the largest and best-preserved Borders abbey and a decidedly touristy ambience. This is the place for ices, Scottish souvenirs – some tasteful, others best passed over – and some serious ladies' outfitters. Not as self-consciously 'tartan' as Pitlochry, Melrose still attracts summer coach tours and on a fine Sunday in August can seem rather overwhelmed. But its townscape has been tastefully developed, its buildings are in good shape and the town certainly exudes prosperity. **Melrose Abbey** itself is well interpreted by Historic Scotland and for those not inclined to vertigo, the climb up the breezy tower offers fine views. A short walk to the footbridge over the Tweed can be rounded off with a pub lunch or, a little further on, the village of Gattonside has the excellent Chapters Bistro (☎ 01896 823217; open 18.00–21.30 Wed–Sun, also noon–14.30 Fri–Sun).

Arrival in **Galashiels** was for long something of an anticlimax, ending at a decidedly down-at-heel bus station adjacent to the High Street with too many empty shops. But with the reopening in 2015 of the railway line to Edinburgh, a smart interchange has appeared, and this could well spark a reversal in the town's fortunes, bringing an interjection of Edinburgh money now that Galashiels is less than an hour from the Scottish capital. Whether it will change the pattern of bus routes is not yet known but, if you want to enjoy route 67 at its best, head to the border country sooner rather than later. ∎

ABOUT THE AUTHOR | **RICHARD WEST** is a retired civil servant and keen reader of *hidden europe* magazine. He likes seeking out under-publicised journeys by train, bus and ship. He often travels route 67.

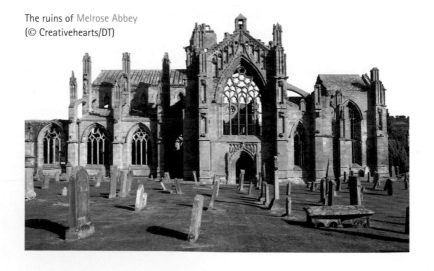

The ruins of Melrose Abbey
(© Creativehearts/DT)

ESSENTIAL SCOTLAND

Deirdre Forsyth

Glasgow

Service no. 926 | Journey time 4hrs to 4hrs 15mins.

OS Landranger 64, 63, 56, 55, 62, 68. 4–5 journeys daily.
Operators: West Coast Motors & Scottish Citylink.

Campbeltown ←

With Journey 45, we take in a great sweep of West Highland landscape including Loch Lomond and magnificent Kintyre. For 18 years, the 926 was my local bus route and also a lifeline link to Glasgow and the wider world. Although this is a longer-distance route, Scottish National Entitlement Cards are recognised for free travel.

If you are riding the 926 on a quiet day, make the most of opportunities to swap sides along the route. For the stretch along Loch Lomond, shortly after leaving Glasgow, the right side is the best bet. Then left gives the best views around Loch Fyne, but you'll certainly want to be on the right again south of Tarbert for the glorious run south down the Kintyre coast to Campbeltown.

The 926 cruises authoritatively past local city buses as we head out from **Glasgow**. Speed is the theme on this bus that serves only a very limited number of stops in the first 45 minutes of the journey. But once we get to the shores of **Loch Lomond**, this is just like any local bus and the driver has to be prepared to stop for passengers at any point along the road – even if they are not standing at the bus stop.

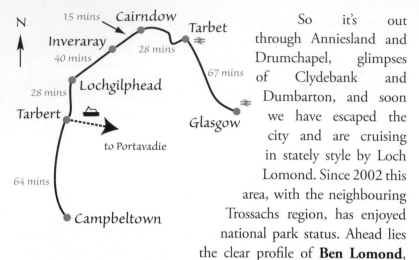

So it's out through Anniesland and Drumchapel, glimpses of Clydebank and Dumbarton, and soon we have escaped the city and are cruising in stately style by Loch Lomond. Since 2002 this area, with the neighbouring Trossachs region, has enjoyed national park status. Ahead lies the clear profile of **Ben Lomond**, said by some to have been the inspiration for the Paramount Pictures' logo. This stretch of the route is at its best on a crisp winter's day: skeletal trees, heavy frost and bright sunshine make a magic combination.

Tarbet marks the point when we leave Loch Lomond and cut over a low hill to the head of Loch Long. You'll run across places called Tarbet or Tarbert all over western Scotland. The name comes from a Scottish Gaelic word that refers to a place where it was possible to haul boats between one loch and another. Later on our journey we'll stop at another such spot: Tarbert (this one with an 'r'). The bus just glances **Loch Long**, pausing for a crowd of hikers to alight, and now starts the haul to the top of 'Rest and be Thankful' – a pious name that recalls that this was once a difficult climb. Even nowadays, landslides or heavy snow quite often lead to the closure of this main road.

Over the top, and dropping down to the west, I know that **Loch Fyne** will be my companion for the next 90 minutes. I think spring, when the primroses and harebells are out and the air is clear, is the best season to enjoy this part of the route. We stop at **Cairndow**, a wee slip of a place, but well known as the home of Loch Fyne Oysters. From modest beginnings in 1988 on the shores of this remote Scottish loch, the company grew to include over three-dozen restaurants. You can still visit the original Oyster Bar on the shores of Loch Fyne (☎ 01499 600482; open from 09.00 daily).

INVERARAY AND LOCH FYNE

Inveraray, a conservation village founded by the Duke of Argyll in 1745, is next and here the bus stops for a few minutes. Just enough time to stretch my legs and enjoy the view over Loch Fyne to St Catherines in Cowal. This Inveraray stop on the 926 is always a nice moment. It is as if all aboard have been conspirators in a plot to escape from Glasgow. And now, here in Inveraray, we can take a breath of Highland air, look at each other, and rejoice that 'we've done it'. If you are tempted to stop off in Inveraray, the George Hotel (☎ 01499 302111) is a good bet for rooms. Don't be deterred by the inscription in the hotel, written by Robert Burns, that tells how unhappy the Scottish poet was with the service.

Heading on south, we leave the loch shore just briefly, returning to the water at **Furnace**, a village that once made a decent living from the gunpowder industry. A mile or two south of the village is **Crarae Garden** (☎ 0844 493 2210; open 09.30 until sunset daily, but note that the visitor centre is open Apr–Aug 10.00–17.00 daily, Sep–Oct 10.00–17.00 Thu–Mon). The bus driver will stop on request at the gate if you are minded to explore this Himalayan-style woodland garden. Before long we are in **Lochgilphead**, a place with more of a buzz than many Argyll towns for it is the administrative centre of Argyll and Bute Council.

The next village is **Ardrishaig** with views of Arran to the south. The nine-mile Crinan Canal starts here and the parallel towpath makes a pleasant walk. The canal was started in 1794 to cut out the 120-mile sail round the Mull of Kintyre from the Firth of Clyde to the Atlantic Ocean. Then on down the banks of Loch Fyne, past the South Knapdale road to Kilberry and Ormsary, until the fishing village of **Tarbert** – the one with the 'r' – comes

EXPLORING KINTYRE

Campbeltown is a little down at heel these days, having lost its regular car-ferry service over to Ireland about ten years ago. But it is still a good base for travel adventures. In 2011, the local bus company West Coast Motors set up a summer speedboat link to Ballycastle on the Causeway Coast of Northern Ireland (details on www.kintyreexpress.com). Landlubbers might prefer the West Coast Motors buses to the sands and golf course at Machrihanish (9 buses daily Mon–Sat, service 200/442), the southern tip of Kintyre at Southend (5 buses daily Mon–Sat, service 444/400), or the beautiful 40-minute run up the east side of Kintyre to Carradale (5 buses daily Mon–Sat only, service 300/445).

into view. From here you can take the ferry over to Portavadie to connect with the previous journey in this book.

South from Tarbert the scenery changes, and now the views are westward towards Gigha, Islay and America. The bus stops near the quays at Kennacraig (for ferries to Islay) and Tayinloan (for the short hop by ferry over to Gigha). By now our bus is emptying out. We have dropped off folk here and there, and only those bound for the southern reaches of Kintyre remain. This is Britain's longest peninsula, or, as our bus driver nicely puts it 'Britain's longest cul-de-sac'. Long it may be, but it is anything but boring. I catch a glimpse of seals on the sunny foreshore at Bellochantuy, see Rathlin Island off the far-distant Irish coast and then we are in **Campbeltown**. End of the journey for our driver, but gateway to a good network of local bus services connecting villages in this far-flung corner of Scotland (see box above). ∎

ABOUT THE AUTHOR | **DEIRDRE FORSYTH** worked for Argyll and Bute Council for many years. During that period she lived in Ardrishaig, right on the 926 bus route. Visitors could alight at her front door.

JEWEL IN THE CLYDE: THE ISLE OF ARRAN

Helen Hughes

46 Brodick 🚌

Blackwaterfoot ◀

Service no. 324 | Journey time 80mins.

OS Landranger 69. 6 journeys Mon–Sat, 4 on Sun.
Operator: Western Buses.

As the CalMac ferry from Ardrossan steams into Brodick Bay, you will see the buses waiting by the pier – if you can tear your eyes away from the hills. Few terminals can be in such a picturesque setting. The older houses are traditional red sandstone, there is a castle hiding among the trees across the bay, and just north of the village is Arran's highest peak, **Goat Fell** (2,866ft). The visitor information centre (☎ 01770 303774) is also at the pier. It's best to get on the bus at once as it can be very busy in summer and the bus may well be full when it sets off. Sit on the right for the sea view, on the left for the hills.

For first-time visitors to the Isle of Arran, the 324 bus gives a fine introduction to a fragment of Scotland that has always punched far above its weight. Along the way we visit Glen Chalmadale, then skirt the shores of lovely Kilbrannan Sound with enticing views across to the Mull of Kintyre. Our destination is Blackwaterfoot, a village that by the direct road (called 'the String') is less than a dozen miles from where we start at Brodick Pier. But it is worth making this great loop around the northern half of Arran.

So we are off, leaving **Brodick** and already we realise this island is packed with history. Just after the golf course, look out for our first standing stone on the right. The island is littered with these stones which date back 4,000 years to the Bronze Age, a reminder that people have been coming here for ages. Shortly after the Arran Heritage Museum (☎ 01770 302636; open Mar–Oct 10.30–16.30 daily), the route diverges from the direct road over to Blackwaterfoot. Viewed from the top of Goat Fell, you'd see why that latter is called the String. Our route is briefly lined with beech trees and with luck you might see a red squirrel. Their grey cousins have never made it across the water so the reds are relatively flourishing.

Heading for the hills

Once past the castle, the road plays hide-and-seek with the shore, where sometimes seals bask on the rocks. Approaching the pretty village of **Corrie**, in clear weather there is a good view of the hills with Glen Sannox and its dramatic peaks. The glen was once home to a barytes mine and the track provides a pleasant walk. As the road turns inland and climbs up Glen Chalmadale, the line of hills on the left is broken by the jagged gap of the 'Witch's Step'. On the right are the old peat banks, once an important source of fuel for the islanders.

Then we drop down to **Lochranza** and pick up the coast again. There's a useful ferry link from Lochranza over to Kintyre. Lochranza is home to a distillery that makes Arran's celebrated single malt whisky (☎ 01770 830264; open Mar–Oct 10.00–

BRODICK CASTLE

Brodick Castle, built in 19th-century baronial style, is invisible from the bus. Ask to be dropped off at the gates. There are landscaped gardens (especially lovely in spring when the rhododendrons are flowering), waterfalls, ten miles of woodland trails and a Bavarian summer house. Ranger services, a shop and a tea room are also available (☎ 01770 330202 for opening times of the castle).

17.30 daily, Nov–Feb 11.00–16.00 Mon–Sat). A less appealing aspect of the village is that it is starved of sunlight, kept in the shadows by the surrounding hills.

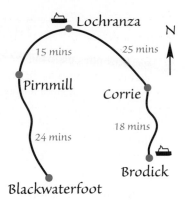

Arran seems so very Scottish but the demography is actually quite dynamic. Young folk from the island move away to the mainland to look for work and affordable housing. And migrants come in. Nowadays, the bus driver on this journey is as likely to be Tadeusz as Tam.

Past the end of Lochranza lies the lonely grave of John McLean, dated 1854. A cholera victim, the sailor was refused burial in Lochranza or Catacol in case the disease spread. In the end, he was buried between the two communities.

The next bead in the string of coastal villages is **Catacol** where we pass the Twelve Apostles, a picturesque row of 19th-century cottages built for tenant farmers who were cleared from the glen to make way for sheep. Sad to think their descendants can no longer make a living here either.

The bus bumps over a set of switchbacks, another result of Arran's remarkable geology where the rocks have been folded over on themselves. Unless you have a cast-iron stomach, I wouldn't sit at the back of the bus – the Arran road surfaces in general leave something to be desired. For the bus drivers, it's part of the fun. 'I love the job,' said one. 'The roads can be challenging. Not exactly single track, but still narrow. We get a lot of tour buses and camper vans on the island in summer. Meeting those can be interesting!'

We rattle into **Pirnmill**, once the home of bobbin makers for the weaving trade, another long-gone source of income on the island. The hill at Whitefarland takes the bus away from the shore up to a view across to Carradale on Kintyre. Then, from the bottom of Imachar Brae, it's a flat run by the sea to **Machrie**, which is more a scattering of farms and cottages than a village. There are numerous ancient sites in this area, once home to Bronze Age communities. The most spectacular circles on **Machrie Moor** were excavated in the 1970s and are about a mile from the road. It is an easy walk and you can get off the bus at the start of the track.

The last three miles run through pleasant farmland, mainly populated by sheep. The hedgerows in spring are bright with gorse and honeysuckle. The final view is, I think, the best of them all: across the silken Kilbrannan Sound to the Mull of Kintyre, Sanda Island and, on a clear day, the thin flat line of the Antrim coast. The bus draws to a halt by the harbour in **Blackwaterfoot**.

You can enjoy local produce for lunch at the Kinloch Hotel (☎ 0844 387 6093) and watch grey seals on the rocks at low tide. Alternatively, if you want to stretch your legs and are wearing stout footwear, it's a brisk half-hour walk to the **King's Caves**. Here, Robert the Bruce is said to have seen the spider whose repeated attempts to complete her web inspired Robert to try once more to defeat his foes. Pictish symbols are carved at the back of the main cave (take a torch). In spring, there are nesting fulmars and black guillemots on the cliffs. You'll see oystercatchers on the rocks and gannets diving out at sea. There is plenty of time for a walk to the caves and a picnic lunch before heading back to the bus. ∎

ABOUT THE AUTHOR | **HELEN HUGHES,** originally from Yorkshire, now lives in Glasgow. She has been going to Arran since before she was born.

THE 456 TO INVERLUSSA: A JURA JOURNEY

David Hoult

47

Feolin

Service no. 456 | Journey time 75mins.

OS Landranger 61. Twice daily Mon–Sat, no service Sun.
Operator: Garelochhead Minibuses.

Inverlussa

S eparating the Inner Hebridean islands of Islay and Jura is the
Sound of Islay, a narrow stretch of sea which is notable for
its powerful tides. Just after three every afternoon the MV *Eilean
Dhiura* whisks passengers across from Port Askaig on Islay to
Feolin Ferry on Jura, where a minibus is waiting by the concrete
slipway. This is the 456 to Inverlussa. The journey will take us
some 25 miles along a single-track road, making a ten-minute
stop *en route* at Jura's main settlement of Craighouse.

Of our four fellow passengers, two are island residents,
heading for home with bags of shopping from Islay's capital,
Bowmore. The other two are American visitors, Betty and Jean
from Slippery Rock, Pennsylvania. We pile our luggage on board,
Mike the driver starts the engine and our journey gets under way.

CRAIGHOUSE: CAPITAL OF JURA

From **Feolin Ferry** the road clings to the shore, and Mike tells us
to look out for otters, which can sometimes be seen playing on the
rocks here. Soon the road slants inland and climbs steadily, before
descending after five deserted miles to the first sign of habitation.
This is **Jura House**, ancient seat of the Campbells of Jura, who

dominated the island for 300 years until they sold the house in 1938. Three empty miles later, a road sign welcomes careful drivers to **Craighouse**, and we arrive at Jura's only village. Betty and Jean have booked in at the hotel, so Mike stops outside and helps them down with their luggage. Then a few metres further on we come to a halt outside the Jura Community Shop, and Mike disappears inside.

It is now becoming clear that the 456 is no ordinary bus. Mike emerges from the shop with boxes of groceries, a couple of newspapers, and a huge bag of dog meal, and these are all stacked on board. Betty and Jean rejoin the bus, having dropped off their bags at the hotel. We resume our northward journey.

Craighouse is a linear village, straggling for a mile along the shore northwards from the village centre. On the left there is a line of houses and cottages, with Jura's whitewashed parish church among them, and behind them in the distance stand the island's three famous peaks, the Paps of Jura (see box below).

To our right, the shore is lapped by the sheltered waters of **Small Isles Bay**. As we drive along, people we pass wave a greeting. Here and there we stop to allow Mike to make a delivery. If no-one answers the door, he walks in and leaves the newspaper or groceries inside – no-one locks their door on Jura. At the north end of the village we pass Small Isles School, the island's tiny primary school.

THE PAPS OF JURA

The Paps of Jura are three mountains on the west side of the island. The highest point is 2,575ft. They are steep-sided quartzite hills with distinctive conical shapes.

The word 'pap' is an Old Norse term for the female breast – despite the fact that Jura has three of them rather than two! They are very conspicuous, dominating the island landscape as well as the landscape of the surrounding area. They can be seen from the Mull of Kintyre and, on a clear day, from Skye and Northern Ireland.

THE ISLE OF JURA

Jura's population is small, but it is a large island. In a list of Scottish islands by size, it would come eighth, just behind Arran. But while Arran supports a population of over 5,000, Jura has barely 200. There is only one proper village, Craighouse, where you will find the island's only shop, the Jura Community Shop, the Antlers tea room, bistro and restaurant (☎ 01496 820496; bistro is open 08.00–17.00 daily and the restaurant from 18.30 – the latter requires advance booking), and the convivial Jura Hotel (☎ 01496 820243), which is the lively hub of island life. But the village is dominated by the Jura distillery; if people have heard of Jura at all, it is usually because of its delicate single-malt whiskies.

Normally we would stop here to collect the schoolchildren, but today is a school holiday, so we cruise by without stopping.

Now the road is ours – there is no other traffic. After another mile or two we cross the Corran River by **Three Arch Bridge**, which was built in 1810 by the great Scottish civil engineer Thomas Telford. Next stop is at the tiny hamlet of **Lagg**. Two hundred years ago this was an important place, with ferries to the mainland coming and going from Lagg Pier – also built by Thomas Telford – but only a handful of people live here now.

Mike drops off his last box of groceries, and then the bus pulls noisily up Lagg Brae to reach open country. Until recently this was Lagg Forest; the felling has left a few scars on the hillside, but there is compensation in that it opened up glorious views across the water to the Kintyre Peninsula and the Isle of Arran beyond.

After the forest, the road descends sharply to **Tarbert Bay** with its sandy beach. Mike points out a white

house, half-hidden by trees away to our right. 'See that house over there?' he says. 'It belongs to the prime minister's father-in-law.'

'Does he ever catch the bus?' asks Jean, but the noise of the engine drowns Mike's reply as he accelerates uphill for the last five miles of our journey, until we arrive at Ardlussa. Here is one of Jura's few road junctions: if you turn left, you can drive for three miles, and then walk another four miles on a track to Barnhill, the isolated house where George Orwell wrote *Nineteen Eighty-Four*.

TEA AT THE END OF THE WORLD

But we turn right, and head down to **Inverlussa**, surely one of the UK's most far-flung bus stops. The afternoon sun glints on the sea. The views across the Sound of Jura to the hills of Kintyre are splendid. A lone yacht is moored in the bay. There are a few stone cottages, and next to the beach there is a trestle table with a hand-written sign announcing 'tea on the beach'.

On the table, an old biscuit tin contains a two-way radio, with instructions on how to order. However, we have cheated: we phoned ahead from the bus (Mike knew the number), and our tea and cake is already waiting on the table. We sit on the rocks for ten minutes, enjoying the tea, the lemon-drizzle cake and the utter peace of this remote spot.

Then it's time to go. We leave money in the honesty box, climb aboard the 456, and head back to **Craighouse**. It has been an amazing journey on this beautiful and virtually deserted island. There are young children living here at the north end of Jura, and the bus is needed to transport them to school in Craighouse. Without the children, it is hard to see how this bus service could possibly survive. So don't delay – go there while you still can! ∎

ABOUT THE AUTHOR | **DAVID HOULT** is a musician and island lover, who regrets that his English bus pass does not entitle him to free travel in Scotland.

FOUR FIRTHS
IN THE FAR NORTH

Eric Newton

48 Inverness

Service no. X99 | Journey time 3hrs.

OS Landranger 26, 21, 17, 11. 5 journeys Mon–Sat, 3 journeys Sun.
Operator: Stagecoach Highlands.

Thurso

W hen we board the X99 bus on an April morning, we are
nearing the end of a two-week journey by bus across
Britain. Archie and I had set out from Land's End. Archie, it
must be said, is smart, intelligent and much-travelled. Few other
eight-year-old terriers have seen as much of Britain as Archie. Like
another of the Scottish routes in this book, namely Journey 45,
the X99 has an ambiguous status. It is more than merely a local
bus, but not quite an express coach. However, Scottish National
Entitlement Cards do allow free travel on the X99, and you can
even reserve places in advance (go to www.citylink.co.uk for
bookings or call ☎ 0871 266 3333).

Starting point for our final big hop north is **Inverness**, the
city at the top end of Scotland's Great Glen, and the spot where
the River Ness reaches the Moray Firth. And that sets the tone for
this bus journey to the northern reaches of the Scottish mainland,
for our route has firths aplenty: Moray, Cromarty, Dornoch and
Pentland. Inverness is solid and reassuring, its 19th-century red
sandstone castle standing on high ground overlooking the neo-
Gothic Episcopalian Cathedral of St Andrew's on the opposite
bank. Imposing stuff.

DORNOCH

The improbably small cathedral town of Dornoch deserves a stop. The original 13th-century cathedral dedicated to St Gilbert has since been replaced by the present 19th-century building that is more like a large parish church. In the churchyard is a flat stone of fixed length, known as the Plaiden Ell, once used for measuring cuts of plaid or tartan cloth. On the way down to the beach is a memorial recalling how, in 1727, Janet Horne was convicted of witchcraft, rolled in tar, placed inside a barrel and burnt alive. Life in Dornoch seems altogether tamer these days. No witches, no executions. If you are tempted to linger, you'll find many good cafés and pubs. Luigi's on Castle Street (☎ 01862 810893; open from 10.00 daily) draws a lively local crowd.

Inverness's road links with the north were transformed in 1982 when the splendid new bridge at **Kessock** opened, making redundant the ferry of the same name. And that impressively graceful bridge is our fast getaway route on the X99. Within a few minutes of leaving Inverness bus station we are speeding across the fertile grazing of the Black Isle. We drop down to the Cromarty Firth, crossing the water by a low-slung structure that seems more causeway than bridge. What a far cry from Inverness this is. Now there are wild moors ahead, remnants of winter snow on the hills, and we have a sense of leaving civilisation far behind us. Archie is duly attentive to the unfolding landscape, and so am I.

Following the northern shores of the firth, we bypass the small town of Invergordon that is dominated by towering steel megaliths: three oil rigs undergoing repair and maintenance within the safe anchorage of the firth. Continuing along the A9, we reach the historic town of **Tain**, the oldest of all the Scottish royal burghs. The elegant sandstone buildings of the town centre and the Gothic-style market cross are dominated by a tall tower known as the Tollbooth. On past the whisky distillery at **Glenmorangie** located on the southern shores of the Dornoch Firth, and then our bus crosses the newly constructed road bridge that now spans the firth, saving a 20-mile trip around its head. On a stormy day in 1809, a ferry's passengers and crew, 100 people in all, drowned when the vessel sank while crossing Dornoch Firth just by the site of the modern road bridge. Perhaps modern travel has become too easy. Once over the bridge our bus, which has kept up a cracking pace all the way from Inverness, leaves the A9 to serve Dornoch.

THE WILD NORTHEAST

Back on the A9, Archie is attending to the gulls outside the window and I am swapping notes with a local man who cannot quite believe that I have travelled so far across Britain by bus. 'From Land's End,' he says, a little incredulously. 'So far... so far.' The man points out Loch Fleet, a little sea loch which is home to ospreys. The countryside is now becoming quite barren and rocky with few trees visible. And what trees there are have been mightily distorted by the fierce winds that taunt this wild coast. We stop at the fishing village of **Golspie**, with its little harbour and attractive sandstone buildings. Not far beyond Golspie is **Dunrobin Castle**, the ancestral home of the Dukes of Sutherland; the formal gardens

Dunrobin Castle
(© Juliane Jacobs/DT)

are said to be based on those at Versailles. From the bus we get no more than a fleeting glimpse of this horticultural oasis in the wilderness.

NORTH TO CAITHNESS

Now the road and railway share a narrow stretch of flat land – to our right the sea and to our left the land rising up steeply. **Brora**, once the industrial powerhouse of Sutherland, is the next place of note. For 200 years coal was mined at Brora, which was used in the evaporation of sea water to extract salt that in turn was used to preserve the landed herrings, at one time so abundant in the nearby seas. Today, no coal is mined nor herrings landed.

We continue up the sparsely populated coast to the small fishing villages of Portgower and **Helmsdale** before crossing into Caithness. Here the A9 climbs up to the Ord of Caithness. The scenery is wild with tortuous climbs and descents along the A9 road as it negotiates its way across the Berriedale Braes. I can only imagine how the buses fare when travelling this route in winter snowstorms.

This is a land that has been defined by emigration, its residents not always leaving voluntarily. There are signs by the side of the road pointing to **Badbea**, a village that was cleared by ruthless landowners who wanted to introduce sheep farming to this area some 200 years ago. The last residents clung on to their lives and their history, staying until 1911. Today Badbea is a poignant memorial to the Highland clearances. We drop down to Langwell Water and the small fishing village of **Berriedale**, guarded by two crenulated towers that were used as lighthouses to guide the local fishermen. Berriedale, like Dunbeath and so many other places on this coast, prospered during the herring boom.

We have, by and large, stuck to the coast from Inverness. But at **Latheron**, our bus turns determinedly inland, heading north across eerily empty blanket bog. There are occasional crofts, huge expanses of heather moorland and small lochans. We leave the main road to stop in **Halkirk**, a neat little village with a distillery that closed 100 years ago. In Halkirk, we cross the River Thurso, and then it is an easy run north along a pleasant B road into tamer country as we approach **Thurso**. Most passengers alight in the town centre, and Archie and I do too. But there are a handful of stalwarts on board for whom this is not quite journey's end. The bus continues round Thurso Bay to the ferry terminal at Scrabster where the elegant blue-and-white MV *Hamnavoe* is waiting to ferry them over to the Orkney Islands. As for Archie and me, we are off to explore Thurso (see box above). ■

ABOUT THE AUTHOR | **ERIC NEWTON** is a retired civil engineer living in Lincoln. He enjoys travelling, especially using his bus pass, which has earned him the reputation of a 'freeloading wrinkly'.

LOST AND FOUND

We feared for Archie, Eric Newton's canine companion on Journey 48. Would he remember to alight when his master did? But Archie is a sensible terrier and always took Eric's cue. Not so Chekhov, a lazy labrador who, when his minder alighted, stayed snoozing on the top deck of a London bus, only to awake when the bus reached the end of its journey.

'The issue is more complicated than you might imagine,' a spokeswoman for Welsh operator Cardiff Bus told us. 'Dogs, even cats, opportunely jump on our buses at bus stops, sometimes merely out of curiosity, sometimes looking for a free ride.' Evidently these freeloading pets don't always know where to alight, become haplessly lost and end up in the lost property division office at Cardiff bus station. That was Snowy's fate. She hopped on a number 61 in Cardiff while her owner was distracted by a shop window. Thankfully, Cardiff Bus co-opted a dog-loving member of their team to care for Snowy until her frantic owner claimed her.

In London, it is Sherlock who presides over the difficult business of reuniting lost property with its rightful owners. Sherlock is a computer who lives in Transport for London's lost property office in Baker Street – the very street where Sherlock Holmes was a (fictional) neighbour. Sherlock will process some 200,000 lost items this year, many of them left on London buses. Among the less-probable items that Sherlock processed over the last year were dentures and an empty coffin.

We have always judged Wiltshire to be a very tame county – and all the better for that. But Wiltshire life does have its hazards. Back in 2004, a number 55 bus arrived in Swindon bus station one Sunday afternoon after the one-hour run from Chippenham. On board were a dozen passengers and an 8ft-long boa constrictor. The snake's owner was never traced, and the animal was sent to a new home in Surrey.

Books are of course very frequently left on buses. Last year, Sherlock logged over 30,000 of them. Not to mention lots of manuscripts. Authors are dreadfully forgetful folk and many great writers have left drafts on public transport or at bus and train stations. The first version of *Seven Pillars of Wisdom* suffered just such a fate, when T E Lawrence was changing trains in Reading. Lawrence had to start again from scratch. ∎

Suas Gu Deas:
Going 'up South'

Rhona NicDhùghaill

49

Berneray

Service no. W17 | Journey time 2hrs 40mins to 3hrs.

OS Landranger 18, 22, 31. 3 journeys daily Mon–Sat, no service Sun.
Operators: Grenitote, Hebridean, DA Travel & others.

Eriskay

O ur last two routes in this volume are set in the Western Isles, the long sweep of islands which lie off the northwest coast of Scotland. They form a beautiful breakwater against the wide Atlantic and a final outpost of folklore, traditional culture and of course the Gaelic language. The first of our duo of Outer Hebrides excursions starts from Berneray (or Beàrnaraigh na Hearadh, to distinguish it from its namesake at the far southern end of the Outer Hebrides) and tracks south over seven islands – each linked to the next by a causeway carrying a road.

Bus service W17 makes this marvellous journey. It is part of the longer Outer Hebrides spinal route that involves several buses

HEBRIDEAN CO-OPERATION

No other journey in this book relies on such a multiplicity of bus operators. The W17 section of the Outer Hebrides spinal route alone depends upon the co-operation of nine different companies. This is another world from mainland Britain. Here bus companies co-operate with each other rather than compete for the same business. On many routes, you'll need to change buses along the way – sometimes more than once. But it all works seamlessly with through fares and ticketing.

and two ferries. Schedules are perfectly co-ordinated so that, in summer at least, it is possible to leave the Butt of Lewis (at the northern end of the archipelago) early in the morning and arrive at Castlebay (on Barra, towards the southern end of the island chain) by evening. Taking some ten hours, this is one of Europe's most extraordinary journeys by public transport.

This journey covers one road segment of the entire overland route. We leave from Berneray and end in Eriskay. You can connect into this portion of the journey by ferries from the Scottish mainland and the Isle of Skye. Ferries from Uig on Skye land at Lochmaddy, while the boat from Oban (on the mainland) stops at Lochboisdale. Our bus stops at both piers.

A LITANY OF ISLANDS

I'm the only person waiting for the bus at the hostel in **Berneray**, the very start of the W17 route. The rustic thatched and whitewashed hostel, huddled low on the shore, nicely evokes a sense of isolation. From the deserted bus stop, I can hear the waves crashing on the white-gold beach and see the hills of Harris rising in the distance.

Right on time, a tired-looking white minibus arrives, and I get on. The same vehicle runs right through to Eriskay slipway where it connects with the boat to Barra, the last inhabited island before

LOCHMADDY

The little port of Lochmaddy warrants a stop. There is a hostel (Uist Outdoor Centre; ☎ 01876 500480), which offers wildlife-watching trips, sea kayaking and hill walking. Nearby, Redburn House (☎ 01876 500301), in the centre of the village, has self-catering units and comfortable en-suite rooms.

Make time to visit the Hut of Shadows, just a couple of miles from the village. It is a low, small stone roundhouse with a turf roof that houses a rustic camera obscura. Ask for directions in Lochmaddy.

rock is swallowed by sea. But this route is too good to rush, and many travellers will stop off for a few hours or even overnight at points along the way.

The driver chats easily while steering us down the single-track road to our first stop in Berneray village, where we pause to pick up two ladies bound for the shops in Lochmaddy. Soon after, a causeway takes us off Berneray and onto a desolate road over the North Uist moorland, before joining the main road. In around 20 minutes, we arrive in **Lochmaddy**, the largest settlement in North Uist.

A short walk from the pier is Taigh Chearsabhagh, a gallery and museum complex, which also houses a café, post office, and a Gaelic/English bookshop covering everything from poetry to history, horticulture to cookery, generally with a local flavour (☎ 01870 500293; open 10.00–16.00 Mon–Fri, 10.00–15.00 Sat). After a bite to eat, while the weather's on my side, I spend an hour or two exploring the coastline at the edge of Lochmaddy, taking in the curious Hut of Shadows (see box opposite).

Back on the bus, across another causeway and the tidal island of **Grimsay**, we arrive in **Benbecula**. Something of a halfway house between North and South Uist, the island is also home to local council offices, a small airport, and an MOD centre, which give it a feeling of no-man's-land. In contrast, the school at **Lionacleit** is a hub of local activity, doubling as a leisure centre, cafeteria, library and museum, with almost all W17 journeys stopping here.

A short distance from Lionacleit, the low land dissolves once again into the clear sea lochs, and yet another causeway takes us on to South Uist. Like most of the Western Isles, the east coast here is home to numerous rocky inlets, while the west coast boasts lush machair and miles of golden beaches. South Uist also has mountains, and almost immediately the shapes of the largest,

Hecla and A' Bheinn Mhòr ('The Big Mountain', at 2,034ft) are visible in the distance. I wonder if this is why the locals describe the journey down here as 'suas gu deas' – going 'up south'.

The bus rolls on, and we pass signs pointing westwards where the majority of the villages are, occasionally picking up or dropping off a passenger at a road end. In contrast, the craggy east side is barely inhabited. I ask the driver (once again, we are the only two people on the bus) if he's ever been walking there. 'Oh no,' he says. It turns out he is from Benbecula and a man more taken by windy two-dimensional landscapes. He's not used to hills.

Uist curiosities

There's a shower starting, so I decide to swap a stroll on the beach for a look round **Kildonan Centre**. The bus drops me off, and I head inside. The centre is open from April to October, seven days a week from 10.00 to 17.00, and its museum houses archaeological displays, a collection of South Uist artefacts, and an archive room dedicated to the American folklorist Margaret Fay Shaw, who made the island her home. The centre's café and craft shop also sell local produce, and whether you're in the mood for a bowl of soup or some handmade jewellery, there's lots to choose from.

Eriskay cemetery (© Rhona NicDhùghaill)

POLOCHAR AND KILBRIDE

The Polochar Inn (☎ 01878 700215) is a four-star hotel, recently refurbished, with a sea view from every room. It's also a great place to stop for a drink or a meal on a sunny day, as the tables outside look on to the Atlantic and the hills of Barra. A mile or so down the road at Kilbride you'll find An Gàrradh Mòr or 'the Big Garden', the only traditional walled garden still standing in the Hebrides. Jonathan and Denise Bridge live and work there, and sell produce farmed according to organic principles, including free-range eggs, vegetables dependent on season, chutneys, herbs, delicious jams and homespun Hebridean wool.

As I wait for the bus outside the museum, I chat to two young women who, like me, are heading for Eriskay. They're tourists, and have never been to the island before. 'You'll love it,' I tell them. 'It's small, but perfectly formed.' I also confess to being biased, as it's where my grandfather was born. Soon enough, the bus arrives, and we go on to **Daliburgh** and the port of **Lochboisdale**, before doubling back to the road south. In the falling light, the bleached grasses reach over and touch the ground beside them. From time to time, the tarmac sends out a spindly finger towards the coast and the townships of Baghasdal, Leth Meadhanach and Smercleit.

As we approach the bus stop at **Gearraidh na Mònadh**, my fellow travellers start peering through the windows, exchanging puzzled looks. 'What's that?' they ask me, pointing. The distinctive local Catholic church, Our Lady of Sorrows, has caught their attention. It is a classic example of modernist (some might say brutalist) architecture. The contrast between the building and its surroundings is stark, a rare reminder that each decade has made its mark on these islands, however faintly. The tourists take a photo and the bus drives on, the church's flat face staring defiantly through the rear window after us. Glimpsing the white walls of the Polochar Inn ahead (see box above), we turn left and the road gets narrower still, its edges now gilded with sand.

Over the sea to Eriskay

As our route hugs the south coast of Uist, we look across to **Eriskay**, closer and smaller than Barra, its rugged appearance contrasting both with its diminutive size and with the uncanny azure lagoon in which it sits. We pass the old pier at **Ludag**, its grey concrete arm still outstretched to the sea, awaiting the embrace of the ferry long since discontinued. Soon, we're sailing across on the latter's replacement: a smooth and unromantic bridge and causeway. Today, the community of Eriskay relies on it, and in all weather it remains regular and dependable, as indifferent to our bus on its back as it is to the whales and dolphins that pass below it.

The W17's final destination is the slipway at the southwest of the island, but as I'm spending the night here, I get off in the island's only village. Like the whole island, it is compact, with the school, shop and pub all within shouting distance of each other. Those familiar with the story of *Whisky Galore* will be disappointed with today's Politician pub, which is a converted 1970s-style bungalow. But Eriskay delights in every other sense.

It's almost dark, so I head for the B&B, and think about how I'll spend the following day. A walk along Prince's Beach is a must, where visitors can read about Charles Edward Stuart who landed on the island and went on to lead the Jacobite rebellion of 1745. Then there's the small church of St Michael, sitting on a hill at the north end of the island. Its distinctive altar is based around the prow of a boat, reflecting Eriskay's fishing heritage, the remains of which can be seen at the natural harbour, Acarsaid.

I trudge on, suddenly tired, the day of island travelling catching up with me. Just as I get to the house, I hear a car horn. Sure enough, it's the W17 coming back from the slipway. Squinting into the setting sun, I give the driver a wave, before turning and closing the door on the salt air and sea. ∎

ABOUT THE AUTHOR | **RHONA NicDHÙGHAILL** is from Oban. She teaches Gaelic to adults.

Next Stop St Kilda:
By Bus Across Harris

Fiona Rintoul

50 Tarbert 🚐

Service no. W12 | Journey time 45mins.

OS Landranger 14, 13. Twice daily Mon–Fri (see box, page 273), no service Sat & Sun.
Operator: K Maclennan.

Hushinish ◄

The tiny beach-fringed settlement of Hushinish on the northwest shore of the Isle of Harris is quite literally at the end of the road. The winding single-track B887 peters out here, its final stretch subsumed by fine, silver sand. Stationed at one of Scotland's most westerly points, the four-house settlement has the feel of an outpost; across the sound is the now uninhabited island of Scarp. Climb up from Hushinish on a hillside path and on a clear day you'll be rewarded by a view of the abandoned island of St Kilda shimmering on the horizon.

Hushinish is separated from the main Tarbert to Stornoway road by a majestic landscape of rugged mountains and sodden bog, punctuated by teeming fishing lochs and tumbling, peat-reddened burns. Here the eagle soars, the stag bells – and the feisty W12 minibus bounces gamely past on weekdays. For Hushinish, though remote, is very accessible and the best way to go is by bus. Glance out the window as the W12 weaves round high-perched hairpin bends and you'll see why. The views south across Loch a Siar – turquoise on sunny days, a moodier teal when the heavens glower – are magnificent. It's hard to appreciate the glittering beaches of Taransay and South Harris if you're slumped exhausted over bicycle handlebars. Or positively dangerous if you are grasping a car steering wheel, white-knuckled after a near-death encounter with a kamikaze sheep on a Monégasque-style bend. Better to let a seasoned pro – used to transporting the island's children, post and supplies back and forth – take the strain.

The W12 bus is also ideal for day walkers who want to take on one of the many satisfying routes among the Harris hills that lie off the B887. A good source is *Walking on Harris and Lewis* by Richard Barrett (published by Cicerone Press). Do check bus timings before setting off, though.

ROADSIDE SURPRISES

The bus journey to Hushinish starts at the pier in **Tarbert**, Harris's main settlement. Reached from the Scottish mainland via the Isle of Skye and a one hour 40 minute ferry-journey across the Minch, Tarbert itself may seem remote to mainland-dwellers. There is, though, a certain familiarity to its neat Victorian architecture, small shopping street and two well-appointed hotels.

This feeling of familiarity persists when the W12 bus turns on to the main A859 road to Stornoway, the principal town on the

---

HILL WALK TO A STUNNING BEACH

For fit walkers, I recommend a day walk east over the hill from Hushinish to the pristine sands of Mill Beach (Tràigh Mheilen). The small, abandoned settlement on the island of Scarp is clearly visible from the mile-long beach. Some of the houses are now holiday homes. The beach is a great place for a swim, but don't be tempted to try to swim to Scarp. Powerful currents lie between you and the island.

From Mill Beach, you can make your way across country to Glen Cravadale, enjoying spectacular views of the Uig hills on Lewis to the north, and pick up a clear footpath by the north shore of Loch a' Ghlinne. The path rises steeply through the glen to a *bealach* (pass) at 712ft, then descends to Loch Leòsaid where you can join the hydro-electric power station track road and descend to Amhuinnsuidhe for the W12 bus back to Tarbert.

Isle of Lewis. Yes, the views are breathtaking as you head along the coast from Tarbert to Ardhasaig and the steep, forbidding hills of North Harris come into view. But the A859 is a normal A road. It is not until the W12 bus veers off the A859 onto the cliff-hugging switchback B887 at the foot of Clisham – the highest peak in the Outer Hebrides at 2,621ft and part of the hill range that separates the 'islands' of Harris and Lewis (there's no water involved) – that the fun really begins.

The bus winds first through the settlement of **Bunavoneader**, where you may be surprised to notice a towering chimney down by the shore. This is all that remains of a whaling station established in 1904 by a Norwegian company. The station was taken over in 1922 by Lord Leverhulme, then owner of Lewis and Harris, but his plans to expand the operation failed and it closed shortly after his death in 1925. It was revived briefly in 1950 to support a Norwegian whaler, closing definitively two years later.

As the W12 bus climbs out of Bunavoneader, another surprise waits in ambush. Between the road and the shore, in the middle of a rocky bog, lies an artificial-grass tennis court. Coaching is to be had in Bunavoneader, and the court is 'available for hire every day of the year except Sundays', according to a roadside sign – a toned-down version of a previous one that read 'no Sunday play'.

Harris and Lewis are traditional strongholds of the Free Church of Scotland, and the Sabbath is still observed here much more strictly than in the rest of Scotland. Elderly, black-clad ladies waiting at the roadside to be transported to church were once a feature of island Sundays, though they are dying out, and some relaxation – notably Sunday ferry sailings – has crept in.

From Bunavoneader, the B887 climbs vertiginously before twisting into a helter-skelter, gear-crunching descent to Loch

Miavaig. Sròn Scourst, a strikingly steep rock buttress, can be seen straight ahead.

Eagle's territory

At the head of Loch Miavaig is a path that leads to the North Harris Eagle Observatory, a timber building with a turf roof. Harris has one of the highest densities of breeding golden eagles in Europe with about 20 pairs resident on the island. White-tailed eagles are also regularly seen in Glen Miavaig, especially in winter, while moorland birds, such as the merlin, golden plover, greenshank, stonechat and wheatear, frequent the glen in summer.

From **Miavaig**, the road climbs again, passing the former Cliasmol primary school, which closed in 2008, then **Cliasmol** itself. As the road corkscrews back down to sea level, another surprise awaits: the white gates of **Amhuinnsuidhe Castle**. You may laugh, or possibly cry, when the bus turns into the manicured castle grounds and the Scottish baronial pile, built in 1865 for the Earl of Dunmore, heaves into view. Nowhere do the architectural excesses of the aristocracy look more out of place than against the craggy backdrop of the Harris hills.

Beyond the castle is a small settlement which used to sport a post office shop, now sadly closed. The only amenities along the B887 are at Hushinish itself, where there is a toilet block.

EATERIES

Take a packed lunch with you to Hushinish, as there are no shops or cafés. On the way back, you may wish to try the comfortable Harris Hotel (☎ 01859 502154). It offers excellent bar and restaurant meals (the latter in season only) using local produce, as well as a wide choice of whiskies. If you arrive in Tarbert before 17.30, the Harris Distillery (☎ 01859 502212) has an excellent café with local home baking and tasty soups – and delicious Isle of Harris gin. Hebscape Gallery & Tearoom (☎ 01859 502363; open Apr–Sep Tue–Sun) in Ardhasaig also provides top-quality tea, coffee, soup and snacks.

The W12 bus operates Monday to Friday, and bus times facilitate a day trip. The morning bus leaves Tarbert at 07.20 on school days (07.50 on school holidays and Fridays), arriving in Hushinish at 08.00 (08.35). The return service leaves Hushinish at 16.40, arriving in Tarbert 17.25. An additional early afternoon return service runs from Govig at 15.00, arriving Tarbert 15.40, and on Fridays from Hushinish at 14.35, arriving Tarbert 15.15. The service from Govig must be booked in advance with the operator – call ☎ 01859 822661 before noon to request a ride. At Tarbert, you can connect with other island buses, including the Outer Hebrides spinal route to and from Stornoway.

Amhuinnsuidhe provides an excellent starting point for an ascent of hills such as Tiorga Mòr (2,228ft) and Ullabhal. Get off the W12 bus just before the castle grounds at the track road leading to the hydro-electric power station in **Gleann Uladail**. Very fit walkers may consider a backpacking expedition from Amhuinnsuidhe to Loch Reasort, possibly via Tiorga Mòr and Tiorga Beag. Alternatively, a path leads from the power station as far as Loch Uladail beneath the impressive buttress of Sròn Uladail – a manageable out-and-return route.

The W12 bus now heads along the final stretch, dipping and climbing extensively along the way. The road to **Hushinish** covers a majestic swathe of one of the most rugged landscapes in Europe, but journey's end is the jewel in the crown. With its lush machair grazing lands, sparkling waters and magnificent silver-sand beach, Hushinish, which has a permanent population of just four, is a breathtakingly beautiful spot. It's a place to pause and reflect on the web of bus journeys that criss-cross our islands. ∎

ABOUT THE AUTHOR | **FIONA RINTOUL** is a writer and translator. She lives in Glasgow.

Marking Time

Keeping track of bus services

In the early days of Britain's stagecoaches, there was no guarantee on longer routes that vehicles would arrive even on the day that was advertised, let alone at a specific hour. Just imagine what bus travellers today would make of such imprecision. By and large, bus punctuality in Britain is quite good. Companies operating in more rural areas record impressive levels of punctuality, although their urban counterparts have it harder, for traffic congestion can play havoc with timetables. That's why bus operators in major cities are so very keen on dedicated bus lanes. Measures which give buses priority over private cars on city streets underpin more reliable, punctual services. Some cities on the continent have such good bus networks that car owners think twice before driving to work. Britain could do a lot better, and keeping buses to time in large cities would be a good place to start.

The tyranny of time defines the working life of many bus drivers in our great cities. The drivers, believe it or not, rather like to arrive early. But the computers and managers who watch over the progress of buses on high-frequency routes have other ideas, and favour the even spacing of buses. Novelist Magnus Mills, who for some years drove London buses on his way to literary fame, plays beautifully with this idea in his novel *The Maintenance of Headway* (published in 2009 by Bloomsbury). Talk about breathing life into a dull topic! This is a book full of deadpan humour, one that will surely appeal to many bus travellers.

Checking punctuality

Today's travellers are easily able to check the progress of their buses. A nationwide service called NextBuses (www.nextbuses.co.uk) gives real-time updates on your local bus services. Why leave home now if you can see in advance that the next bus at your local bus stop is running ten minutes late? Instead, enter a postcode or, for example, 'Green Man, Ewell', and you'll get a list of nearby bus stops. Click on your preferred bus stop from the list to reveal the next buses due to leave that stop.

If you are on the move, the same data can be accessed via www. nextbuses.mobi. Technology has worked wonders in improving the lot of British bus travellers.

Real-time bus information is also just a text message away. Many readers will long since have discovered that you can check upcoming departures for any bus stop in Britain. Every bus stop in England, Wales and Scotland has an eight-digit reference code, shown in timetables and usually on the bus stop. Just text that number to 84268 and within seconds you'll receive a message with the times of the next buses coming your way. This is a first-class service, but it does now carry a charge – you'll pay 25p (plus your own phone provider's charge for sending the request) for each enquiry.

JOURNEY PLANNING

The obvious journey-planning portal for travellers in England is Traveline (www.traveline.info), a service run by a consortium of transport operators and local authorities. Sister services covering Wales and Scotland are available at www.traveline-cymru.info and www. travelinescotland.com respectively. These websites allow you to plan local and longer journeys. We have found that, if you are planning a very long journey across Britain by local bus, then you'll have much better luck in securing sensible results by splitting up your itinerary into separate sections. You can call Traveline for timetable assistance for journeys throughout Britain at 0871 200 2233.

Moving to specific regions of Britain, you'll find for most areas other sources of travel planning and bus timetable information that may be vastly superior to Traveline. Individual bus companies often have their own websites and – at their best – they are excellent. But they usually reveal only details of their own services, and say not a word about the offerings of rival operators.

So, for the last word on bus services in many parts of Britain, the best source for timetable information is often the county council or other local authority. Few offer interactive journey planners of the kind hosted by Traveline, but for the savvy traveller they provide something much more valuable: access to the timetable for every bus service that operates within the borders of their council.

Local authority websites

The manner in which local authorities in Britain discharge their duty to provide information about local bus services in their area varies greatly. Some host a 'bus timetables' section on their own websites – you may have to click through a few layers to get there, but it'll surely be worth the search. There are many fine examples of councils that do this very well and also regularly update their timetable listings. These are no frills web services: they may win no marks for slick design, but they work well and provide access to essential timetable resources.

Good examples of the latter are Ceredigion (www.ceredigion.gov. uk), Argyll and Bute (www.argyll-bute.gov.uk), North Yorkshire (www. northyorks.gov.uk) and Cumbria (www.cumbria.gov.uk). Play with those four and you'll see it takes a bit of patience to navigate through from the council's home page to that part of the website dedicated to bus timetables. It is all too easy to be waylaid by the timetable for emptying dustbins or the procedures for reporting potholes.

Other councils have set up a dedicated website for supplying public transport information – but these are still websites that they maintain themselves. A great example of this approach is Suffolk (www.suffolkonboard.com). Some metropolitan areas have developed excellent websites covering all forms of public transport in their region. For example, Nexus (www.nexus.org.uk) covers Tyne and Wear, while Transport for London (www.tfl.gov.uk) gives the last word on public transport throughout the Greater London area.

Good old print

We are great fans of printed timetables, and we are not the only ones. French novelist Marcel Proust loved timetables, using them to plot imaginary journeys linking Paris and the provinces. The fact that he spent long winter evenings poring over timetables may go some way to explaining why there was never a Mrs Proust.

Max Beerbohm's fictional hero Zuleika Dobson always kept a timetable to hand, and so do we. It always makes sense to have an escape route if one is needed. Many local authorities in Britain produce printed bus timetables, usually aggregated into a series of booklets that each cover part of a county or region. In some areas, they are distributed free through public libraries, bus stations and tourist information centres; elsewhere there is a modest charge to help defray the costs of production. The transport sections of council websites will usually tell you if printed timetable booklets are available and how to obtain them. Some authorities also produce good bus maps.

A printed timetable is great for taking with you on journeys, but they do date quickly. It's always wise to check online for service updates.

Calling time

All great journeys come to an end, and it's time for us to call time on our bus tour through England, Scotland and Wales.

Britain can and should be proud of its comprehensive bus network. It really is possible to travel from Lands End to John o'Groats by local bus services. The author of Journey 48 in this volume, Eric Newton, has done just that. There are lots of good tales to be told of local bus travel in Britain, but this is not a time for complacency when it comes to local buses. Savage cuts in government support for rural bus routes have led to the thinning out of timetables and the cancellation of entire routes. Evening and Sunday services have entirely disappeared in some areas. Many innovations in bus services in remoter areas of Britain (and in some old industrial regions) have benefited from European Union support, but with Britain currently reconsidering its relationship with Europe, that funding is in doubt.

A caring, compassionate society values mobility. Those who, for whatever reason, do not possess cars, have as much right to travel as the rest of us, and good bus services are the key to promoting mobility at the local level. We have a sense, as we write these words in spring 2016, that Britain's bus industry is marking time... just waiting for the moment when public pieties and government attitudes become more sympathetic to providers of essential public services. For the village bus is most definitely an essential public service, part of the very fabric of community. ∎

Nicky Gardner and Susanne Kries
March 2016

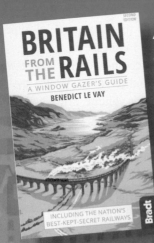

MEET THE TEAM

This second edition of *Bus-Pass Britain* is the product of two community-writing projects that we have co-ordinated for Bradt Travel Guides. This book is very much a co-operative effort, with four dozen writers contributing to this volume, and each bus journey concludes with a short note about the author of that text. Our hearty thanks goes to all those writers. Most would not describe themselves as being professional weavers of words – many are keen amateurs who rose magnificently to the challenge of writing with fluency and enthusiasm about bus journeys which were important to them. Without exception, they have been a delight to work with.

Our role has been as mediators of the enterprise. Susanne Kries was very much the driver of the bus, who kept the engine well-oiled and made sure the project stayed on schedule. Nicky Gardner was the conductor – she neither collected fares nor issued tickets but used her baton to keep our ensemble in order, setting the tempo and ensuring that the results of our collective efforts have a measure of harmony. Our close friend and colleague Tim Locke (author of Bradt's *Slow Travel Sussex* guide) recently joined the editorial collective and has done a handsome job in updating the journeys for this new edition.

We owe a vote of thanks to many who kept us on the road. Were it not for Hilary Bradt, this project would never have left the bus station. It was Hilary's energetic support for local bus services which inspired the *Bus-Pass Britain* project. Hilary's colleagues at Bradt Travel Guides helped plan this community adventure and supported us along the way. In this context, we extend a special vote of thanks to Laura Pidgley, Anna Moores, Rachel Fielding and Adrian Phillips.

Most texts are credited to their respective authors. All unattributed editorial material (such as the scene-setting texts for each region and the bus stop mini-features) was researched and written by the editors.

Nicky Gardner and Susanne Kries

Index of Bus Operators

Here you will find a complete list of all British bus operators featured in this edition of *Bus-Pass Britain*. Some are companies which operate one or more of our 50 journeys, others are interesting bus companies that have deserved a mention in the book. Where the reference is to an operator that runs one of the 50 journeys, we include here only the first page of the route – unless the operator has a further mention in the course of the route. The following list includes only currently operating bus companies.

INDEX OF PLACE NAMES

This index identifies places in Britain that feature in this book.

W

Y

FEEDBACK REQUEST

Here at Bradt, we always love to hear from our readers. Are there things we could have described better? Or perhaps there are some new journeys which you think might warrant inclusion in a new edition or follow-up volume. Don't forget to tell us a little about yourself and include your contact details (ideally an email address).

You can reach us by post as follows: The Editors, *Bus-Pass Britain*, Bradt Travel Guides, IDC House, The Vale, Chalfont St Peter, Bucks SL9 9RZ. If you prefer to email us, please use info@bradtguides.com. You can also add a review of the book on www.bradtguides.com or Amazon.

For the latest news, and updates, please check www.bradtupdates.com/buspassbritain.

Notes

NOTES

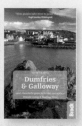

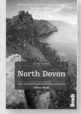
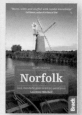
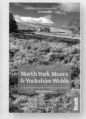